50p

To Steven
With lots of love,
Mum & Dad. Christmas 1987.

GW00458971

THE BRITISH CELTS
AND THEIR GODS UNDER ROME

'perdifficilis . . . et perobscura
quaestio est de natura deorum'
(THE QUESTION OF THE NATURE OF THE GODS
IS . . . MOST DIFFICULT AND OBSCURE)
Cicero:
De Natura Deorum I, i

THE BRITISH CELTS
AND THEIR GODS UNDER ROME

Graham Webster

B.T. BATSFORD LTD · LONDON

To Anne Ross, to whom we owe so much

Typeset by
Servis Filmsetting Ltd, Manchester
and printed in Great Britain by
The Bath Press, Avon
for the publishers
B.T. Batsford Ltd
4 Fitzhardinge Street
London W1H 0AH

British Library Cataloguing in Publication Data

Webster, Graham
The British Celts and their gods under
Rome.
1. Celts—Great Britain—Religion
I. Title
299'.16   BL980.G7

ISBN 0-7134-0648-8

CONTENTS

CONTENTS

LIST OF ILLUSTRATIONS

Figures

7

ACKNOWLEDGEMENTS

Photographs and permission to use them: I am most grateful to Dr David Smith at the Museum of Antiquities, Newcastle-upon-Tyne, for Pls. 10 and 16; to John Dore, Curator of Corbridge Museum, and to the Historic Buildings and Monuments Commission (England) for Pls. 9 and 17; to the Winchester Research Unit for Pl. 15; to Stephen Clews and the Corinium Museum, Cirencester, for Pls. 5, 12 and 13; to Nicholas Moore and the Grosvenor Museum, Chester, for Pl. 4; to John Rhodes and the City of Gloucester Museum for Pls. 6 and 20; to Dr Paul Robinson and the Wiltshire Archaeological Society for Pls. 11 and 21; to Colin Richardson and the Carlisle Museum and Art Gallery for Pl. 22; to Stephen Bird and the Bath Museums Service for Pl. 7; to Miss Catherine Johns at the BM for Pl. 8; to A.A. Round for Pls. 2 and 3; to Robert Trett and the Newport Museum and Art Gallery for Pl. 19; to the owner and to Alan Saville and the Cheltenham Art Gallery and Museum for Pl. 14; and to the Historic Buildings and Monuments Commission (England) for Pl. 18.

For the figures and permission to use them: I am most grateful to my wife Diana Bonakis for the drawings and Figs. 9A and C, 11, 14, 16 and 17; to Weidenfeld and Nicolson for Figs. 1 and 2; and to the Society of Antiquaries of London for Figs. 12B, C and D; to Dr Ian Stead for Fig. 6; to Miss. M. Darling and the Lincoln Archaeological Trust for Figs. 7D and 10A; to Tim Potter for Fig. 12A; to Dr Stanley West and Miss Jean Plouviez and Suffolk County Council for Fig. 10H; to Martin Howe and the Peterborough Museum for Fig. 12E; to Robert Turner, Miss Margaret Tremayne and the Historic Buildings and Monuments Commission (England) for Fig. 13; to the BM for Figs. 9A and 12A; to Dr Alec Detsicas and Maidstone Museum for Fig. 8E; to David Brown and the Ashmolean Museum, Oxford for Fig. 8A; to David Gurney and the Norfolk Archaeological Unit for Figs. 10E, F and G, and to the Cheltenham Art Gallery and Museum for Fig. 14.

PREFACE

I came to write this book through my long-standing research into the Roman Army and the conquest of Britain. I began to realise that all this study had been from the Roman viewpoint and that one ought to consider how the Britons reacted to this sudden and violent change in their way of life. The reason why so little has been done on this subject is that the evidence is almost entirely weighted on the Roman side. The Celts were not a literate society, and, apart from the large collection of wondrous late Irish sagas, have left no records except in their physical remains, recovered by archaeology and by casual finds. It seemed to me that an obvious line of approach would be in the religious ideas and practices, but I little knew at the outset of its daunting complexities. With a great deal of reading and much help from colleagues I eventually began to unravel the main elements in this intricate subject. I am especially grateful to Martin Henig, who has kindly read much of the text and has made many valuable suggestions, in extending my limited knowledge, and correcting errors. I am also grateful to Miranda Green for her help and encouragement, and to the many museum curators for their courtesy and patience, in particular Dr Paul Robinson of Devizes, Stephen Clews of Cirencester, and Malcolm Watkins of Gloucester. I am also grateful to Dr Joan Alcock for reading the proofs and making some useful suggestions, and to Dr Roger Tomlin and Betty Britton for help in proof-reading. By no means least, I would like to acknowledge the hard work of copy-editing by Alison Bellhouse. I would also like to thank Peter Kemmis Betty of Batsford for his great patience and forbearance over a long period of writing and rewriting.

CHAPTER ONE

INTRODUCTION

This is not a straightforward account, or a history, of Roman Britain; admirable studies of this kind already exist and are unlikely to be superseded for some years. This particular volume is an attempt to understand what happened to the Britons at the time of the Roman invasion of AD 43 and in the subsequent occupation. There still remains in the minds of some people the misconception that the Romans came to Britain, occupied it and, just as suddenly, departed, leaving the Britons much as they had been before. This completely neglects the timescale of six centuries or eighteen generations, from the first contact with Rome through Julius Caesar, to the moment when the five provinces of Britannia became independent, which accounts for about a quarter of Britain's recorded history. After this period, the Britons lapsed into a twilight world and, apart from the Celtic west, were absorbed into an English or Scandinavian society.

The study of the impact of Rome and its effects on the Britons has been sadly neglected, although that great scholar F. Haverfield made a brave attempt in his *Romanisation of Roman Britain* in 1912. Since his day, a vast amount of new archaeological and epigraphic evidence has been accumulated, though all the general accounts of the period pay scant respect to the Britons. This may have been due less to a lack of interest than to the heavy weighting of evidence in favour of the Roman point of view and activities. The Celts were not literate and only a tenth-century version of their colourful sagas and heroic myths survives. The only trace of the Britons comes from a study of their occupations and ritual sites, metalwork, pottery, stone and wood carvings.

Studies of the British Celts tend to be of the pre-Conquest period, since it has been considered too difficult to isolate them from the Roman background after AD 43. Investigation into the Britons *after* the Conquest and attempts to understand how their way of life was affected would, therefore, open new ground and provide fresh information. One could carry out this investigation under several subject headings, such as political, social, economic, religious etc. The last appeared the most tractable, and thus a good beginning, when such an investigation was planned. Very soon, however, this proved to be a much mistaken view, for reasons which will soon become self-evident.

The study of the religious ideas and practices of pre-Christian times really belongs to the anthropologists, and in the last 100 years their studies have undergone dramatic changes. The Victorian anthropologists were fascinated by the tales of the primitive myths and magic brought back by the travellers and missionaries venturing into hitherto unknown parts of the world. This was also a period for assembling and publishing great encyclopedias of ill-digested information. The anthropological books of this period tend, therefore, to be collections of travellers' tales assembled regardless of geography or background information and all taken at their face value. They have been rightly castigated by the later anthropologists since none of the writers had ever visited those parts of the world from which their material emanated or become personally acquainted with any primitive people. It was argued, therefore, that all their material was unproven and thus as worthless as the theories developed from it. A great scholar, Sir James Fraser, rose above this and produced a massive number of erudite volumes which still retain much wisdom and hold a great fascination for many readers. The ideas he developed were tempered by his prudence and commonsense, but have, nevertheless, been rejected by modern anthropologists.

In the twentieth century, anthropology was deeply influenced by the work of Freud and Jung, whose research appeared to demonstrate that the deep subconscious of modern man still contained ancestral elements derived from primitive origins. Later, anthropology was invaded by the rapid growth of sociology, a comet that once burned bright in academic circles, only to fade as quickly as it appeared, though the subject eventually settled down and achieved respectability.

Far more important than these changes of fashion was the rapidly growing body of first-hand evidence being patiently collected and published by devoted field workers who integrated themselves into those primitive societies which have survived into this century. By these careful studies and, above all, by understanding the highly complicated social structures of these communities, the foundations of anthropology have been securely laid.[1]

Whilst it is not possible to send a field worker to study the Celts at first hand, it may be possible to gain impressions, albeit vague and unsatisfactory, through the scraps of evidence which have survived in monuments and historical records, to enable comparisons to be drawn from the behaviour of societies which have been studied in the field. Several facts become clear at the outset. The use of the word 'primitive' is highly unsatisfactory, as the field studies have all demonstrated the extraordinary complexities of the social organisation of the so-called 'primitive' peoples. Nor is it possible to isolate religious practices from this intricate pattern. Whilst the modern concept of Western religion is that of a personal belief somewhat isolated from the rest of life, and practised to suit each individual, societies uncorrupted by modern contacts would find this separation of religion from everyday life an alien practice.

The origins of religious beliefs

The origins of religious beliefs and practices are so deeply buried in the remote past that they can only be the subject of speculation. The remains found in the caves in which men lived in Europe as early as the inter-glacial periods are the sole surviving evidence. Animal bones in their debris of cooking and living places give some indication of their meat diet; but, in addition, there are arrangements of stones and animal skulls which can only suggest some purposeful activity not associated with the necessities of existence. Such finds have been made in the deepest recesses of Alpine caves where the cave-bear hunters found shelter.[2] These remains can be categorised only as 'ritual', a word much over-used by archaeologists when given as a label to anything they fail to understand. In the case of the strange cave deposits, it is possible to go a little further with analogies from later discoveries and suggest that these arrangements of the skulls may have been linked with a ceremony directed to securing success in the hunt for more bears and other edible animals. This idea is supported by the famous palaeolithic cave paintings which appear to show hunters killing their prey (Fig. 1). These have been considered as a kind of wish fulfilment, and elements of such scenes are enacted in native dances in many parts of the world. This practice has been given the name of 'imitative magic', with the idea of imitating the events desired to happen, and this still occurs in the form of mental fantasies in the minds of most people today.

It is possible to make backward projections from the later cult practices about which far more is known. Religious beliefs and customs arose out of man's struggle for survival against the forces of nature. Man has inherited animal instincts and drives, especially the dominating will to survive and to propagate his species, which together form the powerful life-force which still compels men and women to undertake extraordinary activities which defy logic and commonsense. It is this illogical element which makes the scientific study of religion a difficult and at times an impossible task. The hunter communities formed a relationship with the animals they hunted, which led to an integration in the ritual in which the hunters closely identified themselves with the animals. This process led to what has been called totemism. It also turned the hunt into a ritual itself which, strangely enough, has survived in shadowy form to the present day. The hunt became a symbol of death and regeneration, since the killing of the animals was necessary in order for the community to survive and regenerate itself.

The life-force manifests itself in other forms, and one of the most powerful and long-surviving of the ancient deities is the mother goddess. She is found in the form of small schematic stone or bone fragments with exaggerated indications of pregnancy, very wide hips and swollen breasts. These representations have a wide distribution and are commonly found on sites of the Upper Palaeolithic period[3] where they are associated with occupation debris, and are found in the dwelling places rather than in any specially constructed context. They are thus thought to be domestic spirits in these fairly settled communities, since they do not occur on sites of a transitory nature, typical of hunters following their game. It would seem that they must have been part of a domestic fertility cult responding to the power of the life-force, and, in this sense, the figures are a form of imitative magic practised in parallel with the hunters and their hunting magic in the cave paintings.

Again, glancing backwards from such powerful deities of later periods as the sky gods Jupiter, Tanaris and Thor, one can imagine that the elemental forces of nature must have been seen as inimical or beneficial powers to which early man was forced to submit. There is buried, deep in the subconscious of the human mind, a desire to rationalise and adjust to overwhelming pressures. The mind, with its delicate system of balance, can screen the active conscious part from the worst effects of disasters by minimising them, or blotting them out altogether. If this did not happen, most of us would never recover from distressing events, such as a sudden loss of someone close to us, or an accident, or a profound misjudgement. Such mental processes ensure that we can sustain these shocks and not lose our reason. One of the more subtle subconscious mental adjustments is to introduce the idea that it was not our fault, but someone else's, or simply a force of circumstance. Thus, rationalisation reveals the basic desire for an explanation to be found which will satisfy us and enable life to continue on its normal course.

The natural progression from this process of mental rationalisation is towards the personification of natural forces – the belief that creatures exist in familiar forms, animal or human, and are responsible for controlling the natural forces. This would automatically lead to the further thought that humans could achieve a certain harmony with these spirits by submission and veneration. In this way, an elementary form of worship could have come into being, and developed from that origin to the establishment of a relationship by means of supplication and gifts. A successful hunting expedition could thus have been regarded as the result of a benevolent act by a spirit; following this, the spoils would have to be shared so that the spirit could be rewarded and so make further successes possible.

The growth of language developed the process of personification, since, once the spirit had a name, he or she could be called upon and specific requests formulated. At a later stage, language also led to the invention and growth of folk tales which related the spirit to the early history of the community. Hunters who had performed great feats of daring and enterprise were remembered and their actions enlarged upon and embroidered with constant recital. Through this medium of the folk tales, which recorded events far beyond human memory that were linked with the intervention of the gods, the ancient heroes were eventually portrayed in an even closer relationship to the gods, thus achieving a semi-divinity. This long process developed through the story-tellers or bards who, by practice, acquired prodigious memories and passed their tales on to succeeding generations.

While all these ideas are highly speculative, it is clear from early evidence of what appears to be ritual or possibly supplicatory acts, that these processes of rationalisation and invention took place from the earliest period when there existed creatures who could be considered human. The belief in the spirit world is universal in primitive communities, and the gods that man created were in his own image or the shape of animals.

Another important factor in the early development of intelligent beings was the recognition of the continuity of the seasonal cycle, so marked in the northern hemisphere. The annual spring birth of vegetation, its summer maturity and death in the winter was seen to be matched by the sequence of day and night and by man's own life-cycle; such a seasonal pattern dominated the lives of the hunters, pastoralists and, later, the agriculturalists. These were the basic, elemental, never-changing forces which must have created mental images and concepts of birth, death and regeneration; this sequence was to become the recurrent theme underlying all religious ideas and practices, but seen always as a complete, though ever-recurring, cycle. Birth, death and regeneration were an integral part of each other, and each stage an inevitability from which there was no escape. The recurrent cycle also affected man's attitude towards his own death, for which there is much evidence of elaborate ritual. This appears in the careful burials and, in some cases, special care for the heads. It has been suggested that communities who lived by seasonal movement to their hunting grounds, returning to better climatic conditions in the winter, carried their ancestral heads with them as if for their preservation, or the protection of the groups. Ancestor worship became an important part of the religious belief of many peoples, not least the Romans themselves, who kept wax masks of their family forebears in a special place in the *atrium* of their houses. The continuity of life in nature gave a strong foundation to the belief in the continuity of human life in a spirit form – a belief which became universal and is strongly held by the vast majority of the inhabitants of the modern world, in spite of a lack of evidence. An understanding of these processes helps towards a fuller appreciation of the ancient deities, which can be studied in detail from surviving images and written accounts.

Early man may have differed from his modern descendants in being slightly nearer to the animal kingdom, and therefore his instincts would have been much keener. The growth of civilisation and mental development, especially through literacy, has tended towards a neglect in man's use of natural instincts and they have become buried in the deeper parts of the brain. Unfortunately, most people tend to mistrust these feelings because they are usually so illogical. In this way, telepathy and water-divining are contemptuously dismissed with all other manifestations of psychic insight as trickery, since there is no scientific proof although many examples are well authenticated.

Animal herds and flocks of birds possess interlocked instincts which make them instantly aware of danger and also give them the ability for instantaneous group movement. This is best illustrated in the flight of birds which wheel and swoop in perfect unison. This fusing of instincts is common to those societies which live together in clearly unified groups, and becomes part of the practice of imitative magic, as anthropologists have observed many times.[4] It survives today, but only at moments of emotional intensity and between people in close attune such as when a crowd or enclosed group is held by strong emotion, especially fear. Crowds panic under the sudden threat of fire, riot or similar happenings, and in these conditions normally sensible individuals lose their self-control and the ability to think logically, and disasters can follow. This loss of an individual's ability to reason or think for himself is also seen at religious and political meetings when the whole audience is caught in a mass emotional response and accepts ideas which, as individuals, they would probably reject. This mass emotion has often been exploited by unscrupulous people who gain satisfaction from having an audience under their control; it can be highly dangerous in the hands of propagandists like Hitler, and less harmful, though still potent, in the hands of advertisers who deliberately use sophisticated forms of mass-hypnosis in order to sell their wares. A remarkable example of the effects of mass emotion is seen in the synchronised outbreaks of singing at football matches, and it is also responsible for much of the crowd trouble, which is accentuated by the lack of outlet for the highly-charged adolescent emotion in modern society.

The close mental interaction in primitive communities results in the groups acting in unison and the development of individual thinking thereby reduced. Religious ritual was always a group activity and, as such, this survives today in the church congregation and service. Many people are more comfortable exercising their religion in groups of like-minded people than as individuals; but in confining themselves to this practice, people have tended to reduce their religion into mere social occasions. In more primitive communities all individuals conformed to group practice, and any individual who failed and took independent action was immediately ostracised, since the group could not exist without total coherence. This fear is still present in people today, and most suppress their natural inclinations for the sake of social conformity. This can, of course, be constructive if the inclinations are anti-social or highly inimical to particular individuals.

To summarise even further, the origins of religion can be seen as early man's attempt to adjust to the forces and annual cycle of nature, in order to survive as communities. The result of the interlocked minds of all the individuals in the group was social cohesion, which was an essential protection against sudden threats. As man slowly developed from hunting to pastoralism and agriculture and thence to permanent settlement and the growth of industry and extensive relations with other peoples, the ancient mental and social ties which bound individuals together gradually weakened, though the fear and respect for the unseen world remained. Any change or break in the ritual cycle was thought to give serious offence to the gods, so religious beliefs and practices continued much in their original form, to the point of becoming fossilised. This rigid conservatism is best seen in Rome, where ancient rituals were carefully repeated every year and hymns chanted in an archaic Latin which no one understood. Even today in the Catholic Church the Latin Mass survives, although many worshippers understand little of the words uttered. However, the benefit from the preservation of ancient practices is that it helps the student of religion to trace surviving ritual back to earlier forms and may even provide a basis for an approach towards an understanding of its origins.

The Greek ethnographers and geographers

Most of our literary evidence for the Celts comes from the Greek ethnographers and geographers, either directly or from extracts copied by later writers. The Greeks were always curious about the world around them; this was partly a result of their enquiring minds, but also had a practical purpose, stemming from their maritime activities in trading and colonising along the shores of the Mediterranean and Black Sea. Their navigators needed detailed information about the coastal terrain and the sea routes taken by their ships. The colonies planted on the shores of distant places had to come to terms with the local inhabitants and establish trading relationships with them; knowledge of their customs and socio-economy were thus essential. Some of the pilots' logs, known as *peripli*, survived into Roman times, and the most famous of these is that of Pytheas, who circumnavigated Britain in about 325 BC. His book, *On the Ocean*, of which fragments survive,[5] is mainly a geography, based on astronomical observations, which continued to be used for centuries. Another, *Ora Maritima*, is only known from a late fourth-century edition by Festus Rufius Avienus, but is clearly derived from a *periplus* of the western Mediterranean of the sixth century BC, though with later additions.[6]

Greek contacts with the great nations of the East followed the conquests of Alexander and brought them closer to the exotic mysteries of even more distant peoples. This new source of information was attractive to the historians and geographers and they regaled their readers with the travellers' tales of remote peoples with strange customs. The accounts of the extraordinary and diverse religions of India show utter bewilderment at their complexity. The Cynics and Stoics were sympathetic towards remote uncivilised peoples, since they detected in them a simplicity of life and lack of interest in material wealth-concepts which appear in the imaginary Utopias created by Plato and his followers. This factor caused the ethnographers to select those elements from their limited information which, adapted to this pattern, would give the greatest delectation to their readers.

This selection and emphasis on particular aspects emerges from the work of the greatest of all the Greek ethnographers, Posidonius (135–51 BC). Unfortunately, only fragments of his work have survived in other writers, namely Athenaeus, Diodorus Siculus, Strabo and Caesar. In some cases the copyists acknowledge their source; in others, especially Caesar, they were not so obliging. (These fragments have been skilfully studied by Professor Tierney,[7] and his conclusions, which are accepted by most scholars, have been taken as accurate for the purpose of this study.) Posidonius was also the greatest Stoic philosopher of his day and it seems only natural that in his ethnographic studies he gave greater space and thought to the religious ideas and practices of the various peoples he described.[8] Diodorus (v, 28, 6) records his view that the Celts believed strongly in the Pythagorean ideas about the immortality of the soul, and supports this with evidence that mourners cast letters written to the dead onto

19

the funeral pyre, which Tierney finds 'incredible' and a misreporting of the rite of placing personal possessions with the burial. Caesar tells us that the Celts of Gaul had considerable knowledge of the movements of heavenly bodies (as would be necessary for their accurate use of a calendar), and also of the size of the earth, of natural philosophy and of the powers and operations of the gods (*BG* vi, 14, 6). This must represent a very heavily compressed section of Posidonius, who could hardly have refrained from an extensive discussion of this aspect of Celtic belief, but who probably rationalised the limited information he had gleaned into a cosmology which Greeks and Romans would be able to identify with their own. This is precisely what Caesar did in listing the Roman deities of Mars, Apollo, Jupiter, Mercury and Minerva instead of their Celtic equivalents. It is clear from our knowledge of Celtic mythology, derived from the surviving Irish legends, that the Celts had no cosmological hierarchy, or a remote dwelling place for their gods, but believed that the human and spirit worlds formed a unity in space and time. While Greeks and Romans may have found this a difficult concept, it was accepted as the ways of life and death by the great illiterate masses of Europe.

The attitudes of the Romans towards the Celts

One of the most important influences on Roman ideas about their barbarian neighbours was the Greek philosophers. It was fashionable for young Romans of noble birth to have a Greek education, although there were those like Cato the Elder who maintained a stern Republican tradition and were bitterly opposed to all Hellenic influences. Many students went to Athens or had Greek tutors, and in southern Gaul was the renowned university at Massilia where the young Agricola was sent. Tacitus, his son-in-law, notes in a significant aside that Agricola's mother was concerned over his growing interest in philosophy, as it was considered a dangerous subject for a young man embarking on a senatorial career. Nevertheless, all we know about Agricola stamps him as a Stoic. Tacitus also held this philosophy but successfully disguised it, although it undoubtedly influenced his thinking and writing.

The main concepts of Stoicism, and its begetter Cynicism, were self-control and independence. The Stoic tried to live in harmony with nature and practised an indifference to all external factors. This meant the control of his emotions, even pity and sorrow. The Stoics rejected the existence of gods and goddesses and taught the presence of a universal life-force, into which the shades of the dead could merge, if a life of virtue[9] had been led (though the word *virtus* had far greater implications for a Roman than it does today).[10] One of the greatest Roman Stoics was Seneca, whose ideas of self-control and self-dependence are revealed clearly in his letters. It was in the times of Imperial tyranny under Gaius, Nero and Domitian that the Stoics were most severely tested, and many forced into suicide. The attitude of Tacitus towards the Celts was largely conditioned by his Stoic training and Republican sympathies: he was prepared to praise those who fought bravely against Rome and especially those who behaved with dignity in defeat. This explains his treatment of Caratacus in his triumph over Claudius in Rome. He tells us that the British king maintained a silent dignity with head held high, never a downcast glance or a plea for pity.[11]

Tacitus also displayed a great admiration for the Germans, even praising Arminius who had lured three legions to destruction, but this may have been to enable him to insert a terse but significant ending to Book Two of his *Annals* with the words, '*Romanis haud perinde celebris, dum vetera extollimus recentium incuriosi*' ([Arminius] has not been given his full due by Romans who, while glorying in their ancient days, care naught for the events of their own times).[12]

The account by Tacitus of the Germans in his *Germania* is one of the few serious Roman ethnographic accounts of a barbarian people. He probably borrowed much of it from the lost work of Posidonius and from another lost book on the German wars by Pliny the Elder.[13] It is difficult to understand exactly why Tacitus chose to write the *Germania*, though the motive most attractive to the leading authority Sir Ronald Syme is the real fear Tacitus had of the Germans as a threat to the Empire.[14] The timing of this book is an important consideration and it can be ascribed with some precision to AD 98, the second year of Trajan's reign. It could be that Tacitus was drawing the Emperor's attention to what he considered was a menace to the most military of all Emperors, at a time when he was in the Rhineland. There is, however, undoubtedly a secondary motive, as Syme states that 'in language . . . heavily charged with moralising' Tacitus was making a sharp contrast between Rome and what he saw as a primitive people unsullied by the greedy commerce of the sophisticated urban society of his own day. He described the monogamous virtues of the Germans, whose unmarried women lived in a state of impregnable chastity, and who punished rare instances of adultery with flogging and public humiliation. The youth were not hurried into matrimony but preserved their strength until maturity, in contrast to the debauchery among the youthful nobility of Rome. A typically pointed epigram was directed at the Romans, who were proud of their legal code but lived such scandalous lives.[15]

Tacitus was echoing an ancient theme one can trace back to the Greeks of a concept of primitive societies beyond the limits of civilisation as innocent children of nature – a theme to reappear in later centuries, especially in the European Age of Enlightenment of the seventeenth–eighteenth centuries, when tales of the North American Indians began to circulate. They were seen as people who had escaped the Fall of Adam and were thus free of original sin. But, as anthropologists were later to discover, these simple natives had a highly integrated and complicated self-perpetuating social-religious system, from which there was no escape.

The Roman from whom we learn much about the Celts is Caesar, who undoubtedly took much of his information from Posidonius. He did, of course, have personal contact with many Celts and was in a good position to describe them and their way of life in detail. He did not regard such aspects as relevant to his main purpose, however, but he was fascinated by methods of warfare, and so we can learn about their equipment and tactics, not forgetting his vivid detailed description of the British chariots in action. But the evidence of Caesar has to be handled with care, since his main purpose in writing was to minimise and justify his outrageous conduct directed to securing a vast fortune for himself to pursue his political ambitions, unaided by his wealthy but uncertain patrons. The information he gives about the Druids must be considered suspect, since he gives them a key role as judges and advisers to the tribal kings. He may have been responsible for instilling into Roman minds a great fear of the Druids as a potent political and religious force. This emerges in a strange incident related by Pliny the Elder, at the time of Claudius, of a Roman knight of Gallic origin who, during the hearing of a law suit, was found to have a 'Druids egg' on his person, and was summarily executed.[16] This object, according to Pliny, was called a '*urinum*'[17] but from his description 'like a round apple of medium size and remarkable for its hard covering, pitted with many gristly cup-hollows', it would seem possible that this natural object was an oak-apple. Its growth on oak trees would have given it a special magic symbolism. However, in an earlier passage[18] Pliny describes various kinds of oak-apple, and thus should have known one when he saw it. Druids claimed that the possessors of this strange object were victorious in the law courts, and in gaining access to important people. It may have been the introduction of magic into the law courts which caused so much alarm, rather than any association with Druids, but Tiberius felt it necessary to expel them from Gaul,[19] and Claudius utterly abolished their cruel and inhuman religion.[20]

Another important aspect of Rome's attitude towards barbarians was governed by the Romans' strong sense of law and justice. The breaking of treaties by other peoples was seen as an outrage and created the feeling among Romans that all barbarians were untrustworthy. Nevertheless, there was always an interest in other people's law codes and methods of trial. Caesar describes the Druids in terms his Roman readers could understand, and may have overstressed their powerful and unifying influence to alert Rome to the danger they presented. No other account of the Druids sees them in quite this role.

CHAPTER TWO

CELTIC RELIGION, BELIEFS, PRACTICES AND ORGANISATION

Religion can generally be considered under three main headings: beliefs, practices and organisation, the latter two of which include the special places and structures associated with these functions. It is impossible to know what the Celts actually believed, since there is no surviving original statement in an ancient text. As seen above, the statement by Posidonius that the Celts subscribed to the teaching of Pythagoras concerning the transmigration of souls (Diodorus, V, 28; *BG* vii, 14) is highly suspect. Some Celtic traders must have had personal connections with a section of the commercial dealers in Massilia, but it is hardly likely that such erudite matters would be discussed. Caesar had opportunities to study Celtic beliefs, had he so wished, but he merely stated that all the Gauls were excessively religious (*BG* vi, 16); the word he used, *religio*, covers all aspects of belief and practice, and he may well have observed some of the latter before and after battles.

The only possible approach to this subject may be in the surviving of the myths and legends which were recounted by the bards, but only committed to writing by the early Christian monks, especially in Ireland. Some of their manuscripts were composed in the eighth century, and in all there survives a large body of literature,[1] while for Wales the *Mabinogion* has preserved some of the early legends. The monks selected their material and in some places introduced elements of Christian morality, but it is remarkable how much has been preserved. These tales of dazzling richness, invention and drama, while including eighth-century details and styles, illuminate the Celtic attitude to the great unseen world and clearly demonstrate the love for stories of great intricacy. It soon becomes apparent that, unlike the Greeks and Romans, the Celts had no hierarchical cosmology with a family of gods and goddesses dwelling on a remote mountain top, like Olympus, and engaged in much the same kind of petty squabbling as the mortals. The Celts fully accepted that the spirit world was integrated into their own material one, and there was no separation between man and the spirits, all living together side by side, here, there and everywhere.[2] The dwellings of the spirits are in the natural features which form the landscape, particularly the lakes, rivers and springs, but also the woods and hills. In Ireland every ancient burial mound has its resident spirit and this may explain why they have not been so extensively robbed as in other parts of the British Isles. As all the spirits were individually associated with their place of abode, it follows that each tribe and community within the tribe had their own family of unseen creatures, and a continuous dialogue was maintained by conjuring them by name when needed, and by gestures of placation in the form of gifts and sacrifices. Such a permanent bond and communication implies a total unity between the spiritual and temporal. There were times when the spirits came together, as on the eve of the great feast of Samain which became All Hallows Eve. Interaction between the two worlds was also possible, but only through special mortals such as the tribal hero.

The Druids

The Druids remain one of the most controversial but fascinating aspects of Celtic religion. They have been the subject of much modern fiction, to the extent that when Stuart Piggott wrote his excellent study[3] he felt obliged to devote a whole chapter to the 'Romantic Image'. Yet Posidonius, according to his copiers,[4] gives a picture of Druids as learned scholars and teachers. Diodorus describes them as 'philosophers and theologians who were treated with special honour' (v, 31, 2). Strabo distinguishes the three grades – the *Bards*, the singers and poets, the *Vates*, the interpreters of sacrifice and natural philosophers, and the *Druids*, who studied moral philosophy.[5] Caesar, as related above (p. 22) portrayed the Druids as a powerful political force, and he is the only source of information that they were arbitrators of disputes and judges of criminal cases, with wide powers of punishment. Tierney has shown (his p. 214) that this was derived from Posidonius, but that it happened to suit Caesar's political ambitions to advise the Senate of the threat that the Druids posed to Rome. Posidonius saw the Druids as the Celtic equivalent of the Greek schools of philosophy and teaching, and thus his account was written with the knowledge that his Greek readers would have an instant appreciation of the familiar comparison. Posidonius has received some support from those who point to the famous schools at Massilia, which, it is argued, must have influenced the Druids.[6] It is quite possible that some Druids may have been attracted to Massilia, out of curiosity, but it seems very unlikely that it would have caused them to change the content or direction of their teaching in matters concerning Celtic beliefs. It is interesting to note that the Druids used Greek when it was necessary for them to commit anything to writing.[7]

The Posidonian account differs markedly from that of Caesar, who stressed the political and judicial importance of the Druids, which would have isolated them as a significant group with which Rome had come to terms. The question is whether Caesar deliberately exaggerated to make his point, or did he have access to a source which remains unknown? An argument for his veracity must be based on his undoubted personal experience with actual Druids, and with

Diviciacus in particular. This chief of the Aedui had become acquainted with Cicero while on a diplomatic mission to Rome. The great Roman orator records that Diviciacus could predict the future by augury[8] and refers to him as a Druid. He was of great assistance to Caesar in persuading some of the tribes to collaborate with Rome, and he depended on him to form alliances which enabled him to proceed rapidly with the conquest; but at no time does Caesar ever refer to him as a Druid. He must have known this but chose to suppress the fact, as Diviciacus was so useful to him. Yet he makes a special point about the Druids as political agents capable of inspiring strong anti-Roman sentiments, and organising a resistance movement. This view was more likely to have been based on the character and activities of Dumnorix,[9] the brother of Diviciacus, than the latter, although Caesar gives no hint that he also was a Druid.

The concept of the Druids as a significant political force was perpetuated by the Alexandrian School of the first and second centuries. In particular Dio Chrysostom[10] stressed their role as rather more than advisers to Celtic chiefs and kings, stating that they were not allowed to make decisions without Druidic authority; but this vision of these priests sitting on golden thrones in their palaces is obviously a rhetorical hyperbole. The scholars of the Alexandrian School were more interested in the philosophical concepts of the Druids than their organisation and political status, and were attempting to identify and classify them in relation to Greek, Persian, Egyptian and Indian ideas and practices. This could have stemmed from the statement by Posidonius that the Druids had absorbed the teaching of Pythagoras,[11] especially on life after death.

Pliny the Elder is the one classical source which is at total variance with all the others. The detailed account he gives of a ceremony conducted by Druids is the origin of most of the modern misconceptions of the Druids. He tells us they are called magicians[12] and seems to depict them as shamans or medicine men performing ritual and magical acts, rather than philosophers or high priests and political advisers. This view is in line with a late Irish source where they are classed as magicians or *magi*; there is a vivid account of the chief Druid to the King of Ireland, who wore a bull's hide with the head-dress of a white speckled bird.[13] Pliny's description of the Druidic rites is given as a tail-piece to his book on trees (XVI), and immediately after a section on the three kinds of mistletoe (245–8) and their use as a bird-lime when pounded and made into a paste mixed with oil. He begins in a manner which suggests that what follows is a casual afterthought: 'while on the subject one should not omit the veneration paid in Gaul to this plant and the tree on which it grows, providing it is a hard oak' (249). It is in the groves of these trees that the Druids perform their rites. He adds that it is thought that their name came from the Greek word for oak ($\delta\rho\hat{\nu}\varsigma$)[14] and adds that the Druids thought that the growth of mistletoe on any tree was a special sign from the sky. The plant was gathered with ceremony on the sixth day of the moon, which was linked with the Celtic calendar. A priest in white climbed the tree and cut the mistletoe with a golden sickle.[15] The word used for the priest is *sacerdos*; this may indicate that the Druids did not perform this rite and that it was probably done by the *Vates*, who were responsible for such rituals. There was then a sacrifice of two white bulls, and a feast. Pliny adds that it was believed that a drink prepared from mistletoe[16] gave fertility to a barren animal. The final sentence (251) is almost an apology to the readers for introducing something so worthless, but he adds that some races hold such matters in very great awe.[17]

Another classical source for the Druids' association with woods is Marcus Annaeus Lucanus (AD 39–65), who wrote an epic poem on the civil war (De Bello Civili; also known as the Pharsalia). He describes (i, 450) in highly poetic terms how Caesar's great successes in Gaul, in the early stages of the civil war, were not thwarted even by the wrath of the gods. He refers to the Bards (bardi) and the Druids (dryadae) returning to their barbarian rites and rituals, with the scathing comment that to them also has been revealed the secrets of the universe, inferring rather pointedly that, like many other religious sects, they were the only ones who believed they were right. He then tells us that they dwelt in deep forests with enclosed groves (nemora alta remotis incolitis lucis).[18] Lucan continues his caustic summary with the Druidic belief in the after-life; if it is true, he adds, that death is merely an incident in a continued existence, how happily are these peoples deceived and freed from the terrors of death which gives the warriors the courage to plunge into the fray, regardless of the outcome. This lack of fear is a well-established Stoic concept and it was natural for Lucan, the nephew and pupil of Seneca, to have adopted this philosophy.

Later in the poem there is an episode in the siege of Massilia, which had been seized by the Pompeians. Caesar's plan was to seal off the city to allow him to proceed with his rapid advance to Spain. He decided, therefore, to surround the city's defences with a great circumvallation, and for this he needed enormous quantities of timber, and forests were felled over a wide area. While engaged in this arduous task, Caesar's troops found hidden in the depths of one of the forests an ancient grove which had never been violated by the hands of men. The interlacing boughs tightly enclosed the space in permanent shade,[19] where gods were placated with barbarous rites on altars heaped with hideous offerings (structae diris altaribus arae) and every tree daubed with human blood. Figures of the gods were grimly and crudely carved on felled trunks. There were further signs and portents to strike terror into the hearts of the soldiers. The very ground quaked; the trees seemed to be on fire and serpents glided round them. Caesar ordered its destruction but the troops were paralysed with fear of the instant retribution by these powerful spirits. So Caesar, in a typical gesture, seized an axe and embedded its blade in one of the oaks, crying out, 'If I am guilty of sacrilege, you need never fear'. Although they were not fully convinced, the soldiers set to work with the realisation that the wrath of Caesar was more immediate, and stronger, than that of the barbarous gods. Nowhere in the highly detailed, although over-fanciful, account is there any mention of Druids.

Another Celtic grove which comes readily to mind is, of course, that described by Tacitus in his account of the attack of Suetonius Paullinus on Anglesea, immediately prior to the Boudican revolt. The sombre picture he paints of altars slaked with the blood of prisoners[20] has a distinct echo of Lucan. While it may be necessary to treat the information Caesar gives about the Druids with scepticism, there is little doubt that there was a serious antipathy towards these priests in Rome. This may have been due to their efforts to foster anti-Roman sentiment among the Gallic and British tribal rulers or simply to the rumours that they practised human sacrifices, for which there is no substantial evidence. The fact remains that, according to Pliny, Tiberius expelled them from Gaul,[21] while later Claudius is said to have completely abolished their cruel and inhuman religion which Augustus had merely forbidden to Roman citizens.[22] Pliny also tells us that Britain practised the magic arts up to his own day in such a grand manner that one might imagine she had given them to the Persians.[23] The practice of magic and astrology was much feared in Rome, especially by the Imperial circle, and there are many examples of the expulsion of these foreign elements from Rome.[24] So the Druids may not be entirely to blame in this matter, as in the strange case of the Druids egg related above (p. 22). Any religion which appeared to conflict with the State and the Imperial Cult was anathema and this must be regarded as the basis of Rome's attitude towards the Druids.

The Celtic hero

The world of the Celts was so constantly beset by the hostile spirits in the forms of storms, tempests, floods, crop-failure and pestilence on man and beast that ritual appeasement was necessary, but not enough. The tribe needed its own superman to watch over it and protect the territory from invasion by malignant forces. It was out of this need for a powerful ally who had been one of themselves that the idea of the hero took root and flourished. He had to be a mortal or semi-divine, imbued with special powers to match those of the spirit world.

Sétanta of northern Ireland, known also as Cú Chulainn, can be cited as an example.[25] He was reputed to be the son of Lug, one of the most powerful of all the Celtic gods and a late-comer linked with the introduction of agriculture into pastoral communities. Sétanta formed a union with the King's sister, Dechtine, in strange and confused circumstances – another common feature of Celtic stories. Some thought the union had been between King Conchobar and his sister, in itself by no means unusual and held in high regard as a sacred act in some parts of the world. The child had to pass initiation tests with the other male children, firstly into manhood and later to gain warrior status. The child hero was highly precocious, especially with weapons; Sétanta was attacked by 159 young boys who threw their hurley sticks at him, but he prevented any from striking him. To become a warrior he was obliged to pass through a series of ordeals against strange demons and phantoms, armed only with his hurley stick, which was, nevertheless, adequate to chop off the head of one of the monsters, and drive it furiously across the fields as if it was a hurley ball. On becoming a full warrior he was given special weapons and armour, often with magical properties.

The hero had quite extraordinary attributes, including being able to turn round in his skin – a strange phenomenon which may be associated with cataleptic fits, practised by shamans or witch-doctors, especially when prophesying or truth-seeking. When in this condition, the hair of the hero stood on end and a drop of blood or a spark appeared at the tip of each hair, a gush of fire came from his mouth and a fountain of black blood from the top of his head. One of his eyes receded into his skull while the other swelled to enormous size, and what is described as the 'Hero's moon' emanated from his skull. When the hero entered a meeting of the tribe he always did so in a violent manner against all custom, often on a horse. He broke all normal patterns of behaviour and acted with an exaggeration of the Celtic traits, especially that of arrogance. He was the quintessence of all the qualities held dear by the Celts, but magnified into super-heroic form. In appearance, to quote Sjoestedt (1949, p. 67)

> He is beautiful, of a beauty rather baroque than classic, which corresponds in some points to the ideal suggested by the figurines on Gaulish coins, and the descriptions given by ancient historians of the continental Celts. His hair, of three colours, brown on the crown of his head, red in the middle and fringed with gold, forms a triple braid before it falls in ringlets on his shoulders. A hundred strings of jewels decorate his head, a hundred collars of gold glitter on his breast. His cheeks are flushed with four colours, yellow, blue, green and red. Seven pupils shine in each eye, his hands have seven fingers, his feet seven toes. Thus the sacred number is inscribed all over his person. Holding nine captured heads in one hand and ten in the other, he juggles with them, parading happily before the people and offering himself to the admiration of poets, craftsmen and women.

The next stage of his life was his marriage, but, a choice having been made, he was forced to undergo more ordeals in the course of a long journey into remote regions inhabited by powerful spirit rulers. The purpose of the journey was often to seek and bring back some unobtainable object, and Sétanta had to subdue by force and magic a series of queens and female monsters. When eventually he returned to collect his bride, the castle was barred against him and he had to make a forcible entry and abduct her. The seizure of women is a recurrent theme in primitive society and probably necessary to bring fresh blood into a closed community. The classical story of the rape of the Sabine women is an example.

An important characteristic of the hero is his vulnerability, since he is mortal. He has to die, but always under spectacular circumstances. The hero is often rendered vulnerable by breaking a tribal taboo. Sétanta, for example, was cunningly trapped by the three daughters of Calatin, who had been slain by Sétanta with his twenty-seven sons. His wife, Queen Medb, had produced six posthumous babies at a single birth and she turned them into sorcerers to exact revenge. One taboo prohibited Sétanta from crossing a hearth without eating and another from eating dog-flesh. The three women were roasting a dog over a hearth, forcing him to eat the forbidden animal in order to pass. Even so, he continued a struggle of epic dimensions until he was eventually slain, after being disarmed. His head was presented to his wife, who was then obliged to die and be buried with him.

Religious practices

Caesar tells us that the Gauls were much devoted to ritual practices, especially in making vows and offering sacrifices to appease the gods, both in public and private (*BG* vi, 16). He was obviously seeing the Celtic practices in the light of his knowledge of those regularly enacted in Rome. Caesar even gives a list of the most popular Gallic deities as Mars, Mercury, Apollo, Jupiter and Minerva (*BG* vi, 17), but here again he was guilty of interpreting Celtic religion in Roman terms and he could not possibly have made this simple equation if he had really understood the Celtic mythology. Yet while there were undoubtedly fundamental differences in both beliefs and practices in the two different worlds, there were basic links which can be applied to most early religions. People were much closer to the spirits, especially in the rural areas, than we are today.

The lives of both Romans and Celts were governed by sets of rules and prohibitions. The latter is a form of negative magic which has been given the Polynesian word *taboo* by modern anthropologists.[26] Some of these prohibitions, to which the Romans gave the term *castus multiplices*, were a form of imitative magic, as in the examples given by Pliny the Elder of clasping the hands with interlaced fingers, or crossing the legs, which must never be done in the presence of pregnant women. Such postures were also forbidden in councils of war or official business, since it prevented any conclusions being reached; nor was it allowed at attendance of any religious ritual.[27] There were also severe restraints imposed on the *Flamen Dialis*, one of the highest priesthoods in Rome associated with Jupiter.[28] He was not allowed to ride a horse, or wear a ring unless it was incomplete, or even have a knot in his girdle or any part of his clothing. His hair could be cut only by a free man, and all the nail trimmings and hair cuttings must be carefully collected and buried under a healthy tree. If a prisoner was brought in chains into his house, he must be released and the chains hoisted through the *impluvium* of the roof onto the roof-tiles and cast into the street below. The wife of the *Flamen* was also subject to a number of strange prohibitions. There were special purification ceremonies people had to undergo. New-born babies had to be purified, girls on the eighth day after birth and boys on the ninth, and at the same time names were given, as in the modern baptism. On reaching the age of puberty, another purification was needed, and after a death the whole family and the house had to be given purification, even the funeral procession by stepping over fire. Thus Romans protected themselves by a kind of disinfection, as Warde Fowler put it.[29] All these practices were derived from primitive magic, but such was the extraordinary conservatism of the Romans in religious matters that their rituals were perpetuated over centuries.

The Celts called taboo *geis* (*geasa* in the plural). The most common *geasa* were often related to food, and such rigorous prohibitions must have had an origin in bad or tainted meat being eaten with dire consequences to a community, especially if it had occurred at a ritual feast. Some of these food taboos are purely sympathetic or imitative magic, such as that prohibiting the eating of horse flesh before setting forth on a chariot. These food prohibitions may also be linked with the tribal totems of animals and birds. Another practice was the taboo on straightening out a spear with the teeth; this must go back to the period of untempered iron,[30] but the significance is that spear-tips were often poisoned. Daily life for the Celts must have been considerably inhibited by needful, positive and negative acts of appeasement and avoidance. Many of these taboos survive in modern societies, especially those which still closely adhere to traditional customs, like the Jews and some of the Islamic sects.

At a somewhat lower level, certain objects and actions were lucky or unlucky (*matis* and *anmatis*) to the Celts. Certain movements always had to be in the direction of the sun, and it was very unlucky to go in the reverse way – 'Widdershins' or 'Withershins', as it became known. This governed the serving of drinks at the feasts, and is still observed in the circulation of port. It also applied to certain days which are those designated on the fragments of bronze plates, known as the Coligny Calendar,[31] the largest single Celtic written record. The Romans had precisely the same idea and their calendar had days which were *nefas* (unlucky) and on which no public functions could be held. Even today, some people regard Fridays as unlucky, especially if they are on the 13th, and carry out acts of propitiation, like bowing seven times to the new moon and saluting magpies. This continuation of very primitive rituals is still deeply rooted in many societies, however 'civilised' they may claim to be.

The seasonal festivals

The public rituals were very closely related to the seasonal festivals. The progression of the earth in its orbit round the sun, with the regular changing of the seasons, has been recognised and observed by similar rituals all over the world. Man has always been deeply affected by the daily turning of the earth on its axis, and the changes from day to night with the progress of the sun across the sky and the monthly cycle of the moon. But above all, it was through the awesome majesty of the heavens seen in clear Near Eastern desert conditions that man first came to be affected by the powerful sky elements beyond human reach, but which could seriously influence him. It was, therefore, natural that early man should begin to imagine within the starry constellations, shapes of recognisable creatures. Observations over a long period of time led to the knowledge of the annual pattern of movement, apart from the independent orbits of the planets. Add to this the monthly cycle of the moon, and a calendar is created, which would make evident the fact that the seasons followed the same annual pattern.

Later the Chaldean astrologers developed the zodiacal system and laid down the basis of astrology.[32] The Near Eastern priests soon appreciated that this knowledge could provide them with powerful magic, since it was possible to calculate in advance the times for the control of the agricultural seasons, the grazing and procreation of animals and the planting and harvesting of crops. This knowledge was a closely guarded secret and the priests appointed themselves as agents of the major celestial and earth spirits, which provided them with power over the whole of the community. In predicting the times for seasonal husbandry and crop-management, they were able to persuade the people that they were actually creating the seasonal changes. This is best seen in the case of the flooding of the Nile, which brought the richly silt-laden waters to rejuvenate the soils in the valley floor every year.

With the growth of knowledge of the seasons, there also developed the pattern of rituals, rigorously followed and directed by the priestly craft to show thankful appreciation to the appropriate unseen powers. Chief among them was undoubtedly the sun – the fount of heat, life and energy – which, in conjunction with the earth spirits, was responsible for the annual rebirth of vegetation and animal fecundity. The seasonal rituals take much the same form in many societies. The spring festival is a joyous time of new life springing from the ground, so it is a period of renewal and purification, of which Lent in the Christian calendar is an excellent example, linked with Easter and the resurrection myth. Autumn in north-western Europe is harvest time, or, in a pastoral society, the movement of the animals from the summer grazing ground to the settlement for protection in the winter. It is a period of thanksgiving for the food supply and fire-lighting to help the waning sun renew its power.

The Celtic calendar and the festival of Samain

The four principal Celtic festivals embody elements of an earlier pastoral society and the later introduction of agriculture. The Celtic year begins on the autumnal equinox, 1st November, with the great festival of Samain[33] which became the Christian Martinmass. It is the time in many parts of the world when annual contracts or agreements are ended or renewed and it is also time to give thanks for the harvest now gathered in and the grazing animals brought down from their upland grazing for the winter; the old and diseased animals are slaughtered and eaten in the great feasting, or salted or pickled down for the winter. The Celts believed that on the eve of Samain all the spirits emerge from their dwellings in the hills, springs, lakes, rivers and ancient burial mounds (*síde*), an idea which became the Christian Hallowe'en. Some spirits in human form turn into birds, often linked together with silver or gold chains – an idea closely associated with bird migration and the extraordinary flight patterns, as if all the birds are physically linked. There are some beautiful Irish legends about these birds, such as the wooing of Óengus[34] and Cáer Ibormeith, who eventually came together on the eve of Samain by the Loch Bel Dracon, where Óengus 'saw three flights of white birds, with silver chains and golden hair about their heads'. He called to Cáer and she came to him and 'they slept in the form of swans until they had circled the lake three times and they flew away together'.[35] It was at this time too that the tribal god Dagda had intercourse with the earth and water spirit Morrígan, Queen of the Demons, by the River Unius in Connaught.

The great feasts of gargantuan eating and drinking were closely linked with

31

the enormous cauldrons of the gods which could never be emptied. At Samain a hole was dug and food for the gods poured into it. This is reflected in the tale of Dagda in the camp of his enemy, the Fomorians, on the eve of Samain. They filled the king's cauldron, which held twenty measures of milk and many more of flour and fat, and into it put goats and sheep, halves of pork and quarters of lambs, boiling the whole mixture and then pouring it into a hole in the ground. Dagda's ladle was large enough for a man and a woman to lie in it together. He ate the whole meal and ran his fingers round the gravel bottom to catch the final drops.

The winter solstice

The Celts apparently did not have any festival for the winter solstice when the Romans held their Saturnalia, which was replaced by Christmas under the early Christian fathers. The next festival in the Celtic calendar was Imbolc or Oímelg, celebrated on 1st February. It was based on the old pastoral lambing season and therefore had powerful fertility associations. Little is known about it, presumably as it was mainly practised by the women and carried out in secret, away from profane male eyes. The festival was sacred to Brigit, the daughter of Dagda. She was a powerful and widespread native goddess linked with fertility, healing and wisdom, presumably of sacred matters. She became the titular goddess of the Brigantes, the largest confederacy of tribes in Britain; the name is also found of the Brigantii near Lake Constance, thus giving the name to modern Bregenz.

A hint of the Celtic practices comes from Kildare in Ireland, where the Christianised St Brigid was venerated by nine virgins, who tended her perpetual sacred fire in the Middle Ages.[36] Fires were an important part of the mid-winter rituals, and this continued into Victorian times, symbolised by the yule log, and even today by lights on Christmas trees. Others are preserved in our harvest festivals and bonfire night, oddly now connected with a very minor historical figure. At the winter solstice, when the sun is at its lowest heat and point of the heavens, the ritual demands more fires to help magically restore its strength; hence the yule logs and revelry of Saturnalia, wisely appropriated by the early Christian fathers as Christmas, displacing the birthday of Mithras, an Eastern deity, and later *Sol Invictus*, which had previously taken possession of this important part of the Roman calendar.

The spring festival of Beltine

The vernal equinox was, and still is, widely celebrated, as new vegetation suddenly appears and living things all feel a great upsurge. The constant theme is renewal and resurrection as the world wakes from its winter death. It was a great Celtic May Day festival, associated with the god Belenus, and was called Beltine, Beltaine or Cétshamain, which means Bel's fire.[37] The rituals included fire-lighting, in imitation of the sun's growing power and purification, and cattle being driven through lanes of flames before being taken out to the summer pastures. It is closely paralleled with the Roman festival of Parilia or Palilia, the worship of Pales on 21st April, an early pastoral ritual for the shepherds and herdsmen.[38] As Fraser has indicated, this festival survived as St George's Day in

England and Russia and he quotes Thomas Pennant, as late as 1769, giving details of the 'Bel-Tien' ceremonies in the Highlands, in which milk, eggs and butter were offered, and special oatcakes, each with nine square knobs, were part-eaten and part-offered to the spirits.[39]

While it was basically a pastoral festival, closely linked with the animals, including, in some areas, horses, it was also a vegetation and agricultural ceremony involving the Green Man, the Green George or Jack on the Green, with the dancers jumping and leaping to encourage the fertility and growth of the crops, helped by men and women coupling in the fields. This probably goes back to the Celts and would have been part of the great feasting and sacrifices.[40] May Day continues to be celebrated, but has now degenerated into political rallies, though the true survival is in the Christian adaptation of the Easter resurrection myth; it is also comparable to the Jewish Passover, in itself a spring festival.

The mid-summer or harvest festival of Lughnasa[41]

The mid-summer festival celebrated on 1st August was Lughnasa, which became the Christian Lammas (or loaf-mass).[42] It was a time of great assemblies lasting a month, usually starting in mid-July with much feasting, mock fighting (a vague echo, perhaps, of the great battles of early legend between mortals and spirits), and horse races. The name derives from the Celtic god Lugos, who was one of the most important and widely revered gods in the Celtic world. As the name means 'light' it can be assumed that Lugos was the Celtic sun-god and accepted by the Romans as the equivalent of their Apollo. The name was incorporated in a number of place names,[43] of which the most important was Lugdunum (Lyon), the principal Roman city of Gaul, where the provincial *concilium* met, and 1st August was set aside for the celebration of Augustus and the Capitoline Triad. Lugos was a magician and the god of the craftsmen, and also became linked with Mercury.[44] It is evident from the legends that Lugos was a newcomer and had to win his place in the Celtic hierarchy. There are clear indications that Lug (or in the Irish form, Lugh) introduced agricultural innovations into Ireland, including the planting and sowing of crops. These came from the legends of the three Battles of Moytura, of which several versions survive.[45] Lug is introduced as a young stranger who had travelled far,[46] arriving in time for the second battle. At first he was not admitted to the Tuatha Dé Danann, a group of powerful spirits embued with magical powers. But he claimed to be master of all the arts they possessed individually, and was then given command of their forces. The battles were initially against the Fir Bolg, who were the earlier inhabitants of Ireland, but, after their defeat in the first battle, they had allied themselves with the Fomoiri, strange sea monsters who were then driven back into the sea. Lug killed their enemy champion Balor, but spared their King Bres, on condition that he introduced crop cultivation.[47] These highly detailed legends, rich in splendid magic, enlarged and embroidered in the constant telling, must have been based on folk movements which are very difficult to arrange in any historical context, although T.R. O'Rahilly has made a brilliant attempt.[48]

Maíre MacNeill has shown the remarkable survival of the festival into recent times, although heavily disguised and changed to suit the harvesting of potatoes. The date has been shifted slightly to the last Sunday in July, known as Garlic Sunday, set aside for the ceremonial lifting and gathering of the first of the potato crop; and although people went hungry if they had exhausted their store, they never advanced the day since it could have brought disaster to the crops. It was also set aside for a special feast, the new potatoes usually being eaten with white cabbage and bacon, if any was available. It was also a time for assemblies on hilltops or by springs, wells and lakes, but now respectably converted into Christian pilgrimages or meetings, often associated with St Patrick, who evidently replaced Lugh in these miraculous tales.[49] There are many records of people gathering at lake sides and of horse races in the lake itself, which may have originated as a Celtic sacrifice or purification ritual. Other possible examples of survival are in the contemporary Puck fairs – the name being derived from the male goat. There are records of these animals and rams being paraded and decorated and kept well fed on a high platform and later sold by auction. There may be a propitiation ritual in this, or, as Maíre MacNeill suggests, it was a symbol of a period of licence (her p. 296).

There are many records of the celebration of Lammas in other parts of Britain. The word itself is significant, as it means the loaf made by the new bread from the first of the harvest crop. The day was also known as Glove Sunday, and gloves were given as presents or exhibited on poles; though this practice could not have been of Celtic ancestry, as hand coverings were not known in the classical world.[50] Details of other feasts, fairs and local events are collected together from widespread areas of England by Maíre MacNeill, all suggesting that there were Celtic survivals, often only in faint outline, well into the last century, which could only have been possible if this festival had survived the Roman period.

The survival of the seasonal festivals
The ancient festivals were so deeply engrained in the fabric of rural society that it is hardly surprising that they survived either in their original or in a Christianised form. The British Celts would certainly have continued their practices throughout the period of Roman occupation, and, providing they were done peacefully and avoided human sacrifices, this would have been allowed. Furthermore, the great majority of the newcomers to Britain would have easily identified these festivals with their own. Many of the soldiers of the Roman army had been recruited from Celtic parts of the Empire, and even northern Italy had a large Celtic population. The Roman government would have required the celebration of the main Roman festivals by the army units and the officials of the administration, but these had, for the most part, become days associated with past and contemporary members of the Imperial house.[51] In Rome itself a large number of festivals were, and still are, strictly observed, since the inherent conservatism in legal and religious matters obliged this annual continuity, although the meaning of many of them and even the words of the hymns had long been forgotten and had often been given Christian overtones. The Roman

Fasti[52] is an extraordinary collection of ancient rituals springing from the seasonal rotation of a pastoral society with the additions of those based in agriculture and viticulture. Very similar festivals would have been celebrated with many local variations throughout Italy. An inhabitant of Italy doing service or living in Britain would not have felt entirely out of place in witnessing or taking part in the Celtic festivals, although the calendar would not have been the same. An innovation which would doubtless have been welcomed by the Celts was Saturnalia, a period of eating, drinking and much licence between the sexes and the different social classes.

Sacrifices

The gods had to be appeased also by sacrifices, but evidence for the origins of this practice is vague and very unsatisfactory. There was probably a time when human beings were offered and there are hints of this in the legends.[53] A sign of gradual enlightenment is seen in the substitution of animals for humans, rationalised by such legends as that of a priest, or a wise woman appearing at the crucial moment with a cow, commanding the change in old ritual as a direction of the gods, since innovation so radical must have unmistakable divine authority. There is a strong implication of animal sacrifices at Celtic festivals from the large number of legends which nucleated round St Patrick. These must reflect the changes he and other priests made in the translation of barbaric pagan rites into respectable Christian festivals, linked with appropriate saints. One of the most favoured stories which abound in many variants in Co. Mayo[54] tells of Patrick and his workmen building churches and seeking donations of food. The local landlord cunningly selected his fiercest bull, expecting it to run wild among the strangers and drive them away, but Patrick calmed the animal and it was killed and formed the basic food supply. The saint, however, insisted on keeping the hide and all the bones. The landowner, furious that his scheme had failed, demanded the return of his animal, whereupon Patrick miraculously restored the beast to life from the parts carefully retained, and presented it to the astonished owner.

There were, naturally, exceptions in the use of humans; when available, prisoners and criminals would be used at times when a major propitiation was necessary. On the other hand, the extraordinary story told by Caesar of large burning wickerwork cages full of men (VI, 16) can be seen as part of his anti-Druid propaganda, and in Strabo's version these *colossi* also contain cattle and wild animals (IV, 4, 5). Yet, as Powell has indicated, it is reminiscent of the Irish tales of timber houses full of people being set alight.[55] Lucan dwells on the same theme and links human sacrifice with the Celtic deities Teutates, Esus and Taranis (*Pharsalia*, 445–8); his source appears to have been independent of Posidonius. If one also considers the custom of head-hunting, to which the Celts were addicted (p. 39, below), one can more rapidly appreciate that human sacrifices were presumably carried out on special occasions; but it is clearly a theme exploited by Caesar and others to arouse Roman antipathy against the Druids, and this has been discussed in more detail above (pp. 22–25).

Although Rome allowed all kinds of bestialities in the amphitheatre and showed little mercy to condemned criminals and enemies of the State, human sacrifices was considered an abhorrent practice. At the Ides of May, as part of the spring festival, the Vestal Virgins assembled on the *pons sublicius* in Rome and threw twenty-seven (a magic number from three times nine) effigies of men made of rushes into the Tiber. Fraser considered this practice a substitute for human sacrifice.[56]

The Celtic Shangri-la

The brilliant inventive imagery of the Celts is nowhere more vivid than in the wondrous tales of other worlds of promise and plenty. In these places, often far out to sea beyond the horizon, there is no shortage of anything; good drink and beautiful obliging young maidens are in plenty, and there is no illness, anger or any of the normal irritations and annoyances of everyday life. Time stands still, no one ages and happiness is for ever. One of the finest tales of the never-never land is in the voyages of Bran,[57] who, with his twenty-seven[58] companions, was lured away to the Land of Women, an island supported by four pillars of gold. There were coracle and chariot races; a great tree full of sweet singing birds was permanently in blossom; the air was full of music, and everywhere was ablaze with colour. As Bran approached the island, he was reluctant to land, but a woman threw him a ball of thread which stuck to his hand and she drew his boat ashore, where they were all taken to a great hall. There was a bed and a wife for each man, and food and drink were constantly replaced. They stayed in this paradise for what they thought was a year, but here 100 years was but a day.[59] When he eventually returned home, no one believed he was Bran, whom they only knew as a distant legend; one of his companions set foot on shore and was immediately turned to ashes. Bran and the rest of his company sailed into oblivion.

There are many, similar, magical tales of voyages to supernatural worlds, not all of them over the seas. In the Connacht tale of Nera, the entrance was through a hole in a rock found by the hero who was following a raiding party of dead warriors into the *sid*; but, having entered this place, he had to stay there, since he had become one of the dead.[60] Another tale is based on the *sid*-mound or *Bri Leith*, Co. Longford, a fairy hill where there was neither death nor transgression and everlasting feasts were enjoyed without their needing to be served, and there was goodwill without strife.[61] Other voyages, such as that of Maeldúin,[62] are not in this category; they are tales of wonder and it has been suggested by Alwyn and Brinley Rees that these voyages were originally taken from an oral Celtic 'book' of the dead.[63]

These remarkable tales are fantasy projections of the fertile imagination, wishfully carrying the teller and his listeners away from the miseries and tribulations of human existence. They are echoed in many other cultures and places. The Greeks visualised Atlantis; the Romans the golden Age of Saturn; the Moslems the gardens of paradise for the true believers, and the Christians the image of a heavenly paradise where those without sin dwelt for ever in constant bliss. The idea of instant escape from the problems of our own making is a dream which has always haunted men and women. It thus forms a common bond between peoples of different ethnic origin, and Romans and Celts would have little difference in a joint understanding of this need for a translation to a better life through a religious experience.

The Irish tales clearly fascinated the early Christian monks, who recorded many of them, occasionally giving them a Christian twist. They were even converted into moral tales of voyages by the saints such as St Brendan, or into pilgrimages undertaken to expiate serious crimes, like those of the three brothers, the Ú Chorra and the Men of Ross.[64] The voyages were usually started by small boats being set adrift without rudders or oars, the fate of the condemned being determined by the state of wind and weather; nevertheless, they often managed to reach islands where they found people 'living without sin'. In the same theme are the stories of infants born out of incest, being cast into the sea or rivers in baskets – an idea adapted, no doubt, from the Old Testament story of the infant Moses in the bullrushes. The Romans would have had no difficulty in identifying with the Celtic myths, since they already had the idea of the voyage of the dead across the waters to the Isles of the Blessed, and dolphins were often a feature of tombstones. It was the theme of medieval romances like those of the Arthurian Cycle which may have helped to inspire the real voyages of discovery of later centuries; although at this period there were other potent factors, including the constant thirst for gold and silver, but these were thinly disguised as the need to proselytise the Christian faith.

The images of the Celtic deities

Before considering the Celtic and classical deities, their attributes and pairings, and attempting to assess the range of their powers and functions as seen by their supplicants, it is necessary to consider the images early man had of the unseen world around him and how they affected his life. To arrive at any firm conclusions would be impossible, since we are so remote from these ancient ancestors that what follows can only be a highly speculative approach to an insoluble problem. With the alarming advance of modern technology it is very easy to fall into the trap of thinking that because early men were primitive, they were simple people, leading uncomplicated lives. Studies of so-called 'primitive societies' which have survived in remote parts of the world into recent times have shown clearly that they have a highly structured framework governed by an elaborate set of rules. Their total social integration creates stability wherein individuals have an assured place throughout their lives. This makes a striking contrast to our present disintegrated society in which individuals may appear to have freedom of choice, considered by some as a precious advance. But this freedom is usually so restricted by circumstances that it has created deprivation for many to the point of desperation. Modern society also has a submerged stratum of the dispossessed and discarded, a state of affairs which could never occur in a primitive community.

A well-educated modern man thinks in a highly compartmentalised manner, putting facts and ideas into neat logical spaces and linking them into patterns and themes. Much of this is due to many generations of literacy and the effect of written or, perhaps even more significant, printed words and grammatical constructions on the thought processes. But earlier, illiterate peoples thought entirely in images, just as young children do until they can read, or those who are born deaf. In the remote past, images of the unseen world were shaped by long tradition in communities upset only by natural disasters. In stable conditions the changes took place very slowly. Society was totally integrated in a complicated pattern of inter-related families and, perhaps, of specialised crafts. The minds of early men must have held a succession of pictures of the visible world, but behind this were their concepts of the unseeable, but ever-present forces imagined as beings who shared every aspect of their lives and could influence for good and bad the activities of the group as a whole and all its members as individuals. These mental projections of the spirit world naturally took the shape of creatures, both animal and human, with which they were familiar.

From the earliest periods in the Near East, the lion was regarded as a solar symbol, a likeness based on his large yellow mane and undisputed superiority over all other beasts. A pair of lions flanked the throne of Cybele, the great earth-mother goddess, although these would have been lean mountain lions and not the more glorious African species. The symbolism is clear: the mother goddess represented fecundity of the earth and all the creatures on it. The sun brought new life as its warmth increased and caused the crops to grow, and thus the goddess combined the life-giving forces of both earth and sky. The lion also appears on Etruscan, Greek and Roman tombstones as 'death the devourer' while at the same time symbolising regeneration in the continued life after death. Although the two aspects may appear in two different contexts, the basic theme-cycle underlies both. The same is true of the dog which had two apparently differing roles: one as the guardian of the underworld, as personified by Cerberus, and the other as a healer. It was believed that the lick of this animal had healing properties, and, as such, was the centre of a cult of Aesculapius at Epidaurus. Dogs attended Nodens at the Lydney healing temple in Britain, and Nehalennia at Domberg in Holland. The basic life-death-regeneration is the underlying theme of both aspects.

The difficulties in identifying particular deities are compounded by their metamorphic abilities; such sudden transformations are common to folk tales the world over. Spirits often undergo shape-changing when in combat in order to elude the grasp of an opponent. This ability of the same spirit to appear in different forms is sometimes reflected in the representations in stone and metal, thus creating difficulties in identification. Fortunately, with classical deities, although changes in shape are often found in the Greek myths, the sculptors had by constant repetition achieved a generally accepted pattern for the representatives of the deities and their attributes. Some gods and goddesses appear in different forms in different places. Diana, for example, in the Western world is seen in the role of *Venatrix* (huntress), but in Italy and the East she was *Nutrix* (nursing mother); so she was depicted with bow and arrow in the former role, and in the many-breasted form, such as Diana of the Ephesians, primarily concerned with child-birth and rearing.

In copying the classical forms in Celtic lands there was a general tendency for the craftsmen to simplify by the smoothing of lines and omission of detail. This may not have been merely a matter of technical skills, but rather a deliberate attempt to produce images of the gods more acceptable to the Britons. The images of the purely native deities appear at first sight to be extremely crude, but as one studies them in more detail they begin to produce a sense of power and performance. Some, like the reliefs of the mother goddess, are highly stylised to the point of being hieratic. This is also seen in the portrayal of the heads (*têtes coupées*) of which there are a considerable number. Details of the face and head are minimal, but special attention has often been given to the eyes, which are large, sometimes projecting and lentoid in shape or hollowed and filled with coloured paste. In the right setting of a cunningly lit shrine these images would have projected power and authority. These Celtic sculptures may enable us to see the gods as they were imagined at that time, as powerful forces capable of exerting their authority and commanding the submission of their devotees, whilst at the same time, with the correct approach and appropriate gifts, being forces which could be used for protection and defence against human predators.

The cult of the head

This cult associated with a veneration of the head is of very ancient origin. Preservation and ritual treatment of human skulls has been found in some of the earliest human remains, and through such evidence Professor Zeuner has dated the Dragon-bone hill caves near Pekin to somewhere about 500,000 years.[65] There is evidence in Europe of special ritual association with skulls in Neanderthal and Upper Palaeolithic deposits. In Egypt, where the cult of the head became an obsessive preoccupation, the skull was singled out for special treatment. It seems evident that from the earliest times man had regarded the head as the very essence of a person. This universal belief is seen in ancestor worship and head-hunting in many parts of the world. The noble Roman families did not retain the heads of their departed members, since a corpse was a taboo object; they did, however, have wax casts made of the face and these effigies were treasured in special cupboards and brought out and worn by relatives in funeral processions.[66]

The Celts also held the head in high reverence. They saw it not only as the whole essence of the being, but also as the 'soul-substance' which made the head a symbol of divine powers and a close link with the spirit world of ancestors.[67]

The Celts were devoted head-hunters, a practice which stemmed from the belief that killing a brave enemy and taking his head transferred his fighting qualities to the victor. Diodorus Siculus (V. 29), no doubt copying Posidonius, in giving a graphic account of the Celts in battle, tells us that they cut off their enemies' heads when they fell and fastened them about the necks of their horses. He adds that they selected the heads of the most distinguished foes, embalmed them in cedar-oil and preserved them carefully in a chest, displaying them on special occasions (no doubt with much exaggeration and boasting). Some heads were set on poles at the gates of Iron Age fortresses, perhaps with the war-gear as trophies and to add a symbolism of divine protection.[68]

The Romans found this Celtic practice barbaric, although, strangely enough, Caesar failed to mention it. It was not entirely suppressed, and the Celtic auxiliaries in the Roman army were allowed to continue the practice, provided that the heads were always those of Roman enemies. There is evidence of this from Trajan's Column (Pl. 1),[69] where Trajan is being offered two Dacian heads by dismounted auxiliaries; he turns his head away, since to all Romans corpses were taboo objects, and especially to the *Pontifex Maximus*.[70]

The strength of the head cult in Gaul and Britain is demonstrated by the large number of representations of the *tête coupée*, especially in the shrine at Entremont and Roquepertuse in southern Gaul. Heads also abound in Britain on metalwork and carved in stone[71] and on pottery (Fig. 7). The difficulty with some of these is that they may represent local deities, especially if they are provided with a neck and shoulders, as at Wall, Staffordshire (Pls. 2 and 3). There are also examples where the head is the terminal top to a shaft, as is the case with one from Guiting Power, Gloucestershire.[72] This figure also appears to have shoulders and, on one side, the upper part of an arm, the rest being worn or damaged; the description of this as 'phallic' appears to be over-imaginative. A small carving from Broadway, however, distinctly gives that impression,[73] but another from Camerton is too broken and appears to be merely a rounded head.[74]

Another form of these carvings is that in which only the face is shown in a circle or oval, as on examples from Eype in Dorset,[75] Maryport in Cumberland[76] and Port Talbot in South Wales.[77] This type of head is also considered as phallic, though with more justification. The link of the powerful head with the phallic life-force would greatly strengthen the potency of these symbols as protective forces at the entrances to shrines and sacred places. Many of these stones were probably grave *stele* and some have been found marking burials in Württemberg.[78]

The assimilation of Celtic and classical deities by the Britons

Rural beliefs and practices were universally based on the daily cycle of day and night, expanded into the annual cycle of the spring resurrection, summer growth, autumn harvests and the winter death, with its human counterpart of birth, maturity, decay, death and re-birth in the new generation. Despite this common ground, there was, however, a basic difference between the concept of Celts and Romans and this was the existence of a classical pantheon of deities closely interlinked by family relationships, and an enormous accretion of legendary tales, invented mainly by the imaginative Greeks in their epic poems and later grafted on to the Roman traditions. As shown in an earlier chapter, the inspiration of the age of Augustus was towards a reconciliation with the mythical past in the forging of Rome's destiny. Although this may have helped to rekindle the old Roman virtues, it probably did more to strengthen the Republican tradition, especially among the Stoics. No one of education and intelligence could be expected to believe in the great farrago of nonsense told of the dwellers of Mount Olympus, least of all the peasant population of Italy.

The sources of evidence of early Roman practices are surviving pieces of inscriptions and the works of antiquarians like Ovid, who preserved much antiquarian lore[79] in his *Fasti*,[80] one of our main sources. The work of M. Terentius Varro (116–27 BC), *Antiquitates rerum divinarum*, alas, only survives as discrete fragments, selected for quotation by St Augustine in his extensive anti-pagan polemic, *De civitate Dei*. There are a few more surviving scraps and inscriptions providing ancient formulae, calendars and sacred songs, and the information they give clearly indicates that, like the Celt and the Greek, the religions of Italy were the result of slow development and external influences both inhibited by conservatism over millennia, all carefully formalised (or one could say fossilised) into a sacred tradition, scrupulously preserved, although not always understood. The rituals were based on the constant need for fertility of the soil, the animals and the humans themselves, and for protection against the hostile and malignant forces, which were feared because they were not understood, and which in earlier times had been rationalised into human and animal shapes, capable of human and animal behaviour and emotions. Rome herself took over much of the Etruscan religion, but it was many centuries before she created a great nation out of the miscellany of tribes of different origins occupying Italy, each with their varying rural traditions and practices which continued unabated, regardless of what happened in Rome.

The classical deities

From the body of epigraphic and figural evidence that survives, it would seem that the Roman deities were totally absorbed by the Britons and that their native gods and goddesses took second place. But this evidence is deceptive, since the inscriptions, and to a lesser extent the sculptures and bronzes, are concentrated on the frontier zones. They represent official Roman attitudes and cannot, therefore, be regarded as reflecting the aspirations of the Britons. It is also clear that the newcomers, whoever they may have been, and many would have been Celts from other parts of Europe, showed great respect to the local deities, and their ancient right of tenure was fully acknowledged. Also, as discussed earlier, the religious practices of the Celtic and Roman peasantry had much the same origins. Under the influence of Greek mythology, prominence was given to a number of gods and goddesses one might term the Olympians. This group might appear to have replaced the older and local spirits, but it becomes evident from Ovid's *Fasti* that the rural population of Italy continued to respect their ancient spirits, some with general powers, but some attached to specific places. The Celts also had their universal deities, but each community placed more reliance on the spirits, each of which had permanent occupation of rivers, springs, lakes, woodlands and hills. The classical deities brought to Britain by the Romanised invaders could not replace the old spirits, but instead shared the holy places, the two names being linked together, provided that the same powers were recognised in each. This does not mean that there were two deities instead of one, since the 'new' deity represented a new 'face' of the same god or goddess; the Britons continued to acknowledge the time-honoured name, but the new people saw the deity in classical terms.

Thus, it is not surprising to find deities of each culture linked on dedications, as were Sulis-Minerva and Lenus-Mars. In these two cases it is noteworthy that the Celtic names precede the classical, as if they were considered to have superior status. This is not unexpected at Bath, where Sulis presided over the remarkable hot springs and where the largest and most prestigious healing temple and baths in Britain were erected. Lenus, another healing deity associated with water, was a very important Rhineland god from Trier. One is reminded of the remarkable relief from Rheims where the horned god Cernunnos is shown seated cross-legged in the Buddha position, attended by Mercury and Apollo, who are shown as smaller figures on either side. This leaves little doubt that the Romans never attempted to force the superiority of their deities onto the Celts, but were even prepared to acknowledge the greater powers of those of the peoples they conquered, especially if the veneration was associated with a particular place.[81] Cocidius and Belatucadrus were gods associated with temples on Hadrian's Wall. The continued acknowledgement of these deities was due to the presence of the garrisons in the forts and the practice of including some on the altars annually consecrated on the parade ground. The distribution pattern of these gods is a purely military one. The classical deities, on the other hand, were universal and represented particular powers, so one finds these linked with a number of local deities; Mars, the protector-healer, is linked in Britain with no less than sixteen Celtic gods.

With statues and other sculptured reliefs there are more occasions of pairings and even triplications. The classical god may have been a consort, like Mars and Rosmerta, or there may be groups of deities. This multiplying of deities is common to Roman monuments, but normally each one is shown separately, as on four-, five- or six-sided blocks, where they appear one on each side – a feature particularly noted in the Rhineland. Celtic deities are also found in groups, the most common being the *Deae Matres* and the *cucullati* who were often in the magic number of three.[82]

A close study of the reliefs brings another aspect to light: those carved by Celtic masons lost their classical appearance and sometimes reached extreme stages of barbaric crudity. This process often frustrates attempts to identify the figures, and one becomes aware that classical originals have been transformed into Celtic deities, although they may still have their original attributes. There are very few accompanying inscriptions in Britain to resolve this difficulty, and, in any case, since most Celtic deities are very local, only a small number of their names are known. There were undoubtedly many hunter or woodland spirits equated with Silvanus, but with a very barbarised relief of this god, the description is merely 'a local hunter god' or, as of the Chedworth relief, 'more probably depicts a local Hunter God than the Roman Silvanus'.[83] From Wall, Staffordshire, comes Hercules only identified by his club, but he may equally well be a Celtic hero god, (Pl. 3).

When the Celtic name is known, as in the case of Rosmerta, whether her name or that of her counterpart Fortuna is given is dependent on the degree of barbarisation. When doubt exists and perhaps only the cornucopia is recognisable, it becomes a *genius*. But the attributes are shared, except the wooden tub which is peculiar to Rosmerta. There are heavily Celticised versions which show this goddess with the cornucopia, the rudder, the wheel and the globe, so that the conflation is complete. There is only one goddess who can change a person's fortune or provide instant plenty, and the name by which she was known would depend on whether the supplicant was a Briton or a Romanised inhabitant from another part of the Empire.

The degree of popularity of the classical deities in Britain can be judged by the extent of the copying and subsequent barbarisation. Dr Claire Lindgren selected Mercury, Venus, Minerva and Mars as examples,[84] but her lists are by no means complete and omit, for example, the ultimate in crudity, the outline reliefs of Lenus-Mars at Chedworth (Fig. 9D and E),[85] and some of the cruder Celtic versions of Mercury (Fig. 8A). There are many stones on which the figures, because of their poor quality of carving, and as a result of damage and weathering, totally defy identification. However, the Celts imparted new life and vigour in the process of copying, as is shown by the fine bronze plaque from Lavington, Wiltshire, and now in the Devizes Museum (jacket illustration).[86]

Hunting

Survival for early man depended on successful hunting, and, in their quest for food, the hunters followed the animals through their seasonal migration. In order to be able to approach near enough for their short-range missiles to be effective (Fig. 1), they dressed in the skins of their prey and imitated their movements, as is clearly illustrated in the Palaeolithic cave paintings (Fig. 2). This dependence and imitation created a profound affinity between men and animals which developed into totemism.[87]

The kill provides the essential food for primitive survival, thus creating the

Fig. 1 Palaeolithic hunters on a cave painting in Spain (after J. Maringer, 1956)

concept of the life-cycle. This basic image was also seen as a direct exchange of death for life: the killing of the animals provided the essential food to keep the human group alive and enable its members to perpetuate their species. Thus the act of slaughter and the spilling of blood, regarded by primitive people as the very life substance, created new life.

The hunt was a sacred act and subject to strict rituals. It also had sexual connotations, associated with the penetration of the animal by the missile. Thus it is significant that in many societies there was a taboo against sexual intercourse before hunting.[88] (There was a direct connection between a sacred act and a taboo and the Latin *sacer* could mean either, i.e. 'holy' or 'cursed', since the breaking of the ritual immediately negated it.)[89] This sexual connotation can be seen echoed in many classical myths.[90] The hunter was often depicted as a

Fig. 2 A man dressed in animal skins and antlers from a cave painting (after J. Maringer, 1956)

grotesque superhuman figure with abnormal sexual prowess, as with Orion and Hercules, and similar characteristics were attributed to the Celtic gods and heroes such as Dagda and Cú Chulainn. In the Near Eastern myths, the object of the hunter's desire was a goddess or nymph, who was vowed to chastity. There was normally a long and difficult chase, as with Actaeon and Leukippos, or the hunter may accidentally surprise the goddess while she is bathing, thus breaking her self-imposed taboo. Retribution on the part of the goddess took the form of changing the hunter into an animal (Pl. 4) or tree and eventually, in a few cases, out of pity, by catasterism into a heavenly constellation. It is also evident from the myths that hunting was not regarded primarily as a pursuit – either for the pleasure of the chase or even for food – but as a means of fulfiling a purpose; thus the hero became a hunter to clear the lands of wild animals for cultivation, and so was seen as the protector of the farmer and the herdsmen. More basically still, however, the hunt symbolises the powerful sexual urge or life-force in the urgent and desperate need for satisfaction, heightened by the grotesque appetite of the hero-hunter inflamed by his rejection by the frigid virgin. J.E. Fontenrose has extended this theme to the suggestion that hunting 'connotes both an uninhibited life of sexual indulgence and a sexless life. One goes to the forest either to satisfy sexual desires or to escape them. The forest represents all in one, "licence and innocence"' (his p. 253). This may take supposition too far; but it is clear, nevertheless, that the myths arose in the earliest period of man's emergence from his animal ancestry, and sprang from his elemental life-force harnessed to the urgent need to sustain and continue his species by the constant hunt for food.

The hunt as a death-regeneration theme is found in many ancient Near Eastern cultures. Although most of the earliest and most powerful deities are the earth-mother goddesses, they are often also associated with hunting. Thus, in Lower Egypt, the ancient hunter goddess Neith became the greatest of all the divine beings and mother of all the gods.[91] The great mountain-mother goddess of Minoan Crete was depicted on clay seals with a lioness and dog at her side. Her domination over the beasts clearly signifies her role in hunting the animals of the wild.[92]

The symbolism of animals is a complex subject, as individual beasts developed a particular imagery of their own. The lion, for example, was regarded as the most ferocious of all the wild animals, and was, from the earliest times, linked with the earth mother, Cybele; she was depicted flanked by a pair of lions over which she exercised complete control, even using the beasts as lap-dogs or a footstool.[93] It is not difficult to see how the power of the lion and the savage way in which it claws down and devours its prey became identified with the image of death itself.

Hunting scenes are thus directly associated with the major human themes of the life-force, death and regeneration. They became associated with the worship of particular deities in the Eastern cults, such as Orphism and, ultimately, Christianity. Hunting scenes were depicted as reliefs on tombstones as early as Mycenaean Greece.[94] and although they have been interpreted by art historians as showing the pleasures to be enjoyed beyond the grave,[95] they are also symbols of death and resurrection. The hunt also appears on Etruscan tomb paintings, and this basic image was adopted by Rome. A theme in parallel with the hunt was that of an open parkland in which animals, both wild and domesticated, roamed freely and were often depicted drinking from the springs and streams of the waters of life. This was a projected image of the golden age of paradise,[96] a state of bliss and innocence awaiting the souls of the departed.[97] To the Romans this was also the golden age of the remote past when Saturn ruled; but the Augustan poets[98] projected it into a future when the old virtues of Rome would once more triumph. It was also adopted much earlier from Near Eastern imagery[99] by the Jews in the Garden of Eden. The serpent maliciously, or by intent, gave Eve what Frazer termed 'the perverted message';[100] for, had they eaten of the Tree of Life, which also grew in the Garden, they would have become immortal as the gods, but instead Eve was directed to the Tree of Knowledge which was the Tree of Death. Thus all human beings are mortal, but there always has to be a rational explanation for mortality; and, unfortunately, the result of this need was the creation of the Fall of Man and the subsequent concept of original sin. This sad distortion of the image of the life-force, from an act of joyous release into a necessary evil subject to severe taboos has caused untold misery, violence, death, corruption and sheer frustration on a prodigious scale ever since. (The Gnostics rightly rejected this dreadful twist to the myth, but the Christian Church, with its political support, was much too powerful, and the sect was crushed and its members persecuted.)

Scenes of the hunt remained favourite themes in sepulchral sculpture but became increasingly popular in the fourth century, especially in mosaics and sarcophagi. The reasons for this development have to be understood from the evidence of the scenes themselves. The most detailed studies of these pavements have been by Professor Toynbee and Dr Katherine Dunbabin. Professor Toynbee has drawn attention to the lion hunt as a death and regeneration symbol and, as such, these animals are seen on Roman tombstones and *mausolea* signifying 'the ravening power of death and of man's victory over it'.[101] Dr Dunbabin, however, suggests that in the second and third centuries the hunt was treated in a more secular manner and that the wealthy landowners and villa builders wished to have themselves depicted at their favourite sport.[102] This may have been true in some cases, especially of those mosaics on which the actual houses and the various activities in the fields and vineyards are shown; but there is undoubtedly a religious element in some of the scenes, the most striking of which is one from the Khéreddine suburb of Carthage.[103] The dominant feature of this large pavement is a shrine to Apollo and Diana in which the two deities are portrayed with the offering of a crane on what appears to be a large altar. On each side of the shrine stand three huntsmen with their long spears, and above and below the hunting scenes are tigers, leopards and a stag. Diana also appears in a central panel in a large second-century pavement at El Djem.[104] The goddess stands in her shrine, surrounded by vegetation, indicating a woodland which has a large assortment of animals roaming freely over the landscape.

This scene is reminiscent of Orpheus, who became very popular in the fourth century and is usually depicted on mosaics in the centre of the encircling animals he had tamed with his music, or is sometimes shown in the middle of an open space. Orpheus was equated with Christ by Eusebius[105] on the grounds that Orphic teaching was that man's existence is but a trial run in preparation for everlasting life, which is only for those following the prescribed Christian rituals and observances. The association appeared to be strengthened by comparison with King David, who was also a gifted musician with his harp and, it was claimed, an ancestor of Christ. Orpheus was also associated with fountains,[106] the symbols of the springs of the waters of life in the paradise scenes, so bringing this concept into a wider context. Diana was able to exert similar influence over the creatures of the wild. The goddess is shown at the centre of a scene from Bir-el-Ksour[107] in which a horseman and his dogs are chasing a hare and fox. The names of the two dogs, Unicus and Aquila, ensure the goddess's protection with the additional power of the naming of names, Dr Dunbabin also draws attention to a curious scene on a Byzantine pavement at Carthage[108] where a hunt is shown in front of a threshold with an inscription *Bide vive et bide ut possas plurima bidere*, which appears to be a garbled attempt to prevent evil spirits from entering through the symbol of the hunt.

It is difficult to understand precisely what hunting meant to the wealthy landowners who paid for these elaborate pavements. The early scenes tended to be naturalistic, but from the third century exotic animals were introduced and, with this introduction the scenes acquire the atmosphere of the *venationes* of the amphitheatre. There are also fewer examples of the killing of the hunted beasts, though more frequently they are captured in nets and traps. No North African landowner could possibly have found such animals on his estate, and they had presumably been imported from Africa or the Near East. It is possible that these exotic animals could have been purchased or hired to be let loose on the estate for the excitement of the chase and capture. The more naturalistic might simply display the *venationes* as on a mosaic from Cherchel[109] in which a richly apparelled horseman is riding above a speared stag. A scene often shown on cavalry tombstones portrayed the deceased riding over the prostrate foe, often a barbarian cowering on the ground, which has been accepted as symbolising victory over death.[110] It is possible that the scene at Cherchel had the same meaning, directly linking it with the basic hunting symbolism.

These themes of kill, regeneration and victory over death as symbolised in the hunt had great appeal to the early Christian iconographists, who absorbed much of the pagan imagery, but with amended identifications. The Old Testament was intensely studied for references which could provide suitable linkages between the pagan and the Christian. Origen, the theologian, found in Psalm 103 and The Song of Songs (2–9 and 17) references to the hart, which he deduced were sufficient for the identification of this animal with Christ[111] in his Passion and the Martyrdom of the Saints. Another scene which was acceptable to the Christians was that of harts and stags drinking from the waters of life or from a *cantharus*, now translated into the living water of paradise. Even the stags' horns were appropriate enough to represent the horn of David; it seems, however, too fanciful to imagine that the Chi-Rho cross-saltire behind the head of Christ also represented antlers. However, the powerful horned gods of the ancient world could still cast their long shadow. E.J. Erikson, who has made this suggestion in the case of the Hinton St Mary pavement,[112] has also drawn attention to the legend of St Eustace, who was converted by the vision of a shining cross between the antlers of a stag while hunting. It is probably stretching the imagination too far to attempt to see the antlers as the branches of the Tree of Life, although by the end of the first century the symbols had become so inextricably mixed that much of the original meaning had long been forgotten. There have been many attempts by Christian theologians, from Origen[113] in the third century to Father Hugo Rahner[114] in the twentieth, to reinterpret classical myths and symbols in Christian terms. But the difficulty with all of this is that they are based on the assumption that Christianity is an unanswerable truth, whereas it is as loaded with primitive survivals and accretions of myths from many sources, as are many other ancient religions.

Diana and the various forms of earth-mother goddess became the Virgin Mary, while the mantles of Hercules, Mars, Mithras and the other divine and semi-divine salvation and protector deities were placed over the figure of Christ. The agony and death of the hunt were not only seen as a symbol of the resurrection, but the dreadful fate of Actaeon, who unavailingly called upon his own dogs to recognise their master,[115] was equated with the passion of Christ on the Cross crying in his agony. The parallel theme of the wild creatures in a landscape, an image of nature in a state of innocence, was used as the fulfilment of Isaiah's prophecy (ci. 6–8) of the time 'when the wolf shall dwell with the lamb and the leopard lie down with the kid'.[116] The scene could also have been used for Noah and his Ark,[117] an early Christian symbol of salvation through repentance, although the animals could have been copied for the Diana-Orpheus scene with the simple substitution of Noah for either of these deities. The widespread popularity of the hunt and the wild creatures in a landscape in the fourth century was probably due to the growing influence of Christianity and its close relationship with the Orphic cult.

One of the most direct links between the hunt and Christianity is in the Hinton St Mary pavement, which is dominated by the centre of the head of Christ identified by the Chi-Rho monogram.[118] There are five hunting scenes, two in adjoining rectangular panels and three as lunate panels in the pavement itself. In the fourth panel is the Tree of Life and in the corners the four seasons, now symbols of the four evangelists.

Popular interest in the hunt stemmed from the *venationes* of the amphitheatre. These were carefully staged episodes consisting of various kinds of wild animals being let loose in the arena, converted into an artificial park. Men and dogs acted as the huntsmen chasing the animals and slaughtering them. The men (*bestiarii*) were well paid and trained for this work, but captives and criminals were also used, and the spectacle was 'enriched' by the sight of men being torn to pieces as well as by the butchery of the animals. It is difficult for those living today to understand the kind of pleasure induced by such barbaric carnage. Revulsion was expressed by occasional writers, usually the Stoics, but the cruelty was relished by the proletarian mob of Rome and it may have had the advantage of giving an outlet for the violence and aggression which are part of the human make-up, often emerging only under stress.

The origin of this practice is obscure, but rituals associated with hunted animals must have continued from the remote times when men depended on them for their very existence and continuity. Their performances of ritual dances in animal skins were very common and still survive, but the kill would probably have become a sacrifice in many places. The survival, however, of bull running, baiting and fighting strongly suggests that there were widespread festivals in Europe and the Mediterranean. In Crete it is evident that there existed elaborate games around the capture of the bull in the Minoan period. Similar events probably took place in ancient Italy, and it may have been from these that the Romans developed the *venatio* as a public spectacle linked to a religious festival.

While bull running and baiting were practised in the open, the more elaborate *venationes*, involving numbers of savage beasts, required special structures to protect the public. These shows were first performed in the *forum* and *circus*, but these places had serious disadvantages. The idea of putting two theatres together, face to face, to create a suitably enclosed arena with banked seating did not seem to occur to anyone until C. Scribonius Curio built one in 50 BC, in timber, to stage his father's funeral games.[119] Timber amphitheatres proved to be highly susceptible to fire, and collapsed under the weight of the packed crowds, causing serious accidents.[120] In 30 BC, stone was first used for an amphitheatre erected by Statilius Taurus in the Campus Martius, but all the seats and stairs were in wood and it was destroyed by the great fire of AD 64.

The first recorded *venatio* was celebrated by M. Fulvius in 187 BC, in fulfilment of a vow made to Jupiter Optimus Maximus when he captured Ambracia in the Aetolian War.[121] These shows became increasingly spectacular. Julius Caesar staged a *venatio* lasting five days. At the consecration of the great amphitheatre started by Vespasian and completed by Titus, now known as the Colosseum, 5000 wild and 4000 domesticated animals were killed. Trajan celebrated the completion of the Dacian Wars with spectacles lasting 123 days during which 11,000 animals were killed.[122] All these enormous and wasteful shows were in honour of the gods as a repayment for splendid victories and conquests. To this extent they can be considered to have had a religious basis, though there does not appear to be any hint of the death and regeneration symbolism. In another sense, they may have been considered as sacrifices on a grand scale with all this blood-letting being for the benefit of the Emperor and people of Rome, assuming that the gods relished these events as much as the populace.

It was, of course, only in Rome that such lavish *venationes* were performed. The Emperors were always jealous of any potential rivals currying favour by similar means in the provinces. Elsewhere these events were on a much reduced scale, and one can imagine that in Britain it would have been confined to bull- and bear-baiting, with the occasional exotic beast exhibited but certainly not slaughtered.

There is a source of evidence which may help to indicate the type of *venationes* enacted in Britain Beakers made of pottery at the factories of Colchester and in the Nene Valley[123] were decorated by figures applied to the surface of beakers *en barbotine*, or made in moulds and applied as casts (*appliqué*; see Chap. 4 below). These vessels are known as hunt-cups since they commonly show deer, stags or hares being chased by dogs.[124] There are, however, more complicated scenes which include hunters.[125] A small bowl with a lid from a Colchester grave[126] shows a variety of animals including a hare or stag and a bear (?), but there is also a man with a long hunting spear dressed only in a loin-cloth being attacked by a lion. Another vessel from Bedford Purlieus in the Nene Valley[127] depicts a *bestiarius*, also with a long hunting spear, dressed in a tight-fitting tunic with fringed tights (Fig. 3); and a sherd from another vessel shows a man similarly dressed, with his left arm protected by a leather buckler like those usually worn by the *bestiarii* (see Figs. 4 and 12).

The most remarkable of these vessels is the so-called 'Colchester Vase' which is complete (Fig. 5).[128] This has a mixture of the amphitheatre and circus in three different scenes; the one on the left has a properly equipped *bestiarius* with whip, buckler and armoured legs and arms with a bear, perhaps a trained bear, and he is assisted by another man in a loin-cloth who has a cudgel and small stick. The

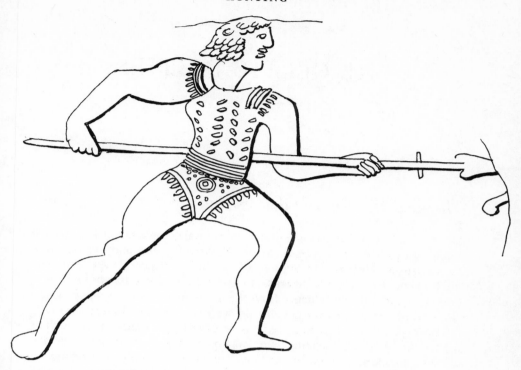

Fig. 3 A *bestiarius* with a hunting-spear on a Nene Valley pottery vessel (after Roach-Smith)

central scene is with a *secutor* and a *retiarius*, while the rest of the vessel is covered with stags and a hare being chased by a hound. Another interesting feature of this vessel is the inscription carefully incised over the figures probably by the owner of the pot. Above the men with the bear are their names, Secundus and Mario, and over the fighters, MEMNO SAC (i.e. *secutor*) VIII; the number, as Professor Toynbee suggests, may be that of his victories, and the name of the defeated *retiarius* is Valentinus. There follows LEGIONIS XXX, which is more difficult to explain as this legion was never in Britain, but at Vetera on the Rhine, in the second century. Maybe a troup of legionary gladiators were on tour in Britain, as Professor Toynbee indicated (1962, p. 190).

It seems most unlikely that potters in Britain would have depicted in such detail scenes unfamiliar to the public. They reflect popular taste much as our modern souvenirs of boxers and footballers do today, and perhaps reflect the actualities of the amphitheatre and circus, which were part of the entertainment provided by the larger cities. Their religious significance is, however, minimal, except for those vessels which appear to depict scenes of a possible ritual nature, which are described below in Chapter 4.

CHAPTER THREE

THE CELTIC DEITIES

The evidence for the deities and their relationships

The Celts had no hierarchy of deities such as quarrelsome families on Mount Olympus, invented by the Greeks. Some scholars, J-J. Hatt and others,[1] have attempted to establish a Celtic mythology based on the scenes on the Gundestrup Cauldron and the Gallic monuments, but they are little more than brilliant feats of the imagination. The evidence from the monuments and epigraphy clearly demonstrates that some of the Celtic deities were acknowledged over a large area and must, therefore, have possessed powers over basic human needs such as fertility, child-birth and healing. Some may have been more tribal or regional, but the vast majority were peculiar to particular places, often sacred springs. Dr Joan Alcock has advanced the idea that there existed greater divinities who were basically concerned with the forces of nature and were of a tribal character, but who appear to have been seen in differing images by each tribe, thus assuming different personalities according to the territory in which they were venerated.[2] This fascinating concept helps to explain many variations. The choice made by a community in selecting a particular deity was probably restricted by tradition, but it could also have been the result of a successful appeal in the past, still remembered in folk history.

The evidence of the Celtic deities has survived in a variety of forms – literary, epigraphical and archaeological. The only literary sources are the Irish and Welsh sagas and the classical writers. The sagas and folk tales have been handed down in literate form because the Christian monks of the tenth century AD copied them from the bards. They thus include details, especially of dress and equipment, which belong to this late period rather than the first century AD. They contain many names of the creatures of the unseen world and of the great folk heroes, themselves often semi-divine. This great collection of material unfortunately provides few links with the evidence from other sources. Its most important value is in the information it provides about the social organisation of Celtic society and some of the religious rituals and, to some extent, concepts of the unseen world.

Classical sources are not only scanty but highly prejudiced, as was seen above, and the number of names of Celtic deities mentioned are surprisingly few. The poet Lucanus gives three names, Teutates, Esus and Taranis, in his description of the sacred grove deep in the forest near Massilia which was cut down to provide Caesar with timber for his siege-works. This is a highly poetic description, emphasising the horrors of the sacrifices.[3] The three names, Teutates, Esus and Taranis, are a most unlikely combination and would appear to have been chosen by the poet for scansion and the sound of such outlandish names to Roman ears.[4] They happen to be important deities in Gaul, and Lucanus would have had no difficulty in selecting them.

Caesar must have had a fair knowledge of Celtic religion, but he wrote his commentaries for a Roman audience, so he lists Roman equivalents when he stated that the Gauls worshipped Mercury, Apollo, Mars, Jupiter and Minerva (*BG* vi, 17). The people of northern Gaul would certainly have had no knowledge of these gods at that time, but in the Roman province in the south, there had been sufficient time for the inhabitants to have become familiar with the deities introduced by the Roman colonists and traders. Caesar would have realised that a list of Celtic gods would have been meaningless to readers. He makes this clear in the following sentence: 'they (i.e. the Gauls) have the same views as other people about the deities, that Apollo dispels disease, Minerva controls the arts and crafts, Jupiter holds the empire of the sky, while Mars rules over war'.[5] This is a somewhat divergent opinion from the reality, since Minerva and Mars were mainly protective deities and venerated for that purpose.

There is little help, therefore, for any enlightment on Celtic deities from classical literature, and one must turn to the other sources, sculptural, epigraphical and archaeological, where there is a positive *embarras de richesses*. When Emile Espérandieu produced his great work on the monuments of Gaul and the Rhineland[6] it appeared in eleven volumes with a number of subsequent supplements. Although Britain appears to be much poorer in this material, there is a considerable number of reliefs and sculptures, often very fragmentary, which have not received the detailed attention they deserve.[7] One must add to this the large number of figurines in bronze and pottery, which supply valuable images of the deities as portrayed by craftsmen in both the classical and Celtic tradition. It is not always possible, however, to offer an identification of the deities when many significant details have either been eroded or damaged, or were never there in the first place.

Epigraphic evidence

The only satisfactory evidence for the identity of a deity is when there is both a figure and an inscription, but this is not a common occurrence in Britain. The epigraphic evidence comes mainly from altars which rarely have any representation of the deity invoked. One can, therefore, in many cases, only draw conclusions from comparisons with the somewhat better evidence from Gaul and the Rhineland. The inscriptions, especially on altars, often give the names of Celtic deities, and when this is the only known appearance of the name, there is no possibility of knowing what the deity represented or what was its image. Some examples of this problem in Britain are described below.

An altar from Bitterne is dedicated to Dea Ancasta, and there is no doubt about the letters (*RIB* 97), but this is the only example of this name and no meaning has been suggested. Andraste also appears only once, but not on an inscription; it was recorded by Dio (lxii, 7, 3) as the goddess invoked by the victorious Boudican rebels after the sack of Camulodunum and Londinium.[8] Dr Ross considers that this may mean 'victorious or unconquerable' and could be analogous with Andarta, worshipped by the Vocontii of Gaul. A strange altar made into a medieval water stoup stands in the nave of the church at Michaelchurch in Herefordshire, dedicated to DEO TRIDAM, which has also defied interpretation (*RIB* 304). Another deity with a single dedication is Setlocenia at Maryport (*RIB* 841), set up by a German, although the goddess is Celtic and means 'the long-lived one'.

Epithets

The practice of adding adjectival epithets to names was very common in the classical world. Often they were descriptive of the powers of the deity, like Apollo Acesius (i.e. the healer), and sometimes related to a place, like Apollo Milesius (i.e. of Miletium in Crete). In Celtic lands it would have been natural to add Celtic adjectives enhancing the powers of a classical deity. In Britain, Mars received several such epithets, such as Mars Alator, 'the nourisher' (*RIB* 218, 1055); Barrex, 'the supreme' (*RIB* 947); Rigas, 'the kingly' (*RIB* 74), or Rigisamus, 'the most kingly' (*RIB* 187). Apollo on a *patera* from South Shields is called Anextiomaro, which has been interpreted as 'the Great Protector'.[9] At Colchester there is Mercury Andescociuoucus, the first part of which has the meaning of 'The Great Activator' (*RIB* 193), a suitable epithet for Mercury. Also at Colchester is a dedication to Silvanus Callirius, or possibly Calliriodaco (*RIB* 194), which may be an epithet. The most extraordinary collection of names, which it has been suggested are epithets by Professor Kenneth Jackson, are added to the name of the god Faunus and inscribed on the silver spoons of the Thetford hoard.[10] The names and the possible meanings he has given to them are: Nari, 'the Mighty'; Auseci, 'Long-Ear'; Blotugi, 'The Fosterer of Corn or Spring Blossom'; Saternio, 'Giver of Plenty'; Tugi, 'Protector', and Medugeni, 'Mead-begetter'; but Crani and Andi Crose have so far eluded interpretation. This prolificacy of adjectives appears on a set of spoons which also has the names of the devotees inscribed on them. It could follow that these epithets were chosen by or were in some way peculiar to each individual, or even formed part of the ritual.

Name pairing

The names with the greatest potential information are those which are paired with classical equivalents. It is then possible to understand the particular powers of the Celtic deities from the known abilities of their classical counterparts. There is little doubt, in the case of Sulis-Minerva and Lenus-Mars (Fig. 9D and E), that these were healing deities, and the fact that the Celtic partners took precedence would appear to indicate that they were recognised as the more powerful of the two. The use of two names does not imply two separate deities, since there is never more than one image of the deity in sculpture or metal. The one deity had two names and the one by which he or she was addressed depended on whether it was by a Celt or a Romanised inhabitant from another part of the Empire.[11] When the Roman soldiers moved into an area, they would have felt the immediate need to make contact with the local spirits so that they could assuage their fears of a foreign invasion into their terrain. A ritual would have been performed, or a vow taken sealed by an altar, when the characteristics of the diety were known, so that a pairing could be made with the most suitable classical god or goddess, in order to obtain the best of both unseen worlds. In this way the established deities in the area of Hadrian's Wall appear on official military dedications. Cocidius was paired with Apollo on four altars and with Silvanus on two; Maponus was paired with Apollo on four out of the five altars, but Belatucadrus usually stood alone, though he was paired with Mars twice. From this evidence one cannot deduce any particular pattern except a preference for either Mars, Silvanus or Apollo, all three of whom were associated with healing and protection from harm of all kinds, although Apollo may have specialised in diseases.

Another type of pairing was with male and female partners. In the classical pantheon this was usually based on a family relationship, but this can hardly be so when the two deities are Celtic and classical. This is, however, rare in Britain, and the most noteworthy occurence is that of Rosmerta with Mercury, both deities of plenty, which is also common on the Rhineland. Mercury, the god of commerce, could provide a good profit, as his purse betokens, and Rosmerta, with the magic mixing-bucket, was also a provider, as indeed her name states. But how were they seen by their devotees? It could be argued that, while Mercury provided for men, Rosmerta acted for women, sharing with them the contents of her bucket, which represented regeneration, and thus fertility and children. The only other pair is that from Ad Pontem (East Stoke) on the Fosse Way.[12] The two very stiff figures, the male holding a knobbed staff and the woman what appears to be a bowl of fruit, would appear to be Celtic deities, the names of which are not known.

Some of the powerful Celtic deities of Gaul and Britain

Taranis

Taranis was the Celtic sky-god equated with Jupiter. The only epigraphic record in Britain is an altar at Chester,[13] dedicated by a *princeps* of *Legio* XX, the second most senior centurion in the legion. The name of the god derived from the Celtic *taran* (thunder)[14] and, like Jupiter, Taranis holds a lightning-flash and has a wheel, the solar symbol,[15] at his side. Although there is only one inscription in Britain, Taranis is depicted on a pottery mould from Corbridge[16] where he carries a shield and a crooked stick, representing the *fulmen* (lightning-flash) (Fig. 9F).

Similar figures are shown such as the Smith-God, and it is obvious that there was an early connection between the hammering and fire of the forge with the sun and sky phenomena. The universal importance of the sky-gods arose from the great powers they were able to unleash from the heavens, which were thought to indicate celestial anger directed against human activities on the earth's surface.

Blacksmiths retained their aura of magic through the ages on the basis that they had access to these powers, and so earned great respect. Their tools were often depicted in use by the sky-gods; Thor, for example, the northern god, had his hammer and heavy blacksmiths' gloves. The powerful magic of the smiths' tools is demonstrated by their frequent appearance as reliefs on pottery vessels (see p. 99 below), although the function of such vessels is a matter of conjecture.

Cernunnos (the horned one)

The horned god was not only powerful but very ancient, as is implied by his normal posture of sitting in the Buddha position. On the Gundestrup Cauldron he is surrounded by animals and holds a torc, a symbol of authority, in his right hand and a serpent with the head of a ram in his left hand. The most important relief of the god is from Rheims (Esp. 1907, No. 3653) where two classical deities, Apollo and Mercury, stand at his side in subservient positions; Cernunnos is holding a large bag from which pours a stream of coins, and below is a bull and a stag, which may represent the domesticated and the wild animals, over all of which the god held sway. In a similar scene from Vendeuvres in the Châteauroux (Esp. 1907, No. 1539), the god has two youthful figures as his attendants, identified as his Dioscuri, with a pair of serpents.

Another important representation of this god is in Paris on the Boatmans Pillar (la Pilier des Nautes), which was erected in the reign of Tiberius (c.AD 17).[17] It consists of square blocks of four stages with a total of sixteen scenes, with the classical and Gallic deities in about equal numbers, although the pillar was surmounted by a seated figure of Jupiter. The classical deities are Jupiter, Vulcan, Mars, Mercury, Venus, Fortuna, Castor and Pollux, and four goddesses, and the Celtic deities are Esus, Taurus Trigaranus, Smertrios and Cernunnos. The special significance of these Celtic deities is that their names are inscribed at the top of each stone,[18] and, in the case of Cernunnos, it is the only known epigraphic record. Only the upper half of this relief has survived and it shows only the head and shoulders of the god. His horns are bent upwards like a pair of brackets, and from each hangs a torc. The face is full and fleshy and not that of a young man, nor does there appear to be any indication of a beard. He also appears to have two pairs of ears, one human and the other animal.

There are some rare figures from Gaul of a female form of the god. One in the BM[19] shows the goddess with a *patera* and cornucopia and sitting with legs crossed, as if the modeller was attempting to portray the Buddha position. The origins of Cernunnos are lost in the mists surrounding the hunting rituals of early palaeolithic man, but the earliest representation of the god is probably on a rock carving at Val Camonica in northern Italy,[20] on which is depicted a tall standing figure with antlers and what may be torcs on his arms, and there is probably also a serpent. The Celts clearly saw him as an earth god of fertility and plenty. The snake or serpent symbolises the life-force and powers of regeneration, hence its representation on the staff of Aesculapius and the *caduceus* of Mercury. It is only in the Garden of Eden that the serpent became evil.

Horned gods appear in Britain in sculptured reliefs, often in very crude forms. Anne Ross illustrates five (1967, Pls. 49–51), mainly from the north and one from London; they are all standing figures and hold spears, and one, a shield, thus having little affinity with Cernunnos. There has been a tendency to identify any knobs or spikes on a male head as antlers, whereas sometimes it is no more than a barbarised version of the winged hat of Mercury. This has been the case with a small crude altar found on the site of Smithfield in London; the figure is holding aloft a forked stick which is presumably his *caduceus*, but he has a purse in his left hand and there seems little doubt that it is intended for a figure of Mercury.[21] The most remarkable and undoubted Cernunnos from Britain is on a small plaque in the Corinium Museum, Cirencester[22] (Pl. 5) where the god is shown in his usual posture, although his legs are not visible, holding, one in each hand, a pair of serpents whose bodies writhe in vigorous S-shaped curves. On each side of the god's head is a rosette in a thick border. As Professor Toynbee remarks, 'it is a rough but bold and vivid piece of work'. A similar figure in bronze has been found at Southbroom, Wiltshire, but here the god is standing and holds the ram-headed serpents, which are coiled round his legs, and he wears a helmet with a crest. This bronze was found with a group of eight, all in the same barbarised style, the only other clearly recognisable deity being Mercury.[23] Dr Ross has also drawn attention to a remarkable Pictish carving of the eighth century from Meigle, Perthshire, which depicts a horned deity holding an intricate pattern of coils derived from the pair of serpents and with coiling legs ending in fish-tails. The god is flanked by two animals which are difficult to identify.

The ancient rituals performed by men dressed in animal heads persisted in Roman times and, of course, to a much later period. The evidence may be seen in the strange figures on pottery vessels decorated *en barbotine* or painted on large beakers, one from Colchester[24] shows four men with masks; one of them has been arranged like a radiate crown and the others appear, from the surviving fragments, to have been bird masks (Fig. 12D) (p.98 below).

Although the surviving evidence of horned deities in Britain is slight, it seems evident that it was widespread, even in the civil areas, and their power and significance far transcend any close association with hunting; they are part of the death and regeneration cycle.

Rosmerta

This Celtic goddess and her male equivalent, Smertrios, were seen, as their names imply, as 'providers',[25] and the goddess had the intensive prefix Ro- which signified 'great' or 'big'. While there are many inscriptions[26] and sculptures of Rosmerta, those of Smertrios are more elusive.[27] The concentration of inscriptions and reliefs of Rosmerta is in the Rhineland, especially at Mannheim,

Trier, Metz, Wiesbaden and Heidelberg; and there seems little doubt that it was from these areas that the goddess was brought to Britain. All the inscriptions and many of the sculptured reliefs link Rosmerta with Mercury,[28] and it would seem to follow that both were thought to provide the same kind of assistance when it was needed. Mercury was the god of the market-place, and traders looked to him for continuing profit for their businesses. One of his important attributes was a heavy purse, which was presumably equivalent to the cornucopia of Fortuna. This also applies to the name of the Celtic goddess, 'the great provider' (la grande purvoyeuse), and a remarkable relief from Wiesbaden[29] shows Mercury pouring the contents of his purse into a patera held by Rosmerta, while at her right hand is a cornucopia held by a small Eros. In some scenes the goddess has her own purse, as on a relief in the museum at Mannheim[30] where she holds in her right hand a crested serpent, the head of which rests on a purse held firmly in her left hand.

On another stone, found at Nöttingen, the goddess is holding a patera in both hands and a purse hangs from her girdle.[31] It is probable also that Rosmerta is holding a purse in her right hand, thus imitating Mercury on a stone from Montiguy.[32] These representations give a clear indication that Rosmerta was the deity one could call upon for commercial success. That her interests were much wider than this is obvious from her close affinity to Fortuna, whose cornucopia could contain anything one desired. To the gamblers it was the winnings,[33] but there was plenty for everyone. Fortuna also held the sphere, the rudder and the wheel, all of which could be turned or directed in the suppliant's favour. When the figure of Fortuna lost her classical appearance and became 'Celticised', she was often identified with Rosmerta, presumably on the grounds that the Celts would have seen the figure as their goddess, an aspect of assimilation considered above.

There is another goddess who is often associated with Mercury, and she is Maia, the god's mother. She was one of the deities of the seven Pleiades, but she never became a major figure in the classical pantheon. An argument has been advanced on the basis of an obscure passage of Macrobius (Sat. 1, 12, 16) that the name was an early priestly invention to account for the month of Maius (May).[34] The goddess to whom sacrifices were made on the first of May was Bona Dea;[35] but the animal selected, a pregnant sow, was more appropriate to Tellus, who, in spite of the suffix, was a primitive earth goddess of fecundity bearing a likeness to the eastern Cybele, and certainly more applicable to the period of crop growth. Whatever may have been the obscure origins of Maia, she was recognised as a minor figure, and, as his reputed mother, a suitable female, the Gauls may have felt, to be seen in association with Mercury, although a French scholar has suggested that she was mistaken for his wife.[36]

As a representative of fecundity, Maia was a natural choice for women wanting children, since they could link her with their supplication to Mercury for financial success in life. The promise of abundance and wealth in the form of cornucopiae and purses, which are depicted on some of the sculptured reliefs of the two figures, has led to the identification of the female as Fortuna, Rosmerta and Maia; the only significant difference is that the more barbarised versions tend to be those of Rosmerta rather than her classical counterparts. Espérandieu clearly favours Rosmerta rather than Fortuna, and in his general index he lists forty stones where there are two figures as Rosmerta (or Maia). The evidence for Maia comes from at least nine inscriptions from Gaul and Germania, where she is linked with Mercury,[37] and six where she is honoured on her own,[38] including a stone from Lyon (CIL xiii, 1748), where she is sitting on a chair holding the fruits of fecundity, like the Deae Matres. One of the most critical reliefs which has a bearing on this problem is on the famous Jupiter Column at Mainz.[39] This gave rise to a scholarly debate in which Körber, von Domaszewski and Oxé[40] supported the Rosmerta identification, but the weighty opinion of Salomon Reinach favoured Maia, and this was accepted by Espérandieu on the grounds that with twenty-eight deities, twenty-seven of which were indubitably classical, it would be highly peculiar for only one to be Celtic. The female figure is that of a mature woman holding the attributes of Mercury, a caduceus in one hand and the winged hat (petasus) in the other. Between the two figures, that of Mercury and the female, stands an ovoid object on a plinth around which a snake is knotted. This is identified by Espérandieu as an altar, of which there are four others on the column, all of the normal type. The object is more like a vessel in shape, but it is probably an egg, a life-force symbol. It is too speculative to suggest that this could be Rosmerta in a classical guise. Fortuna is seen on another panel, however, accompanied by Minerva.

Rosmerta also has a special attribute where she appears on reliefs found in Britain, a good example of which is from Gloucester,[41] where the goddess is partnered by Mercury who, unusually, is placed on her right side; she holds a staff in her right hand with a pelta-shaped terminal, presumably a symbol of authority.[42] In her left hand she holds a patera, the contents of which she is pouring into a small wooden tub (Pl. 6). A similar, though cruder, carving has been found at Bath[43] showing Mercury with a female deity on his right, who appears to be carrying a short staff, possibly a very crude attempt at a cornucopia, in her left hand, and she holds in her right, over a small wooden tub, an object which could have been intended as a large stirring spoon. Below the figures there are three hooded cucullati and an animal identified by Anne Ross as a ram, though it could also be a dog (Pl. 7). The same object is seen on a relief from Wellow in Somerset, now in the BM[44] in which there are three figures, the heads of which are all missing. The one on the right could be Mercury with a purse, although Professor Toynbee prefers a cupid with a bunch of grapes. The other two figures are female, the central one holding what appears to be a bunch of rods in her left hand, while the other figure holds a thin sceptre in her left hand and in her right a large spoon with a long handle; at her side is a tall, round bucket or tub, although it is shown here as if it was flat. The appearance of a conical lid described by Professor Toynbee is entirely due to the lighting on her published photograph. The four bands round the top represent the bronze bindings on a typical Celtic mixing bucket[45] and these are repeated at the base, but only the edges of two are visible in the break. The identification of the mixing bucket and stirrer confirms the identification of the figure as Rosmerta and this makes it very probable that the male figure is Mercury, although only his purse is visible (Pl. 8).

There are three and possibly four buckets on reliefs in Britain, one of which is from Corbridge,[46] where there is only one figure, that of a female standing to the left holding a long-handled spoon in her left hand in the act of stirring, while her right hand probably held a *patera*; the wooden bucket has four bronze bindings at the top and bottom. It was once identified as the tombstone of a washer-woman, but the relief is more appropriate to Rosmerta, and the two elaborate rosettes on each side of the head are reminiscent of Fortuna's wheel, though the decoration on the right hand edge is based on the *vulva*, adding the element of fertility (Pl. 9). Another example is a figure in an arched niche supported by columns found at Newcastle-upon-Tyne,[47] holding a cornucopia in the left hand and a *patera* in the right over a bucket (Pl. 10). A third relief with Rosmerta with the mixing bucket is from Nettleton, Wiltshire, and now in the Devizes Museum.[48] This stone is incomplete and in two parts; the goddess stands on the right hand side of Mercury and is holding the purse in both hands, while Mercury appears to be holding a *patera* and is in the act of pouring its contents into the bucket, which is represented by a round column standing on a base. The erosion apparent on the rest of the stone has probably erased traces of the bands of binding (Pl. 11). The act of role-sharing or reversal is shown on some of the Rhineland reliefs; on a stone from Wiesbaden, for example (Esp. 18), Mercury is standing by a seated Rosmerta and emptying his purse into her *patera*; while on one from Nöttingen (Esp. 350), they both hold purses and *paterae*. There is another stone from Gloucester[49] showing the pair, but the lower part has not survived, though there is a possible indication of a mixing bucket, in outline only, between the pair. Another stone with a possible relief of Rosmerta has been found at Stitchcombe, near Mildenhall,[50] on a site which could be a Celtic temple. This stone, now in Devizes Museum, is much damaged, but shows a female deity holding a *patera* in her right hand, pouring its contents into what appears to be a large roll-rim jar with a possible handle. The published illustration[51] clearly shows the outline on the viewer's right hand side.

Wooden barrels or tubs are also shown in Gallic reliefs, such as one from Epinal Museum on which there are six, of which two have legs. The scene has been identified as an apothecary's workshop,[52] and the goddess as an unknown deity of healing. Another wooden tub appears on a relief from Avallon,[53] a nude male figure stands centrally holding a long-handled shovel or paddle in his right hand. He appears to be dipping a cloth into a tub with his left hand. This tub stands on a grid which is clearly for heating the water, the tub presumably having a metal base. It is possible that this deity was associated with dyeing, and the paddle was for turning the cloth in the tub.

The wooden tub must have a special function which Rosmerta was able to utilise, though its significance seems to be confined to Britain. The purse she shared with Mercury provided profits for the merchants and traders, and the cornucopia likewise was a source of plenty for those in need; while the wheel, the rudder and the globe could be turned or steered onto a less weary and burdensome road along which the suppliant was travelling. Yet how could a wooden tub be seen as a symbol of plenty? In the sagas of their god heroes, the Celts had such an image in the magic cauldron. The grotesque Dagda possessed a cauldron which held 80 gallons of milk, and any number of whole goats, sheep and swine, which he stirred with an enormous ladle to make his porridge. At the great feasts such cauldrons could never be emptied. Perhaps there was a similar beer or wine tub and only kings and chiefs could afford large bronze cauldrons. For the ordinary Celt a magic wooden tub could contain an endless supply of drink and food, an assured supply of life's basic necessities.

The closest archaeological analogies with Rosmerta's tub are the splendidly decorated buckets found in the rich, late Celtic burials in Britain. The most famous of these is the one collected from a gravel pit at Aylesford, Kent, by John and Arthur Evans in 1888,[54] and given to the BM, where it was reconstructed.[55] Fragments of twelve buckets have been listed and described by Dr Ian Stead, with a reconstruction of one from Baldock (Fig. 6).[56] The diameter of these vessels varies, but they appear to average about 25cm (10in), and their height is about the same; but some, like the Baldock example, have triple feet, which gives an additional 3.5cm (1½in). On the vessels shown with Rosmerta there are no indications of handles or feet and they have much more the appearance of a barrel, especially the one from Corbridge, and there is the additional feature of the lid on the Wellow stone. Nor is the function of the vessel clear, except that the goddess appears to be pouring a liquid into it, and at Corbridge there is a projecting staff or handle, which may have been for stirring. As Dr Stead has shown, the buckets had a definite religious connotation since they were all, with three possible exceptions, found in graves, and in four cases actually contained the ashes of the deceased. Their primary function may have been wine buckets, or, as Dr Stead suggests, for holding the water used to dilute the wine. The obvious connection between red wine and the life-death-resurrection cycle may have underlain the burial use, a theme explained by Émile Thévenot with relation to the god Sucellos,[57] but it would seem to be extending speculation too far to associate this theme with Rosmerta. In her capacity as the goddess of plenty, her tub/barrel/bucket could mean more than food and drink, and include a more general provision of plenty.

Sucellos

The name of this deity appears on eight inscriptions[58] but he has been identified on over 100 reliefs, statuettes and bronze figures. He is linked epigraphically with only one classical god, Jupiter, on an altar at Mainz.[59] This association, and his bearded face, similar to that of Jupiter, has caused him to be identified as a sky god[60] and the father of the Celtic deities. His name means 'the good striker', or 'he who holds a good striking implement'; the prefix Su- is intensive, with the meaning of 'much' or 'very'. The implement he invariably carries is a mallet, not a hammer, with a very large cylindrical head and a long shaft, which is either thick or thin, in some cases rising well above his head.[61] The mallet head is obviously of wood and the shafts either of the same material or of iron, resembling the modern beetle or tool made for driving a post or wedge, or for hitting anything with a heavy blow. It has been suggested that the implement is no more than a sceptre of power rather than being representative of a particular trade or use.[62]

In the sense of a powerful striker, Sucellos could have been seen as a protector against a sudden turn of fortune, which often gives the impression of a heavy blow. The difficulty here is that such adversities are usually sudden or unexpected, and one is unlikely to seek protection in anticipation. The protection sought must, therefore, be more general or of a different nature. There is also another side to the problem, since Sucellos might be asked to deliver a blow on one's behalf against a person or organisation thought to have inimical designs. A slight piece of evidence is provided by an *appliqué* decorated roundel on a vessel from the Rhone valley which is inscribed SVCELLUM PROPITIUM NOBIS (Sucellos is favourably disposed to us).[63] The god is shown here with his mallet in one hand and a small flask in the other. He is accompanied by his dog, and there is a tree on one side, possibly a symbol of regeneration, if it is intended to be the Tree of Life. Further clarification may emerge from a study of his other attributes and associates.

The god has a female partner on an altar from Sarrebourg, found near a temple and inscribed DEO SVCELLO NANTOSVELTA.[64] (The name Nantosuelta is said by Dr Ross to mean 'winding river'.)[65] The Celtic goddess holds in her right hand a staff, surmounted by a terminal in the shape of a small structure or building, which has been separately identified as a bee-hive (Espérandieu and Reinach),[66] a dove-cot symbolising 'domesticity and maternity'[67] (Dr Ross), and a shrine (Thévenot).[68] The last of these seems to be the more likely, at least in appearance, especially on an altar from Speyer[69] where the goddess appears alone, and the object surmounting the staff has a single central opening. Espérandieu describes this as '*une maisonette*', but she holds in her left hand a censer, which would go well with a shrine.

The other association with these two deities is the raven, which appears on a panel below the two figures on the Sarrebourg altar, and on the wrist of Nantosuelta on the Speyer altar. As Dr Ross has pointed out, this bird is found in Irish sagas with the triple war goddesses[70] who were considered to have been concerned basically with fertility and childbirth.[71] Later, under early Christian influence, the bird suffered the same fate as the serpent, becoming a creature of ill-omen, presumably since both were closely associated with fertility and the life-force. There are mixed attitudes towards ravens in folk tales throughout the world. A persistent one tells how the bird was originally white and was turned black for some treachery to man. The Romans regarded it as a garrulous bird and it was connected with the Sun/Apollo. It appears as a tale-bearer in Ovid's *Metamorphoses* (ii, 547 ff), while Pliny the Elder wrote of a famous talking raven which lived with a cobbler in Rome at the time of Tiberius. When the bird was killed by a jealous neighbour, it was given a splendid funeral.[72]

Sucellos often holds, or has at his side, a jug or large pitcher, and sometimes a *patera*, both of which are considered to be symbols of plenty. He is also shown with a dog,[73] and, on a stone from Toul, there are what appears to be two barrels.[74] Another relief with barrels from Monceau near Autun[75] shows the god holding a short-handled mallet in each hand, and there is a small dog at his side. Whilst the barrels may have a possible life-death-regeneration connotation (as proposed by Émile Thévenot), there is no evidence to support this, and more information might be gained from considering the possible significance of the symbols on garments worn by the god on bronze figurines, which include rosettes, crosses and ring and dot motifs,[76] all of which could be symbolic rather than decorative. It is not, however, certain that all these figures are Sucellos.[77] A bronze figure from Viège (Valis)[78] has two features on his tunic: a large nail above an object with a short staff, with two curved horn-like projections at the top. The nail would be suitable for the good striker, and perhaps symbolises a firmly-held bond. The problem of this object has been discussed by M. Chassaing, who has pointed out that it bears a striking resemblance to ancient anchors of the Mediterranean, and also to some representations of the *thyrsus* of Bacchus.[79] Plausible as these suggestions may be, neither of them has any connections with this deity. A more mundane, but likely, explanation is that it represents a lynch-pin, as seen from the front.[80] This object is vital in holding a wheel in its axle and needs a good blow to fix it firmly in position; as such, it was essential for Celtic chariots and carts. More generally, it has become a universal term for someone or something playing a key role in any organisation or structure. The idea of Sucellos as the lynch-pin god has its attractions.

There is little doubt that Sucellos was a very popular and powerful deity, but it is far from clear what exactly were his powers, or his classical affiliations. In view of this, it is surprising that there are no clear traces of Sucellos in Britain. Professor Toynbee does suggest one possibility, on a small stone from East Stoke[81] (Ad Pontem) on the Fosse Way. This stone, now in the Nottingham University Museum, has two figures, each in a separate niche. One is undoubtedly a beardless male in a tunic, holding in his right hand what is described as a 'long-handled hammer'. It could be a hammer or a club, but the handle is by no means long in comparison with the Gallic images of Sucellos. Professor Toynbee considered the other figure to be female, but there is no indication of breasts, and the upper torso is bare. The figure wears a torc round the neck, and a kind of skirt, and holds a bowl of fruit in both hands; but the details are indistinct. The identification of these figures as Sucellos and Nantosuelta remains a problem. The only positive appearance in Britain is the name Sucellos on a silver ring found at York.[82]

Deae Matres – the mother goddesses
By far the most popular and widespread Celtic deities were the *Deae Matres*. More than fifty dedicatory inscriptions have been recorded, all but four from the military zone, but there are also more revealing sculptured reliefs found mainly in the Cotswolds. What is strange, however, is that the Celtic name is never given.

The worship of the earth-mother goddess can be traced back to the earliest times when men began to fashion images from clay or lumps of stone, and the most obvious features are the grossly swollen breasts and abdomen of advanced pregnancy. Much of the efforts of these early hunter-farming communities was spent in the constant struggle for fertility to maintain their very existence and continuity. In the Near East, this urge was focused on the great mother goddess Cybele.

The deities of the Celts were usually depicted in their potent triadic form and the mother goddesses were present everywhere, not so much in the universal sense, but as belonging to particular places, communities and even households. This is shown epigraphically by the frequent regional epithets. In military units the dedications attempted to give protection to men who originated from or had served in many places. This was neatly overcome by the words *Matribus Tramarinae*[83] (an abbreviation of *Transmarinae*), i.e. 'the mother goddesses from overseas' which included all such deities other than those of Britain. Another cover-all word was the Celtic *Ollototae*[84] which meant 'of the other peoples' (i.e. non-British). A centurion acting as a *praepositus* at Castlesteads[85] on the Antonine Wall overcame the problem with a dedication *Deabus Matribus omnium gentium*, i.e. 'to the mother goddesses of all nations'. Yet another formula used was *Matribus Communibus*,[86] i.e. 'to the universal mother goddesses'. There are two dedications by soldiers who set up altars to the mother goddesses of several countries, and these presumably covered the places from which the soldiers had originated, or in which they had served. A. Antonius Lucretianus, a *beneficiarius consularis*, dedicated an altar[87] to *Matribus Italis, Germanis, Gallis, Britannis*; a river pilot of VI *Victrix*[88] at York set up his altar to the mother goddesses of Africa, Italy and Gaul, whilst a *strator consularis* (transport officer) on the governor's staff at Dover[89] addressed himself only to those of Italy, presumably his homeland. Mounted units often appealed to the mother goddesses of the parade ground (*Campestres*) to protect the area where religious rituals and ceremonial parades took place. For individuals, the deities were the *Matres Domesticae*,[90] i.e. the mother goddesses of the household, showing clearly that every home had its own deities, a concept which came from the Rhineland.

The classical equivalent would appear to be Tellus, known also as *Mater Terra* and *Bona Dea*. She was often depicted with many breasts distended with milk, and sometimes wearing a crown and holding a sceptre and a key with a lion at her feet, as was Cybele. She was also the deity at the Fordicidia, one of the most ancient of all Roman festivals, which took place on 15th April, when the Vestal Virgins supervised the tearing of unborn calves from the wombs of thirty cows, and their sacrifice.[91] This primitive ritual was a crude form of imitative magic to encourage the fertility of the crops.

The power and nature of the mother goddesses is amplified by their association with the *Parcae*, the three classical goddesses known as the Fates who appear on two altars in Britain.[92] The Fates, Clotho, Lachesis and Atropos, controlled the birth, life and death of all mankind, the complete death-regeneration cycle, and although the mother goddesses appear to have concentrated on fertility and birth, it is known from some of their images in Gaul that their power extended far

Pl. 1 A scene from Trajan's Column showing Celtic auxiliaries presenting the Emperor with enemy heads (from a cast published by Cichorius)

Pl. 2 A *tête coupée* in relief from Wall (Letocetum) Staffs

Pl. 3 A *tête coupée* and a barbarised figure of Hercules from Wall (Letocetum) Staffs

Pl. 4 A relief of Actaeon turning into a stag and being attacked by his own dogs, from a tomb from Chester (76 × 61cm)

Pl. 5 A small stone plaque with a relief of Cernunnos and a pair of snakes from Cirencester

Pl. 6 A relief of Mercury and Rosmerta from Gloucester (58.5 × 43cm)

Pl. 7 A relief of Mercury, Rosmerta and three *cucullati* at Bath (28.5 × 22.5)

Pl. 8 A relief of Mercury, Rosmerta and a native deity from Wellow, Somerset
(30 × 33.6cm)

Pl. 9 A relief of Rosmerta stirring the contents of her magic tub from Corbridge

Pl. 10 Rosmerta/Fortuna in an arched alcove, holds a cornucopia in her left hand and a *patera* in her right hand over the magic tub with its bands of binding (44 × 25cm)

Pl. 11 A relief of Mercury and Rosmerta from Nettleton, Wilts. (30 × 22cm)

Pl. 12 A relief of the *Deae Matres* from Cirencester (78.7 × 63.5)

Pl. 13 A relief of three *cucullati* from Cirencester (25.4 × 30.5)

Pl. 14 A relief of three figures, a *cucullatus* and two attendants, each holding a large bag-shaped object, and a seated female deity from Wycomb, Glos. (17 × 22cm)

Pl. 15 A wooden effigy of a female deity (Epona ?) from Winchester

Pl. 16 The head of Antenociticus from Benwell (32 × 20cm)

0   10
cms.

Pl. 17 A typical head of a Celtic god with a *focus* on the top from Corbridge

Pl. 18 A relief of a winged and legged phallus and fist, clenched to ward off the evil eye, drawing a cart full of small phalli from Viroconium (Wroxeter, Shropshire)

Pl. 19 A Celtic head from a shrine at Caerwent, Gwent (23 × 12cm)

Pl. 20 A Celtic-type head as an early medieval corbel from Gloucester (20.3cm high)

Pl. 21 A pottery cult figure from Westbury, Wilts. (11cm high)

Pl. 22 Two views of a pottery cult figure of a male god from Carlisle, in the Tullie House Museum, (14.7cm high)

beyond this. In Britain they are occasionally and significantly accompanied by the *genii cucullati* and other attendants.

The sculptures and reliefs

To understand the full meaning of the *Deae Matres*, one has to study their sculptural representations, and although a fair number survive in Britain, they do not exhibit the great variety, quality and quantity of those from Gaul and the Rhineland.[93] They appear in threes, sometimes sitting, sometimes standing;[94] occasionally the central figure is different from the other two, strikingly so in the case of the *Matronae Aufaniae* at Bonn, where all three are wearing enormous hats like great cheeses[95] but where the middle hat is by far the largest.

The most astonishing example in Britain is from Cirencester (Pl. 12), in the form of a bold relief in a very free style which marks it out as an outstanding work, highly unusual when seen against the other contemporary British reliefs, which rarely rise above a pedestrian level of competence. It is in the local stone and must, therefore, have been carved at Corinium by, one can only presume, a Gallic sculptor with a knowledge of classical form. Haverfield was the first to recognise its unusual quality and he compared it with the *Terra Mater* on the *Ara Pacis* of Augustus.[96] There is certainly a comparison in style but it can hardly be said to have been 'copied fairly closely'. Professor Toynbee has described it with her usual eye for telling detail and scholarly judgement,[97] and charmingly notes, 'They recall a group of human mothers chatting together on a bench in a park or garden while watching their children at play'. The three children are no longer in arms, but sturdy youngsters who are actually standing to suckle.

This group contrasts with another from Cirencester[98] where the three goddesses in a hieratic pose are sitting stiffly in their chairs, holding plates of the usual fruit and bread,[99] and gazing at the beholder with a stern disapproving look, which, Haverfield commented, 'would daunt the bravest of men'. They certainly could well represent the officers of a branch of the Women's Institute, but these formidable figures may have been meant to remind men of the serious nature of fertility and its subsequent responsibilities (Pl. 12). Occasionally there is an extra figure, as on that from the London riverside wall;[100] here the additional figure is holding a suckling infant and is presumably *Dea Nutrix*, who was often represented in the form of a pipe-clay figurine,[101] of which at least six have been found in London,[102] and were especially popular in Gaul. There are, however, examples where one of the mother goddesses is holding the infant, as in one from Cirencester in which the central figure is holding the infant dressed in a little *cucullus*.[103]

Professor Toynbee lists several groups of the *Deae Matres* from the Hadrian's Wall area,[104] including an attractive fragment from Bewcastle,[105] which shows the end figure of the group sitting on a throne with an S-shaped arm-rest at the end and her feet on a footstool. The highly stylised dress almost gives the appearance of an icon, in contrast to the naturalistic group from Cirencester described above. The other groups from the Wall are crude and often badly weathered and damaged. Two from Corbridge,[106] although small, must have had dignity and power. The goddesses are sitting squarely, with their legs wide apart to hold large baskets or plates of fruit in their laps, and in one (No. 63), they appear to be wearing capes covering the shoulders; in both examples the heads are missing. Another found in Newcastle-upon-Tyne,[107] shows the goddesses in separate arched niches;[108] an inscription at the base is dedicated to the *Deae Matres Tramarinis Patriis* (*RIB* 1318) i.e. 'the mother goddess of his native land from overseas'. The carving is in very flat low relief; each goddess is wearing a kind of mantle and, exceptionally, none of them is holding anything. Their mantles fall straight on either side of the body as if they are standing, but the squatness of the bodies and protruding legs of seats must indicate that they are in their usual seated position. This highly stylised treatment adds a strange dignity with an almost Byzantine quality.

Mother goddesses also appear singly and sometimes in a very crude form. There are two examples from Britain, one of which is from Caerwent,[109] where an apparently naked female is seated on a throne, holding a leaf in one hand and a piece of fruit in the other. It is crude work and the form of the head is Celtic, but the solid, stocky figure, although so small, exudes great power and authority. Another nude seated figure was found in a corner of the Carrawburgh Mithraeum[110] on a small stone pedestal; this mother goddess is holding a basket, presumably filled with fruit. This association of the goddess with Mithras may not be so surprising, as he was a powerful life-force and regeneration deity; nor must the nudity of these two figures cause surprise, since the Celts regarded this as very powerful magic.[111]

That mother goddesses were held in great reverence by the Celts is shown not only by the large number of surviving sculptures and inscriptions, but also from the highly formal way in which they were portrayed; however crude the carvings, they are powerful and have a commanding authority. The goddesses controlled the very life-force itself, and are so basic that they could never have been supplanted by a foreign influence. They survived into Christian times, adapted with Cybele and Diana into the Virgin Mary, supported by the Holy Trinity.

The genii cucullati

They are shown as small male figures wearing the *cucullus*, usually in groups of three, which was the Celtic way of increasing the power of their deities. The *cucullus* was a large hooded cape covering the shoulders, or a cloak over the whole body down to the knees[112] – an ideal garment for protection against the harsh winters of parts of Europe. The name appears to be Celtic, or even earlier, and persisted into the Middle Ages in the word cowl, used for the hood of a monk's habit. The hooded shoulder cape was often made of leather.[113] The full garment was in use in Italy in the first century and referred to by Juvenal and Martial usually as a disguise[114] or to cover the face.[115] Columella lists it as a garment suitable for slaves,[116] and by AD 382 it appears to have been restricted by law to this class.[117] The garment was worn over much of Europe, but there is no evidence as to how it developed its special religious significance.

The *genii cucullati* are known as deities worshipped in the Roman Celtic world from inscriptions on two large altars found at a small temple of Celtic form at Walbelsdorf[118] in Carinthia, now part of the Austrian Tyrol. The origins of these hooded spirits are more difficult to trace. It is possible that there is a link with the Greek god of healing, Telesphorus, who wears a similar hooded cloak, but this is tenuous. There are other strange figures wearing the same garb listed by Heichelheim.[119] It is possible, as M.W. Deonna in his major study[120] has suggested, that the phallic shape of the *cucullus* and its all-enveloping quality symbolised mystery and darkness as well as the death-regeneration cycle. He concludes that, in Professor Toynbee's words, 'they were deities of death and after-life, of life through death, of healing and of fertility, as well as acting as protection from all kinds of evil'. Like many other deities, they obviously represent the whole cycle of birth, death and regeneration. Their appearance in groups of three vastly increased their potency, but they are also small, even shadowy spirits, always present but lurking in the background. The very fact that they are classified as *genii* places them in the category of minor spirits present everywhere. Professor Toynbee, in her paper in 'Hommages à Waldemar Deonna',[121] listed and discussed fifteen examples from Britain, at least one of which is doubtful; but more have been found since.

A fine example of the garment is seen on a tombstone found at Cirencester in 1836 and now in the Gloucester Museum.[122] The stone marks the burial place of Philus, a citizen of the Sequani on the upper Saône, on the west slopes of the Jura. A short *cucullus* ending at the waist is seen on a wall painting from Trier[123] in a villa scene, where it is worn by a man with a stick, who may be in charge of the gardeners; and from the same place has come a fine bronze of a man in a hooded cloak with fastenings shown down the front.[124] Another example from Britain is worn by the ploughman in the well-known bronze group of a plough-team from Piercebridge, Durham. This remarkable piece, now in the British Museum, has been the subject of a detailed study by Dr W.H. Manning,[125] who has drawn attention to its fine detail. The man is wearing a leather hooded cape over a belted tunic. The function of this bronze has been a matter of discussion. Professor Toynbee[126] has rather dismissed it as 'a straightforward genre piece, a scene from local country life', whilst Dr Manning points out that such decorative pieces are not normal in the Roman world and argues for a religious significance as a more likely solution. As seen elsewhere (p. 129) the plough was a fertility symbol and used in that sense as a votive gift. The Piercebridge group, as Dr Manning demonstrates, includes a bull and a cow, a combination used when ploughing round the sacred *pomerium* of a new city on the occasion of its foundation. But the ploughman is not a citizen in his toga, and urban development failed to reach the military zone in which the bronze was found. The same team would presumably have been used for marking out the boundary of the sacred *temenos* of a temple when it was founded, a more likely event in this area. It is doubtful even in these circumstances if the wearing of the *cucullus* would have had any particular significance, since it was the garment normally worn by ploughmen in the cold weather.

Four examples come from the Hadrian's Wall area. At Netherby[127] there are three figures standing facing outwards, wearing leather hooded capes which leave their right arms free; each holds in his hand an oval object, thought to be an egg, symbol of regeneration. In 1933 a stone was found at Housesteads[128] also with three standing figures facing outwards, each wearing the full *cucullus* extending almost to the feet. Dr F.M. Heichelheim has suggested[129] that the face of the central figure could be male and his companions female, but this is a highly subjective judgement, since they all have very set and solemn, almost fierce, looks. Another example was found in the Castle Yard at Carlisle,[130] but only two figures survive; they stand in an arched niche, and from the shape of the arch it is clear that the third figure is missing. Like those at Housesteads, their cloaks almost reach their feet. The stone is badly damaged, but enough remains to indicate the base of the stone and one leg, and it is quite apparent from this that the figures are indeed dwarfs. The remaining Wall example was found at Birdoswald, but it is only a single, hooded, cloaked figure less than 20cm (8in) high; it was free standing and worked in the round, and appears to Professor Toynbee to be only a bust standing on an abbreviated pillar. But the drawing in Bruce[131] (if accurate) clearly shows that the bottom of the stone is broken and that there are clear indications of legs.

The *cucullati* in the civil zone seem to be concentrated on Cirencester, where there are four examples, and also two from Daglingworth, near to Lower Slaughter, one from Bath and two from Wycombe, also in Gloucestershire. The Cirencester examples include a small stone with a curved top[132] and three dwarf hooded figures in a recessed panel; although the surface of the stone is badly eroded, the essential character of these *cucullati* is preserved. The angle of the legs, bent knees and peak of the hood seen in profile at the back of the head gives the impression that they are highly mobile and scurrying away rapidly, in contrast to the solid stances of two from the North (Pl. 13). Another small, also weathered plaque[133] has only two figures but is clearly broken, and it is impossible to know how many figures there were originally. The one on the outer edge is wearing the hooded cape over a tunic reaching to the knees, and is holding a round object, probably an egg, in both hands. The other figure is female, with thick hair, holding in both hands what seems to be a plate containing three rounded objects – probably fruit. From the angle of the knees she appears to be seated, and is clearly one of the *Deae Matres*; there may have been two more *cucullati* on the missing right hand part of the stone. A third stone was found at Prices Row, Watermoor Road in 1972[134] with three altars and part of a stone eagle, probably from a nearby shrine. This is another small group of three hooded figures standing in a frontal position; the central one is a *cucullatus* but the flanking figures wear capes open at the front to show a hand holding a stick. A mirror image of this scene is on the Daglingworth stone (see below). The details have been lost through weathering and damage, but the cloaks reach the knees and the faces would have been visible. On the left hand side of the stone is a small seated female, presumably one of the *Deae Matres*. The remaining item from Cirencester is a piece of jet[135] showing part of a nude figure, possibly male, and another in a large cloak with, according to Professor Toynbee, a hood thrown back over the head with the tip showing over his cloak.

The Daglingworth stones were found half a mile south-east of the church in 1951 and 1953 whilst a field was being ploughed where a building was previously known.[136] These discoveries, and an inscribed stone built into the church (*RIB* 130), suggest the presence of a shrine or temple.[137] The first of these stones is a gabled niche in which there are four figures, of which the central one is a *cucullatus*, but the other two wear capes like the Cirencester example above; two of them stand frontally, while the third turns to face a seated female as if making her an offering. The fourth figure, the goddess, holds a round object in her lap which may be an egg or part of a basket of fruit. There is a crude inscription cut on the base (*RIB* 129) which reads CVDAELO[. . .]v, but who the *Cudae* were is not known. The second stone, found in 1953,[138] is only the corner of a plaque with one male standing figure in what could be a hooded cape and tunic to the knees; he is in all probability one of a triad of *cucullati*. The inscribed stone (*RIB* 130) built into the church is a dedication to the *Deae Matres* and the *genius loci*. The shrine belonged to the mother goddess, and the *cucullati*, as the votive plaques show, were clearly attendant spirits.

Lower Slaughter was a large Iron Age and Romano-British native settlement, at least 10ha (25 acres) in extent, which has now been destroyed by gravel workings. Aerial photographs and observations by Mrs Helen O'Neil, over 25 years during stripping have left a partial record.[139] A group of three altars and five sculptures were found in a well (No. 5) in the Farnworth Gravel Pit in 1957[140] and are now in the Gloucester Museum;[141] these include two groups of *cucullati* (*JRS* 48, Pl. VIII, No 1 and Cat. V), three hooded figures standing frontally accompanied by a fourth, which appears to be another male figure, rather more bulky and wearing a kilted tunic; but the details have been lost by weathering. In the gabled top a pair of birds flank a rosette, symbols of life and death. The other sculpture (*JRS* 48 Pl. VIII, No 2; Cat VI) is the smallest and most crude of all; only 15 × 19cm (6 × 7½in), it depicts three *cucullati* only in outline on a flat surface with a minimal amount of carving round the heads. It is evident that these sculptures have been deliberately broken and thrown into the well during a campaign of destruction, and that they presumably came from a nearby shrine, although on the RCHM plan of the site the nearest recorded remains, the so-called 'farm-house', are 50m (164ft) away.

The native settlement at Wycomb, about 21km (13 miles) north of Cirencester, was about 12ha (30 acres) in extent and is known to have a temple in the central area.[142] A number of religious sculptures have been found, including two with hooded figures (Pl. 14). One is a small plaque only 15cm (6in) high,[143] which has three figures in a recessed panel; the central one wears a hooded cloak but the other two wear tunics and hold large circular bag-shaped objects in both hands which may be crude representations of fruits or bread, indicative of fertility. The other stone[144] is very similar, although one of the figures has almost been lost through damage. There are two other even smaller stones. Another Cotswold example has been found at Bath and was mentioned above (p. 68, Pl. 7), where the triad of *cucullati* is on a Rosmerta-Mercury dedication.[145] Here they appear to be walking to the left behind an animal which could be a ram; they are clearly, once more, in a subordinate position.

The strange single figure carved from a chalk block (Fig. 9A)[146] and found on Rushhall Down, Wiltshire, was thought by Professor Toynbee to be a *cucullatus*. It is a very crudely shaped figure with a large head and lentoid eyes, but what was identified as a hood may equally represent hair, and the lightly cut lines on the body indicate arms, in which case the garment being worn is not a cloak.

Another *cucullatus* included by Professor Toynbee is part of a pipe-clay figurine imported from the Rhineland and found at Reculver in 1949.[147] It is certainly a dwarfish figure wearing a short tunic and holding a scroll in the right hand, which in the more sophisticated Greek counterpart, Telesphorus, was thought to hold the secrets of healing. Such figures in pipe-clay are well known,[148] but not common in Britain. Little hooded men also appear on pottery decorated *en barbotine* (see Chap. 4), below.

The *genii cucullati* have been examined in some detail, as they are a typical British phenomenon in their popularity and triadic form, although they appear sporadically all over Europe. They are also evidence of the small, ever-present spirits which must have been an essential part of the everyday life of the Britons. The concentration of the surviving monuments on Hadrian's Wall and in the Cotswolds is due entirely, in the former case, to the military policy of recognising local spirits, and, in the latter, to the ready availability of a good quality stone which was also suitable for delicate carving. The representations elsewhere were in either wood or stone which has deteriorated or been extensively reused. These little local spirits have never been wholly forgotten, and such eminent scholars as Dr E. Egger,[149] K. Kerenyi[150] and Fritz Heichelheim[151] have supplied the idea that hobgoblins, gnomes, elves and leprechauns could be their survivors. It is sad to think that these ancient spirits have degenerated into ornaments which can hardly be said to decorate so many gardens of the 'villas' of today.

Epona[152]

The Celtic horse goddess was very popular in Gaul, where she was regarded as the Celtic *Magna Mater*.[153] She probably survives in Celtic literature as Rhiannon, the wife of Pwyll, Lord of Dyfed.[154] The name Rhiannon was derived from the Celtic *Rigatona*, 'the great queen'. Epona is usually depicted riding side-saddle on a small horse. The Celts were great horsemen, and the animal was an essential part of their way of life. Their wonderfully rich and colourful horse-gear and trappings clearly underlines the significance of this animal in warfare and its role in the highly stratified Celtic society. Specially trained horses were needed for the chariots, the use of which in warfare had survived in Britain, although they had passed out of favour in the rest of Celtic Europe.

The significance of the horse as a cult symbol is evident from the extensive appearance of the animal on the British coins and hill-figures, such as that at Uffington. The coins of the Atrebates range from the uniface staters of Commius to the sophisticated horse and rider of Tincommius and Verica. When these two latter rulers became clients of Rome, they were given skilled die-cutters, and the coins the kings selected from Republican types invariably had an equestrian motif.[155] The coins of the Catuvellauni under Tasciovanus, Addomarus and Cunobelinus repeat the theme,[156] although Cunobelinus soon expanded his types to other motifs. The Dobunni specialised in a stylistic triple-tailed horse,[157] while the Iceni used the horse almost exclusively on their coins.

Used as a decorative feature, there is the remarkable stylised horse-head mount from Stanwick;[158] strange horse-like creatures gambol on the Aylesford wine-bucket,[159] and there are elongated versions on a similar vessel from Marlborough.[160] The wine-bucket had a profound religious function as a symbol of regeneration and rebirth (as seen above, p. 61). The horse represented great fecundity and sexual prowess and, to a people who regarded the animal almost as an extension of themselves, it was seen also as a symbol of the life-force itself.

The goddess is often seen holding a *patera* of fruits, just like the *Deae Matres*, and even occasionally a cornucopia, thus clearly demonstrating that she symbolised fecundity and plenty. It is, therefore, hardly surprising to find that Epona was extremely popular in the lower ranks of society, and this can be judged by the number of pipe-clay figurines of horses with and without Epona, imported into Britain from factories in Central Gaul[161] for placing in domestic shrines. In Gaul over 300 monuments to her are known.[162] Epona obviously appealed to all those associated with horses and the stables and to the men of the cavalry units, many of whom were Celtic in origin, and they spread the worship of Epona along the frontiers of the Rhine and Danube in the Roman army. It is hardly surprising that the only epigraphic evidence of the goddess in Britain is from the military zone. An altar from Carvoran on Hadrian's Wall (*RIB* 1777) was probably erected by a trooper in the *Coh* II *Dalmatarum*, a part-mounted unit, and another from Auchendavy on the Antonine Wall (*RIB* 2177) where the centurion M. Cocceius Firmus[163] attempted to cover all eventualities with the four altars which must have come from the parade ground, and which he erected on behalf of his unit. Epona is here linked with the *Campestres* (goddesses of the parade-ground), Hercules and Mercury.

From the civil zone has come a figure, identified as Epona by Dr Anne Ross, found in a well on the Brookes site at Winchester in 1971.[164] It is a small wooden effigy, 18cm (7in) high, which has survived in the waterlogged conditions (Pl. 15). The goddess has a high pointed hair-style and wears a voluminous cloak with a very large collar, which Dr Ross describes as 'a prominent neck ornament'. She holds in her right hand a typical large key with a ring terminal, and a piece of cloth is folded over her left arm. This is a *mappa* (napkin) and, as it was customary for dinner guests to take their own *mappa* when they were invited to a meal, it was a highly personal object.[165] But, more important in this context, was its use for starting horse races, signalled by the magistrate dropping a *mappa*;[166] though even so, there may be some doubt over this attributed significance. Keys were the attribute of a number of deities[167] and symbolised the opening of the door to the spirit world; they were also seen as the symbol for sexual penetration, and subsequent fertility. Epona and horses, as will be seen below, were always closely associated with death and regeneration, the completion of the cycle. The two attributes of the Winchester figure could thus be seen as the *mappa*, symbolising the start, and the key, the finish, which led to the opening of the way to the underworld in regenerated form. For precisely the same reason, St Peter was given his key to unlock the portals of Heaven. There is yet another aspect of the key in its symbol of the Roman matron. Part of the Roman marriage ritual was the handing of the storeroom key to the new wife, and this was a symbol of her responsibilities, including the production of children. A key was one of the attributes of the ancient Earth-fecundity goddess,[168] Tellus. The identification of the wooden effigy as this goddess may account for her hair-style being a Celtic version of a turreted crown, and normally worn by her.

There is another important aspect of the horse in Celtic mythology which appears on Roman cavalry tombstones. The horsemen are often shown riding over the prostrate foe and this scene has been interpreted as symbolising victory over death.[169] The role of the horse as a regeneration agent is a natural corollary of its potency as a life-force and, as seen in other contexts, it is part of the birth-death-regeneration cycle. Bronze figures of horses with and without saddle and harness are often found in association with Mars in the shrines and temples in Gaul and Britain;[170] whether or not these have any association with Epona also is not known. The only name is on the base of a life-size bronze of a horse found in 1861 at Neuvy-en-Sullias near Orleans with a hoard of temple bronzes.[171] This remarkable horse was originally thought to have had a rider, as it has detachable reins; the name Rudiobos may have referred to him.[172]

The river deities

Rivers, like springs and most other natural features, had their own spirits varying in power and personality according to the characteristics of their waters. Crossing major rivers could have been hazardous at times, and many travellers sought the protection of the river spirit and cast a votive gift into the waters in thanksgiving or placation. Many such objects have been dredged out of rivers and crossing points, perhaps the most famous being the Battersea Shield now in the BM. This magnificent piece of Celtic craftsmanship was almost certainly made to a Roman order, since its pattern is absolutely symmetrical. It may well have been a thanksgiving by a Roman officer for a safe passage across the Thames at the time of the conquest.

Although many of our river names are very ancient survivals, some pre-Celtic, very few are actually the names of the deities. The reason for this, as Ekwall has suggested,[173] may be that the divine name was too sacred for common use. This was a universal practice with many gods, who had several names for everyday speech and for different occasions; his most reverend was always the most secret. Thus most of the river names are simply the Celtic word for water (*esc*) giving Esk, Usk, Axe, etc., or for river (*abona*) giving Avon, or *tam* which could be pre-Celtic meaning 'to flow' and giving Tamar and Tamesis (Thames). Other names may be a characteristic of the river such as 'powerful' (*stur*) giving Stour, or *dubo* (dark) giving us the Dore, or swift (*isa*) from which is derived the Aire, etc. Others may be tree names, such as *derna* (oak) giving the Romans Derventio, hence the Derwent, Dart and Darent, or *lem* (elm) giving the Leam and Lympe. There are several names which appear to signify the sacred character of the waters, as in *deva* (holy) from an ancient root from which has come our words divine and deity. There are no less than six River Dees in Britain,[174] and the Roman name for the fortress at Chester was Deva, a common type of transfer. From early Welsh sources we know that the Celtic goddess of the Dee was Aer, the goddess of war, a bloody and revengeful spirit, as many know from experience in her treacherous waters. *Alauna* was another name signifying 'might or holiness' and there are eight Roman examples and thirteen possible derivatives.[175] Some names have doubtful religious connections, since they could be interpreted in other ways. This applies to the River Cam, which could be derived from the Celtic *cambo* for crooked, hence a winding stream, but Camulos was the god of war, giving his name to Camulodunum. Similarly Lugos was one of the greatest of all the late Celtic gods, and from him has certainly come Lugdunum (Lyons); but how do we interpret the River Lugg and its Welsh equivalent River Llugwy? Ekwall suggests that it comes from the word *leuca* which means 'white or shining' (Leucetios was the god of lightning), applicable to both gods and water and has left us with River Loughar and the Roman fort of Leucarum in South Wales. A similar problem is the prefix *cen* which means 'powerful', giving us the Kennet and Kenn, which could equally have been applied to a spirit.

Direct connections with actual deities such as Verbeia (R. Wharfe, *RIB* 635) are rare and it is sad to record that even the most likely and lovely Sabrina (River Severn) is suspect. It is probably pre-Celtic and may be no more than a word for 'water', although there are scholars who have stoutly maintained the holy image. We are left with a Celtic goddess Belisama 'the bright one' who has given her name to the Ribble (Ptolemy ii, 3, 2), and possibly the spring god Aventius from whom the River Ewenni in South Wales is derived. The only other name which could be included is a place near Gloucester called Magalonium, which actually means 'a noble river' with the prefix *maglos* 'great one', as the god Hercules-Magusanus (Mumrills *RIB* 2140). Unfortunately this is an interpretation of a different name in the Ravenna Cosmography – Macatonium – making it into a more meaningful Magalonium, but the original may be nearer the truth.

Celtic deities peculiar to northern Britain

The best examples of Celtic deities undoubtedly come from the Wall area where epigraphic evidence is abundant. Antenociticus is only known from the Wall fort at Benwell (*Condercum*); there are three dedications of good-quality work (*RIB* 1327–9), but they show no link with any classical deity. The actual temple was found in 1862,[176] although an accurate plan and description was not published until 1941.[177] The excavation produced the head, forearm and part of the leg of a full-size statue of the god in the round. The head is a remarkable example of Celtic vigour with its writhing locks of hair (Pl. 16), and where the stone is broken at the neck there is a groove cut for a metal torc. The god is youthful but his name has so far defied interpretation. Unlike the other Wall gods, he appears to have been restricted to this one site, which has no doubt prompted Charles Daniels to suggest that he may have been introduced by *Coh I Vangionum*, which was recruited from Upper Germany and occupied the fort in the second century.

Belatucadros

Belatucadros was recognised over a large area of the western half of the Wall and Cumbria, as a distribution map of dedications shows (Fig. 4).[178] The name of the god appears in a variety of spellings[179] and appears to mean 'the fair, shining one', probably indicative of a solar origin, with fertility as his prime concern. As Professor Eric Birley has noticed, the dedications are by low-ranking troops and civilians. Dr Anne Ross has commented[180] on the large number of sculptures, mainly crude and in low relief, of horned deities in the area in which

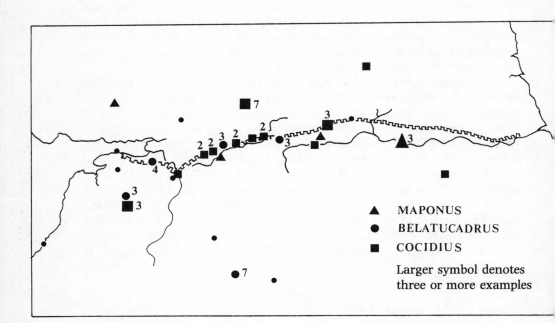

Fig. 4 A map of the Northern frontier showing the distribution of dedications of the deities Maponus, Belatucadrus, Cocidius

Belatucadrus held sway and on the possibility that they may actually represent the god. But some of these could well have been intended for Mercury, especially the ones from Burgh-by-Sands, where the figure holds a staff (*caduceus*) and purse(?). No less than twenty-seven dedications of Belatucadrus have been recorded, six of which are from Brougham. They are all from Roman forts with the possible exception of *RIB* 948 from Carlisle, but there was a military establishment there at least in the Flavian period. The only classical deity linked with this god is Mars, and on only five altars (*RIB* 918, 949, 970, 1784, 2044). This strongly suggests that the Celtic god had protective or healing qualities, and for soldiers on active service the former would have been the most desirable quality.

Cocidius

This was another god on the Wall with a concentration of dedications in the Irthing valley. A place-name FANVM COCIDI is listed in the Ravenna Cosmography, and the most likely site is near the out-post fort at Bewcastle,[181] north of the Wall, and where eight dedications[182] have been found out of a total of twenty-eight. But more critical was the discovery of two small silver plaques in the *sacellum* of the fort *principia* in 1937.[183] Apart from the punched inscriptions DEO COCIDIO, the plaques show the god beaten out in relief. He holds a long staff with a knobbed end in his right hand and, on the larger of the two plaques, holds a shield in his left. The small figure lacks detail, being in the form of a 'pin-man', but the other has a belt and decorated cape. Another representation of Cocidius is shown on an altar from the fort at Risingham on Dere Street, in advance of the Wall.[184] In 1936 only one side was visible, as the stone was walled into the byre of a nearby farmhouse, but then Ian Richmond persuaded the owner to take it out so that he could see the front. On this was the dedication to Cocidius and Silvanus, but above this was a relief of the god in a sylvan scene with a dog and a small stag. Although the stone had been severely trimmed, an outline of the god is visible, but the most significant feature is a bow in front of the figure. This link with Silvanus prompted Richmond to take another look at the famous rock-cut figure, known as Rob of Risingham, although deliberate vandalism has sadly reduced this figure[185] to its legs and tunic bottom and part of an animal, probably a hare, carried in the left hand.[186] The relief is better known from a drawing by John Horsley[187] when he visited the site in the early eighteenth century, the figure then being complete. He identified the figure as Commodus in the form of Hercules, but Richmond thought it was more likely to be Silvanus as Cocidius. There are two other possible rock-cut figures of Cocidius in this area, one, a tiny shrine at Yardhope in Upper Coquetdale, found in 1980,[188] where the figure is unclothed and holds a staff or spear in his right hand and a small round shield held aloft in the left; the other is built into the porch of a farmhouse at a place called the Heads, 3km (2 miles) east of Risingham.[189] The top and right side of this relief are missing, but the rude carving depicts a wide figure with a belted tunic, holding a staff in the right hand; the left is raised as if holding a shield, like that at Yardhope.

Silvanus and Cocidius also appear on a Housesteads altar (*RIB* 1578) erected by a *praefectus* of *Coh I Tungrorum*. On five other altars, however,[190] Cocidius is linked with Mars, who had a very ancient association with Silvanus as protector of the farm, its inhabitants and livestock against disease and predators. Cocidius must, therefore, be seen in a similar light but in a more hostile terrain. These two gods were not the only ones linked or associated with Cocidius. There is a very strange dedication from Ebchester (*RIB* 1102) which has been thought to read *Deo Vernostono Cocidio Virilis* (*Germanus*) *V S L*. It is an old find of 1784, and was rejected by Huebner and Haverfield as a modern recutting. The name Vernotonus is a possible Celtic name, the first part meaning 'alder' or 'marsh', but the precedence of the name over Cocidius makes it doubtful and there is a possibility that the original name, which had been eroded, was Mercurio.[191]

Maponus
Although there are only six known dedications and a graffito to this god, their quality and the rank of the dedicators clearly demonstrate his importance. A shrine to the god is known from the place-name *Locus Maponi* in the Ravenna Cosmography.[192] The place has been identified with Lochmaben where there is a lake, Castle Loch, 1½km (1 mile) west of the crossing of the River Annan by a Roman road. Lochmaben, with its early church and motte, is an ancient site, and it has even been suggested by Ralegh Radford that the medieval earthworks disguises an earlier enclosure which could have been the *temenos* of the temple to Maponus.[193] But there is another significant name – Clochmabenstane[194] – given to a stone monument in a circle which could equally have been the *locus Maponi*. There are eight of these *loca* names in southern Scotland and it has been suggested that they were tribal meeting places, where markets under Roman control could have been established. They would have been valuable for trade and for contact points with the local chiefs beyond the northern frontier.[195]

The connection with Maponus is strengthened by a graffito on a red sandstone slab found at the Roman fort of Birrens, a few miles to the south.[196] The scribble is very difficult to interpret and has been read CISTVMVCI LO(CO) MAPOMI or CISTVM DIO MAPOMI; below it has been scratched an animal which has been seen as either a hound or a serpent. The four legs and projecting ears and snout seem to favour the former and make an appropriate attribute when the link with the healing god, Apollo, is considered.

Three of the altars come from Corbridge;[197] one of them (*RIB* 1121) is badly weathered, as it had been used as the base of the market-cross, where it was seen by Stukeley in 1725.[198] The dedication, like the others from Corbridge and one from Ribchester, is to Apollo Maponus, and there are figures on the other three sides of the altar. One of the reliefs on the side is a nude Apollo with his lyre in his left hand, and on the other side Diana Venatrix, with a bow in her left hand and taking an arrow from the quiver on her back with her right. Unfortunately, the figure on the back is much damaged, but it is presumed to be that of Maponus.

The other two Corbridge altars (*RIB* 1120, 1122) were found in Hexham Abbey; one had been cut to form an arched lintel in the Saxon crypt. Both have fine lettering and on one (*RIB* 1122) Maponus precedes Apollo. All have been dedicated by high-ranking officers, a *tribunus militum*, a *praefectus castrorum* and a centurion of *Legio* VI. The remaining Apollo Maponus altar of exceptional interest comes from Ribchester (*RIB* 583). The dedication is to the holy god Apollo-Maponus (*Deo san(cto) [A]pollini Mapono*) and for the welfare of our Lord (*[pr]o salute (Domini) N(ostri)*) and the mounted *numerus* of *Sarmatarum Bremetenn(acensium) Gordiani* (dedicated by) Antoninus, centurion of *Legio* VI *Victrix* from Melitene, *praepositus numeri et regionis* . . . The remaining four lines are too badly eroded for realistic legibility. The imperial epithet of Gordian dates the stone to AD 238-44 and the dedicator is not only commander of the unit but also a *regionarius*, i.e. in charge of a territory, somewhat like the old British colonial district officer. For a more detailed study of this fascinating stone, see the work of Ian Richmond.[199] More important for our immediate concern are the reliefs on the sides and back. On one side is Apollo with his lyre and on the other would presumably have been Maponus, but alas the relief has been totally cut away, presumably when it was built into Salesbury Hall in 1578. On the back are two elaborate female figures, one in a niche wearing a turreted crown, her companion or attendant handing her a box or basket. According to Richmond, the junior figure represents the local region (*regio*) and she is making an offering to her senior, who represents the province. He further considered that this special gift is being returned, an imaginative interpretation which could have merits though remains unproven.

An altar found at Brampton, south of the Wall (*RIB* 2063), is dedicated by a group of Germans to Maponus, coupled with the *numen Augusti*, i.e. 'the divine will of the Emperor'. A small, silver, crescent-shaped votive inscribed *Deo Mapono* has been found at Chesterholm[200] and is presumably a votive offering to a shrine there. There is also, from the *vicus* of this fort, a relief thought to be of Maponus.[201] In an arched recess, a figure wearing a *cucullus* appears to be making an offering to an altar. At the left hand of the deity is a diminutive figure with spear and shield, possibly intended for Mars, and on each side of the head of the god are busts of two deities, one with a radiate crown identified as solar Apollo, and the other, a female thought to be Diana, both the classical deities on the Corbridge altar to Apollo-Maponus. The identification with Maponus must thus remain a strong possibility, in view also of the discovery of the silver votive, which is evidence for the presence of a shrine to this god at Chesterholm. A rather more doubtful identification was ventured by Ian Richmond of a head from Corbridge[202] on the grounds that 'the site has produced inscribed dedications to only one native god of importance and . . . these give a clear indication of the high standing of the cult' (Pl. 17). This particular head is a remarkable piece of Celtic work, but it is of an elderly male,[203] whereas the outstanding feature of Maponus was his youth. It may be another example of the head cult (see p.39 above). The very name means 'the divine youth' and Maponus occurs in the Mabinogion[204] as Mabon, the son of Modron, from whom he was abducted when he was three nights' old; he was famed for his powers over wild hounds and sought by Arthur, who eventually found him imprisoned at Gloucester, from whence he was rescued. The close association of Maponus with Apollo, a classical god who, as seen above, was primarily concerned with healing and was a protector against disease and plague, aided by his youth and solar powers, implies that Maponus must have been a Celtic solar god with similar gifts. This is confirmed by his link with Diana and hunting – the power symbol of death and regeneration – with the additional healing powers of his hound, an association seen below with Apollo-Cunomaglos (the hound-prince) at Nettleton and Mars Nodens with his dog at Lydney.

Coventina

Coventina, the water nymph, is one of the most famous deities on the Wall. She presided over the sacred spring by the fort at Carrawburgh and is known from thirteen altars, two incense burners and sculptured remains. The well was excavated by John Clayton in 1876[205] and found to be crammed with votive gifts cast into it through centuries of Roman occupation.[206] Over 13,000 coins were catalogued, but many were lost when some local miners, finding the site deserted on a Sunday, had an excavation of their own and took away many finds. The altars are all dedicated to the goddess with no links with other deities.

It is not unreasonable to suppose that this spring was known and venerated long before Hadrian's Wall was built, and the goddess, like Sulis, was peculiar to this one place. But there were many other springs and pools which must have had their resident spirits. They may have come under the general Roman name *loca*, discussed elsewhere as tribal meeting places, which in Ireland were very often by the side of lakes. There is a strange goddess who appears twice on the Wall, the *Dea Latis*,[207] but there is some doubt about the meaning of the name, which could have meant 'a pool'.

The Veteres

The strangest deities on the northern frontier are represented by over 50 small, usually very crude, altars, almost all of them on Roman Wall forts, although there are some at Lanchester, Ebchester and Chester-le-Street in County Durham and an outlier in the form of a silver plaque from the temple at Thistleton, Rutland. There are many different versions of the name – Veteri, Vitire, Vetiri, Vetri, Hveteri, Hvitri, etc. Some are singular, others are plural; most are masculine but a few are feminine. There has been much discussion as to the meaning of the name; an obvious explanation is that they are the 'Old Gods', but this has not been widely accepted. It has long been recognised that the addition of the H is Germanic, and it has therefore been argued that the Germans on the Wall either brought the god with them, or that this is their form of a god they found here. A more attractive idea[208] is that the name stemmed from the old Nordic[209] *hvitr*, which means 'white' or 'shining,' a name often used of solar deities. Another old Nordic word is *hvethr*, an epithet of Loki, the ancient German fire god, and thus a term which could be used of the classical equivalent Vulcan, the Smith-God. It is doubtful if this problem will eventually be solved until a figure is found which could be identified with this god. One has been suggested, on a small altar from Corbridge[210] (*RIB* 1145), one side of which is a standing stocky male figure in a niche, but unfortunately it is in outline only and there are no details. Nor is there much certainty about the inscription which consists of only three letters, v m d. It has been suggested that Veteris is not an unreasonable choice for a deity whose name begins with V.

A few of the altars have other features in relief on their sides. One from Netherby[211] reads DEO HVETIRI in well-cut letters on a small, but exceptionally carved altar with twisted columns and leaf-pattern capitals at the edges and astragal above. On one side is a snake coiled round a tree and on the other the forepart of a boar in front of a tree. These scenes were interpreted by Eric Birley as the hydra and an apple tree of the Hesperides and the Erymanthian boar. But in Nordic times the former would more likely have been intended as Yggdrasil, the Tree of Life at the centre of the earth, with the world serpent coiled round its foot; the boar was an important Nordic symbol associated with Freyr. There may be another boar on the inscribed face of a Benwell altar,[212] but it is too weathered for any certainty. Another from Carvoran has a boar on one face and a snake on the other.[213]

The poor quality of almost all these altars is reflected by the status of the dedicators, of whom eighteen have no name at all. Only one[214] is identified as a soldier, and this is at Carvoran (*RIB* 1795); he was named Julius Pastor, *imaginifer* of *Coh II Delmatarum*, the unit occupying the fort in the third and fourth centuries. Many of these dedicators have single, very ordinary names like Senilis, Facilis, Longinus etc., apart from the two Aurelii, Mucianus and Victor and Aelius Secundus and Menius Dada.[215] There is a strong barbarian element, and Aspuanis and Duithno could be Germans. One man with the curious name Necalames put up three altars at Carvoran (*RIB* 1793, 1794 and 1799). All dedicators appear to be men, except Romana at Greatchesters (*RIB* 1729) and another odd name, Mocuxsoma, who dedicated the Thistleton votive plaque.[216]

The Celtic deities of the civil areas

The permanent presence of the army distinguished the military areas from the purely civil in the distribution of Celtic deities. Every fort had its parade ground with a collection of altars dedicated annually, as well as temples and shrines to special cults. The material was usually stone and therefore the survival rate was good. In the civil part of the province there would have been a concentration of population and also of temples in the *coloniae*, cities and towns. It has become increasingly evident from aerial archaeology and casual finds that, scattered over the countryside, were far more sites of a religious nature than had been appreciated. There is another problem in the identification of the many sculptured figures and reliefs in stone, wood, metal and pottery found on temple sites or as surface finds with no known association. These deserve a special section which has been headed 'The Unknown Gods' (p. 99).

London, as the metropolis and centre of the Roman administration, would have been expected to produce a collection of dedications to imperial cults and classical deities. It is a sad fact, however, that from this great city, the capital of the province, the remains recovered have been surprisingly poor, although much improved by the recent discovery of sculptured blocks in the riverside wall from a monument arch and screens.[217] As would be expected, the classical deities are well represented and there is no Celtic influence here at all. However, there was a separate block with a relief of the three mother goddesses, accompanied by *Dea Nutrix*.[218] While the three goddesses are all upright with erect heads, the fourth figure is distinguishable by the incline of her head and the arrangements of the folds of her dress. Ralph Merrifield suggests that she is the divine empress, Julia Maesa, as she is wearing a veil.[219] Professor Toynbee, however, considers this solution to be unacceptable and suggests that the odd figure is the one on the right, and that this is a worshipper or possibly the donor.[220]

The other Romanised centres were the *coloniae*, Camulodunum, Lincoln and Gloucester. The settlers were legionary veterans who had largely been recruited from the barbarian frontier zones and were hardly shining examples of the sophisticated Roman citizen. More than half the population would have consisted of non-Romans, Britons acting as craftsmen, servants and soldiers' wives, as well as Gallic immigrants. One might expect, therefore, a strong Celtic element in the deities venerated. At Camulodunum there is an altar to *Matres Suleviae*, dedicated by a Briton of the Cantii (*RIB* 191). The Suleviae were goddesses with a wide distribution spreading as far to the east as Dacia.[221] They have been found in Britain also at Cirencester (*RIB* 105 and 106) and Bath (*RIB* 151), unassociated with any other deities. The Bath dedication is on a statue base set up by Sulinus,[222] a sculptor who presumably carved the figures for it, which, alas, has not survived; the same man was responsible for one of the Cirencester dedications (*RIB* 105). Another stone, found at Binchester in 1760 (*RIB* 1035) and since lost, had been read as *Sul[e]vi[s]*, and it would be difficult to suggest any other possible deities. These goddesses were presumably connected with fertility, but no one has suggested a meaning for their name.[223]

A Purbeck marble slab from Camulodunum carries a dedication to the Imperial deities and Mercury Andescociuoucus; this long and complicated name is probably no more than an epithet, the first part meaning 'the great activator' (*RIB* 193), implying that Mercury can make things happen. Another epithet appears on a small bronze plate (*RIB* 194) to Silvanus Callirius, in which clearly the stem *calli* (wood as in Calleva)[224] is most appropriate to Silvanus. The other two *coloniae*, Lincoln and Gloucester, have produced no epigraphic evidence, but the latter is very rich in sculptured reliefs, with several Celtic deities, including Rosmerta.

The epigraphic evidence from the remaining towns of Britain is remarkably small in comparison to Gaul and the Rhineland and consists almost solely of a few tombstones. Silchester has produced from a temple in Insula XXXV a series of dedications by a guild of *peregrini*.[225] One of these fragments bears the name of the god Hercules Saegon [. . .] (*RIB* 67). The Celtic word is probably an epithet derived from *sego-*, meaning 'power or force',[226] and thus applicable to Hercules. A small *Tempelbezirk* was uncovered at Caerwent and later elucidated by Nash-Williams.[227] The dedication was to the healing cults Mars-Lenus and Ocelus-Vellaunus, and the altar had been erected by one of the town guilds (*RIB* 309 and 310). This cult was imported from the Rhineland and is seen again at Chedworth (p. 114 below).

Another town temple to produce sculptured evidence is at Wroxeter, where Bushe-Fox excavated a range of buildings on the west side of the main street in 1913.[228] This temple, with its associated buildings, comprised a typical urban *Tempelbezirk*, and has been described in detail elsewhere. The excavator found a number of fragments of sculpture which had been deliberately broken when the site was destroyed by Christian vandals. These include part of a life-size head of a bridled horse, suggesting a possible connection with Epona (Report, Pl. VIII), and a fragment of a large frieze with two figures in deep relief; one is a three-quarter view of a nude from the rear, and the other is facing and clearly male (Report, Pl. VII). These pieces, however interesting in themselves, give little indication of the deities involved. The most important information about Celtic deities venerated in the towns comes from the sculptures and reliefs which are prolific at Cirencester but not matched by any supporting epigraphy. These gods and goddesses have been described elsewhere under their names (Chap. 3).

The evidence so lacking in the towns can be gathered from the countryside, mainly from the large numbers of temples and shrines which were usually built on the sites of places considered sacred. The largest, grandest and most prestigious of these was undoubtedly at Bath, where the hot springs was sacred to Sulis-Minerva. Bath is often referred to as a town, but the central position of its great temple, with all the large adjacent structures, demonstrates that it was a place of healing, and would have attracted large numbers of civilians, craftsmen and workers, housed on the edges of the temple enclosures, and where there was most likely a market and other facilities, such as hostelries for pilgrims. Although dominated by the powerful healing cult of Sulis-Minerva, other deities were present. A curse tablet from the hot spring appeals to Mars at his temple,[229] and there is an altar to Diana (*RIB* 138). Celtic deities are well represented; apart from the Suleviae mentioned above, the three mother goddesses appear in a relief of a very schematic group;[230] Rosmerta and Mercury are seen above three small *cucullati*[231] (Pl. 8). There is also an altar dedication by a Treveran to Loucetius-Mars and Nemetona (*RIB* 140). These Celtic deities are paired in the Trier area: Loucetius appears to mean 'the fair shining one' and his consort Nemetona is the goddess of the sacred grove.[232]

Another deity from the Trier area in Britain is Lenus-Mars at the healing temple-spa at Chedworth[233] (Fig. 9D and E) but again, other deities are present such as Silvanus and Diana, and there is a bronze votive hand typical of the Sabazius cult. The healing temple at Lydney excavated by Wheeler[234] was dedicated to Nodens-Mars, presumably the local god of this holy place. A dog played an important role in this cult, as is seen from the number of votive bronzes of the animal (Report, Pls. XXV and XXVI). There was also a stone figure of a seated Fortuna (Report, Pl. XXIV), and a bronze diadem, or possibly part of an elaborate vessel, bears a relief of Apollo in his four-horse chariot (Report, Pl. XXVII).

Another temple with a multiplicity of deities is that at Nettleton, Wiltshire.[235] The classical healer Apollo is here linked with the local deity Cunomaglos (the hound-prince) on an altar (Report, pp. 135-6 and Pl. XXXIV), but there is another altar to Silvanus and the *Numen Augusti* (Report, p.136 and Pl. XXXVc). There are also sculptures of a female deity, possibly Diana, with a hound (Report, p. 136 and Pl. IIa), and of a headless female deity in a voluminous but stylised tunic, reaching to her ankles and held with a bronze belt at the waist. She holds a box or basket by the handle in her left hand (Report, p. 138, Pl. IId). A fragment of another figure wears a similar garment and holds a staff in the left hand, which it is thought was for a double-axe, but this is far from certain (Report, pp. 137-8, Pl. IIc). Finally, there is a small relief of Mercury and Rosmerta, described in detail elsewhere (p. 60, Pl. 11).

Although many temples and shrines are known in Britain,[236] very few have produced any evidence of the names of the deities venerated at them. Some have been extensively investigated, as at Harlow, Essex;[237] Woodeaton, Oxford-shire,[238] and Springhead, Kent.[239]

CHAPTER FOUR

DEITIES AND RELIGIOUS
SCENES ON POTTERY

One greatly regrets the loss of all the wood effigies and shrines that could perhaps have helped towards an understanding of the beliefs and practices at the lower levels of society. There is, however, a possible approach through the figures on pottery vessels, which had a widespread distribution and were presumably within the purchasable range of most Britons. Scenes with figures and sometimes single objects are found on several types of vessels; they are either painted or *appliqué* from moulds or squeezed onto the surface, *en barbotine*. Vessels treated by these techniques are far richer and more plentiful in the Rhineland, where they are known as *Planetenvasen*[1] and *Göttervasen*.[2]

The deities whose heads and busts occur on these vessels are recognisable classical deities such as Minerva,[3] Fortuna and Mercury. Although carefully painted, these busts are somewhat removed from the classical form and can be considered to have been 'barbarised', or, more correctly, 'Celticised'.[4] These beakers also have painted inscriptions below the rim, such as ACCIPE ET VTERE FELIX. This classified them as 'motto beakers', for offering toasts or encouragement towards drinking. As these vessels are obviously for drinking, and possessed no religious function, one may well seek the reason for these elaborately painted deities, yet it seems to have been general practice to decorate vessels with deities, mythical creatures, hunting and gladiatoral scenes, erotic practices and many other features. It is doubtful if the purchasers and users ever examined these vessels, any more than people do their plates and tea-cups today.

Gods, goddesses and religious scenes are very common on the moulded bowls and beakers of glossy red slip ware known as samian and manufactured all over the Roman world in the first and second centuries. Later these wares were superseded by black colour-coated vessels produced in factories in the Rhineland and Gallia Belgica, and copied in Britain.

The scenes could not, therefore, be considered to have had any particular significance and this must also apply to all the other pottery. This does not, however, lessen their interest, since the Celtic potters included deities with which they were most familiar, or which they thought would prove to be popular with the purchasers. Pottery decoration may thus offer a means of estimating the relative popularity of the different deities among the lower classes. It may also provide details of local or generally accepted Celtic gods and goddesses, and even

Fig. 5 The Colchester Vase showing a hunting scene and gladiators (from Roach-Smith, *Coll. Ant* iv, 1957, Pl. XXI)

religious rituals. For these reasons, this source of evidence cannot be overlooked. It is unfortunate that the great majority of pottery sherds decorated with figures remain in museum collections, unrecognised and, until very recent times, for the most part unpublished. Many are extremely fragmentary and offer only a tantalising glimpse of what would have been recognisable scenes and figures.

Of the few identifiable figures, Mercury stands out, since his name is usually on the vessel. Excavations in 1957 near the town of Durobrivae at Water Newton produced five fragments of a vessel in cream ware with carefully-cut letters filled with red slip, together with a cock and a goat *en barbotine*, with details picked out in red slip. From the two animals it is certain that the figure of Mercury was also on the vessel, and the surviving letters can be arranged to form part of his name M[ER]CVRIO. The fifth sherd from the same pot has a brush-painted tree. This vessel was clearly large enough for several different scenes and/or deities. The name[5] of Mercury also appears in red-painted letters at the base of a damaged face-pot from Lincoln, now in the BM.[6] There are, however, no attributes to this god on the vessel and the face is very similar to those on other face-pots (Fig. 7).[7] One must, therefore, assume that this was a votive offering made to the god.

British potters made very poor imitations of the Rhineland vessels, and these were in the form of large indented beakers, with crude figures, usually made from

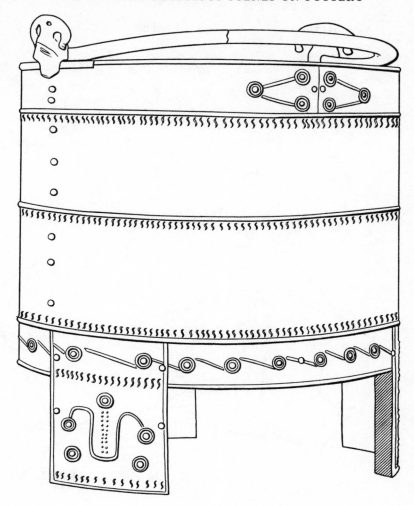

Fig. 6 A reconstruction drawing of a wine-mixing bucket from Baldock,
(31.6cm × 27cm)

moulds, placed in the indents. One of these in a fine grey ware has been published from Richborough,[8] of which fragments of four figures occur on five non-joining sherds (Fig. 8B). Two are described as similarly draped male figures with radiate crowns, one of whom is holding a whip in his left hand and has been identified as Sol; they could, however, as convincingly be Apollo.[9] It is far more probable though that the deities with their long tresses and high-waisted dresses are female. The object held in the right hand of one is round and has the appearance of a mirror, identifying the goddess as a draped Venus, who was far more popular

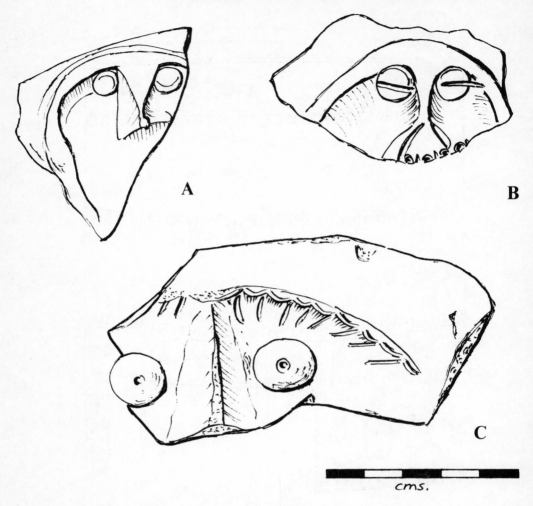

cms.

Fig. 7 Celtic faces on pottery vessels. A, B and C from Viroconium (Wroxeter, Shropshire), D from Lincoln (by Tig Sutton)

with the Celts than Sol, who was worshipped by some of the Roman senior officers and administrators. The third figure is also male and has a bare torso with a nether garment held by a thick girdle; a non-fitting sherd may be a leg and foot of this figure. Of the other figures, only a foot and an edge survives. The latter appears to be part of a shrine, with possibly a seated draped figure which could be a female deity. There are moulded letters at the side of this figure, and they have been read as OGMIA, though this is unlikely and, in any case, depends on which way it is read and whether it is reversed. Bushe-Fox noted a possible connection between his reading and the god OGMIOS, the Celtic god of eloquence, who is

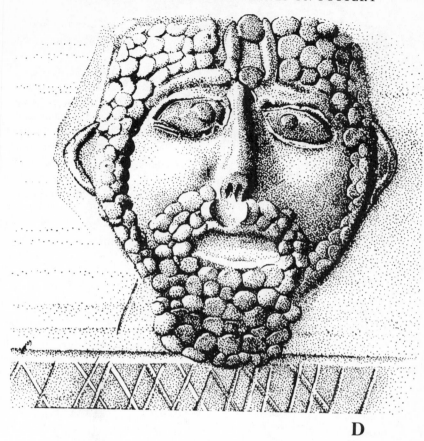

D

depicted in a very strange scene in Gaul, witnessed and described by Lucianus of Samosata.[10] Lucian further tells us that the Celts saw this god as extremely old and bald-headed with wrinkled skin, but dressed as Hercules in a lion skin with a club in one hand and a quiver in the other. It is difficult to associate any of the figures on the Richborough beaker with a figure of this kind. It seems more likely that the lettering gives the name of the potter.

Two fragments of a similar figure, but in a red ware with a dark red colour-coat, have been found in Kent.[11] This is of a nude female deity with long hair, with a long thin object ending in a circular blob at the right side (Fig. 8E). This also has a moulded inscription, but only three letters survive and appear to read [. . .] svs, retrograde. This would appear to give a male name, as in the nominative, and if so is certainly not that of the goddess, who is presumably intended as a Venus who could have been holding a mirror in her right hand. The figures on these vessels have been compared with those on a lost beaker found at Great Chesterford[12] and published by Roach Smith[13] (Fig. 8D). This had

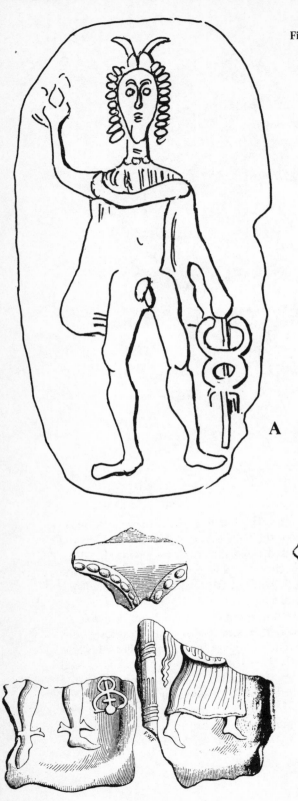

Fig. 8 Deities on large indented
beakers
A A figure of Mercury from
Wantage, in the Ashmolean
Museum
B Sherds from Richborough,
Kent (after J.P. Bushe-Fox)
C A figure of a male deity from
Lothbury, London in the BM
D Figures of Mars and Jupiter
on a Great Chesterford vessel
(after Roach-Smith *Coll. Ant* iv,
1857, p. 91)
E A figure of Venus and part of
a potter's stamp from
Aylesford, Kent

A

D

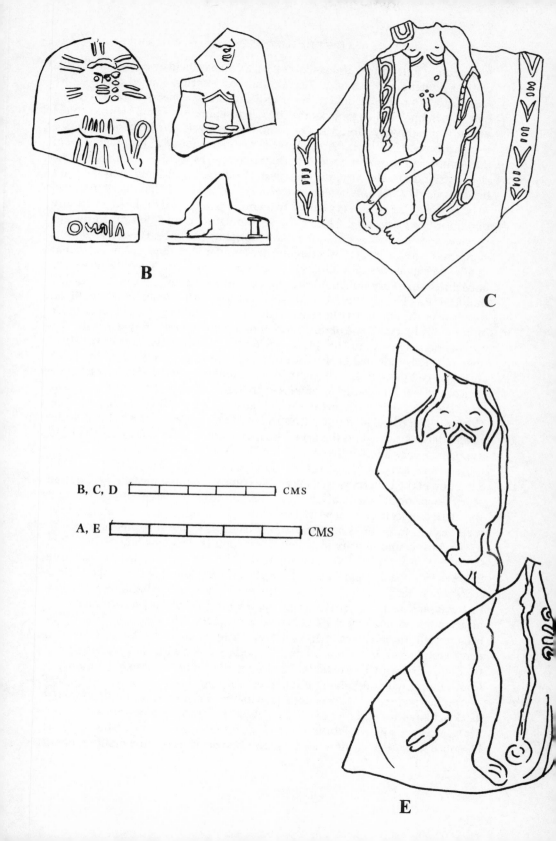

B

C

B, C, D ⊏⎯⎯⎯⎯⎯⎯⎯⎯⊐ CMS

A, E ⊏⎯⎯⎯⎯⎯⎯⎯⎯⊐ CMS

E

fragments of four figures of classical deities; the *fulmen* held by one identifies this deity as Jupiter and the *caduceus* held by another, wearing winged shoes, shows Mercury. A third figure holds a spear and shield and appears to be wearing a helmet, which could suggest Mars. The fourth figure is a female with a shield which is presumably Minerva. The 'dull, brown glaze' on the vessels offers a comparison with the Kent sherds. Another vessel was found at Wantage, now in the Ashmolean Museum, Oxford.[14] Only two figures survive and one has the clear attributes of Mercury: the *caduceus* is held in the left hand, and the right hand is raised. What he is holding in it is not clear, but it may have been intended to be a purse. The *petasus* is reduced to a knob on the top of his head, sprouting two horn-like wings (Fig. 8A). Of the second figure, only a pair of sturdy legs survive, and the lower corner of a garment below the knee. However, what is significant is an object at the side ending in a circular blob almost identical to that in a white slip at the right hand side of a Venus from Kent. These three vessels appear to be in a very similar fabric. There is a link between the Kent figures and that from Richborough in the arrow-like features with a touch of white slip on them under the diminutive breasts on the former, matching an identical feature on the naked torso of one of the Richborough figures. This strange feature also appears on a figure found at Lothbury, London, in 1865 and now in the BM[15] (Fig. 8C). This indented beaker is in a cream fabric with a good quality dark chocolate colour-coat, and the figure is well moulded and the details much finer than any of the other British examples. Although the figure is undoubtedly male, it has carefully delineated breasts which give it a hermaphroditic appearance. The right arm is held aloft bearing a spear, and the left hand holds a shield, while a small bow is carried on the arm. The decoration on the cloak over the right shoulder is very finely executed.

These five large indented beakers have striking similarities, and, with the exception of the London vessel, may have come from the same factory. They all depict the principal classical deities, although the figures are so barbarous that positive identification is not possible in all cases. The figures may ultimately have been derived from late samian vessels,[16] as Chris Going has suggested.

The most common deity found on British pots is the Celtic Smith-God, often linked with Tanaris, the sky-god equated with Jupiter. A mould for making a figure of this god for application to vessels has been found at Corbridge.[17] He is represented here as elderly and bearded, wearing a conical hat and carrying a rectangular shield and a crooked club, representing a lightning flash (*fulmen*); on his left hand side is a wheel, the solar symbol (Fig. 9F). This celebrated figure has become affectionately known as Harry Lauder, after the famous Scottish comedian. The same site has produced a pottery sherd with an *appliqué* figure of the Smith-God with a very similar face and hat,[18] but this example is standing in front of an anvil and holding a hammer and pincers.

Another pottery figure from Corbridge has been identified by Ian Richmond[19] as Dolichenus wielding an axe. This deity, brought from Commagene by the army, was the ancient Hittite sky-god of thunder and fertility. This god was identified with Jupiter, although a separate cult developed in the higher ranks of the army, since the deity was mainly concerned with safety and protection in war, as well as military victories. Dolichenus was especially revered by the Emperor Commodus, and this may have lead to a spread of the cult at that time. With only fragments of these deities remaining it is impossible to make a positive identification, except perhaps by the provenance. Richmond was probably right in assuming that the pottery figure on this Corbridge sherd is Dolichenus, since the cult is well represented here. A small fragment from Durobrivae in the civil zone depicting a bearded man in a conical hat wielding an axe[20] seems unlikely to indicate the spread of the cult of Dolichenus into the area.

Scenes of possible religious ritual on pottery vessels

Scenes on the Nene Valley vessels are cruder and more often in coloured slip rather than *en barbotine*, and they are even more enigmatic. A notable exception to this is a remarkable fragment in the Peterborough Museum,[21] which depicts a duel between two men; one, a carefully modelled form of a *bestiarius*, has a whip in his right hand, and a small buckler in his left, similar to one in a Colchester scene (Fig. 12C). This small protective device could have been a curved wickerwork shield known as a *pelta*, used by the Greeks.[22] The other half of the beaker has a fragmented scene of a pair of animals, probably intended to be leopards. But the most astonishing feature is in three fragments with the unmistakable figure of a female in a short tunic, leaping over animals with the help of her hands, which appear to be on the body of the leopard, reminiscent of the wall paintings of Minoan Crete (Fig. 10D). It is unlikely that such a scene was the result of a potter's imagination, and must, therefore, surely represent an actual event, enacted as an additional item to the normal *venatio* programme, similar to that on the Colchester vessel.

On one of the Peterborough sherds there is a figure of a Smith-God holding a pair of long-handled tongs and standing in front of a stand on which there is an anvil, and trails of smoke come from a furnace. On another, the lower half of a figure wearing a short pleated tunic, carefully indicated with incised and zig-zag lines and high boots, stands before the base of a composite feature, the central part of which looks much like a plough handle; but once again, it is difficult to interpret.

Other enigmatic fragments are four non-joining sherds from the same barbotine vessel found in the excavations at Plants Farm, Maxey, Cambridgeshire, undertaken by Gavin Simpson in 1964[23] (Fig. 10E, F and G). The vessel is a medium-size beaker (c.10cm [4in] in diam.) with a cornice rim in a dark chocolate colour-coat, dull red internally on cream fabric. It has been decorated with thick barbotine depicting a number of enigmatic scenes of which only fragments of three survive. One (10F), near the top of the beaker, with part of the rim moulding included, shows a female with a bare breast and an elaborate coiled hair style to which are attached long plumes; she appears to be holding a

A

B

C

92

E

F

Fig. 9 **A** A relief in stone of a *cucullatus* from Rushall Down, Wilts
B The bust of a female deity with a crested helmet and necklace carved in a
bone plaque from Great Casterton, Rutland (in the Oakham Museum)
C A small bronze figurine of a goddess (?) wearing a torc from a temple at
Yatton, Somerset
D and **E** Crude outline figures of Lenus-Mars from Chedworth, Glos.; E has an
inscription above: L]EN(O) M[ARTI (in the site museum)
F A pottery mould of Jupiter-Tanaris with his lightning-flash (his crooked
stick) and wheel, from Corbridge, Northumberland (in the site museum)

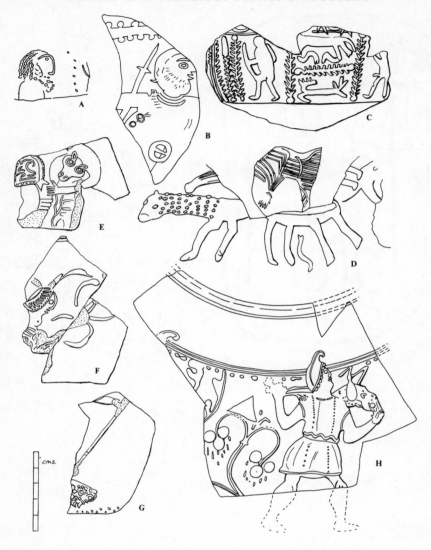

Fig. 10 Figures and scenes from pottery vessels from Britain

    A A bearded head from Lincoln in the BM (Walters M. 2480)

    B A man with a cloak and spear from Sawtry, Cambs.

    C A moulded vessel with animals and an archer from Heddington, Wilts.

    D A scene on a vessel from Water Newton, Cambs. showing a female leaping over a leopard (?)

    E, F and G Sherds of a vessel with enigmatic scenes from Maxey, Cambs.

    H An Eastern archer from Lackford, Suffolk

garland on a staff which bears a similarity to the *caduceus* of Mercury, and which would be unusual in the hands of a female deity. The second (10E) is equally difficult to interpret; a man seems to have an animal mask under his right arm, and holds part of it, the skin falling in front of him; on the left is the left arm of a *bestiarius* to which is attached a decorated buckler based on the Greek *pelta*; the lower part of the arm has the protective binding usual for these men. This is evidently part of a *venatio* scene in which animals were let free to be hunted and killed for the enjoyment of the populace. There are many variations to this basic theme, as the Colchester vessels demonstrate (see p. 98 below).[24] The third fragment (10G) is the most difficult to understand. An arm and hand hold a spear(?) which is being driven into a creature on the ground, of which all that survives is a strange head on a thin neck, but whether it is face up or face down, is not certain, since there are features which could be described as an eye, an ear, or possibly mouth and hair. This bears little resemblance to any particular animal, real or mythical. Dragons are not unknown in La Tène metalwork in Britain,[25] but this seems remote for third-century pottery; an alternative solution is that it is a Celtic copy of a creature of classical mythology, and it could well have been the hydra being slain by Hercules, who was widely recognised in Roman Britain as a salvation deity, especially at the time of Commodus, who identified himself with the god.[26] The vessel was most probably made in one of the Nene Valley factories. There is a striking parallel in the way the nose of the female has been depicted with that of a bearded man from Lincoln[27] (Fig. 10A).

Yet another interesting scene appears on a barbotine scene on a Nene Valley sherd from Grandford (Fig. 12A).[28] On this two men, one unclothed, are holding aloft a deer by its legs. It is quite impossible to hold an animal, alive or dead, in this position and the only explanation is that this is a wooden effigy being offered to the deity as a votive gift. There are examples of actual effigies of this nature from temple sites, such as the large wooden figures from Fellbach-Schmiden, Rems-Murr-Kreis,[29] although a pair of these animals, 90cm (35in) high, may not have been votive offerings but part of the shrine itself. It has been possible to postulate a reconstruction since there are human hands grasping the flanks of the animals, and the stumps of the broken arm indicate that the deity was seated between them. There is also another animal effigy, part of a prancing stag, which appears to be part of a larger feature, possibly a temple fitting.[30] There is no uncertainty about the large collection of material recovered from the source of the Seine.[31] These wooden images are mainly of humans, but there are some animals (Fig. 11).

The Grandford sherd is reminiscent of the strange scenes on the Gundestrup cauldron, where a pair of men are holding up small animals, one in each hand.[32] From the shape of their jaws, these animals would seem to be boars, but have been much miniaturised, as if they are small effigies and not real animals. The men, in turn, are being held by an arm by the giant figure of a bearded deity. It is true, however, as J-J Hatt points out, that the decoration on this extraordinary vessel is in 'an archaic and pre-realistic style' (J-J Hatt, 1970, p. 103) and perhaps one should totally disregard any possible reality in this scene. The same,

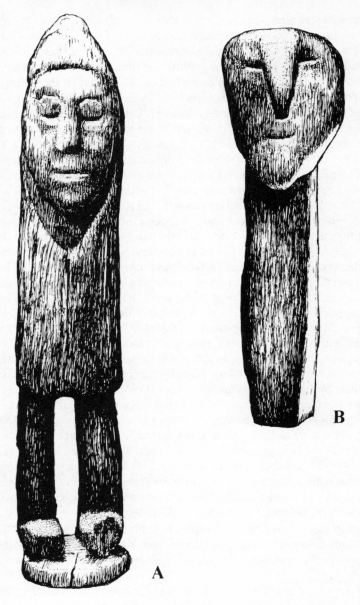

Fig. 11 Wooden effigies found at the source of the Seine (after S. Deyts 1983)
A A figure in a *cucullus*
B and C *têtes coupées*
D a horse

C

D

however, can hardly be noted from some of the later pottery scenes. It could be argued that the scenes depicted on pottery are so crude and fragmentary as to be unworthy of consideration as evidence of religious practice. Furthermore, the so-called circus scenes may have no religious basis whatsoever. But the potters must have had images in mind which their purchasers would recognise, and, whatever they may represent, they must be reminding people of events they had seen somewhere at festival times. The religious elements may have been totally forgotten but they are probably faint shadows of ancient rituals that were transformed into exhibitions of popular amusement.

The finest and most complete pottery scenes come from Colchester and are the products of the local factories.[33] Although far from complete, two barbotine beakers offer fragmentary scenes which are difficult to explain. On one[34] (Fig. 12D) are four human figures, three of which are wearing animal masks; one of these masks has six projecting spikes like a radiate crown, but these may have represented horns. Damage has reduced another to a thin beak-like projection, and it may have been a bird mask, possibly of a crow; the third has a thicker beak, comparable to one on the head of an eagle on a sherd from another vessel.[35] There is a fourth head lower in the scene, probably indicating a child or dwarf; the hair extending down the neck may be part of an animal skin, and there is a strange double knob of hair at the back of the head. The antlered figure is carrying a spray of foliage in each hand, and the other two hold sticks with curved ends in the right hand. This stick is a *lagobolon*, used for throwing at hares.[36] These features permit a possible interpretation of the scene: the men are disguised in animal and bird masks and one has branches or fronds as a camouflage, and it would thus appear to be a hunting scene from a *venatio*, but echoing an ancient hunting practice which has become part of a religous ritual.

The other scene (Fig. 12C)[37] depicts dogs, a hare and a bear with two hunters – one, a *bestiarius* equipped with a whip or small buckler, and the other, his assistant wearing only a diminutive girdle, and armed with a pointed stick. The oddest feature of this scene is the presence of four small hooded figures resembling *cucullati*; they appear to be being chased by the man with the stick, and are threatened by a dog. An explanation could be that they are clowns introduced into a mixed *venatio* scene, to provide an element of low comedy.[38] There is a more enigmatic figure on a sherd from Sawtry, Cambridgeshire, on a Nene Valley colour-coated vessel. This is a bearded man wearing a close-fitting helmet and a garment with possible brooches and a belt-buckle; he holds what appears to be a large boar spear with a cross-bar[39] (Fig. 10B). He may be a hunter-deity or merely a professional *bestiarius* in a *venatio* scene; other hunters are the Attis-like figures on a large beaker from Lackford, Suffolk (Fig. 10H) and the archer on a moulded bowl from Heddington, Wiltshire (Fig. 10C).

Other features on pottery

Blacksmith's tools are very commonly found as applied reliefs on large jars,[40] but what ritual function they had, if any, is a matter of conjecture, although one with a crude face mask was found as a foundation deposit at Chester-le-Street.[41] A blacksmith or Smith-God at work on a forge is painted in very inferior work on a vessel in the Wisbech Museum;[42] it is possible that another figure is holding a piece of iron on the forge or anvil.

Fertility and the powerful life-force is an ever-recurrent theme on pottery and stone. The phallus was a very potent amulet protecting the wearer, or building on which it was carved, from evil influences. According to Pliny (N.H. XXVIII, 36), babies and infants were especially vulnerable, and if a stranger looked at a sleeping child, it was customary for the mother to spit three times at its face, since human saliva was also efficacious against the evil eye. But more powerful was the protection of Fascinus, the *genius* of the phallus, amulets of which were hung around the necks of infants. It is hardly surprising, therefore, that it is found on pottery from the Colchester[43] and Nene Valley factories,[44] occasionally taking strange forms, like the one from Colchester of a phallus with a pair of legs and possible wings (Fig. 12B), reminiscent of a stone carving from Wroxeter (Pl. 18).[45] The oddest form comes from the Nene Valley[46], in which a man is running towards a woman, who is clearly indicating her genitalia, but the hurrying man is having a premature ejaculation (Fig. 12E). There is obviously an element of humour in such a scene, but, even today, it might be considered too crude for general viewing.

The unknown gods

Wealthy votaries no doubt offered silver and bronze busts or figures of deities, few of which have survived. Most of those known to us are carved in stone. The widespread pratice of the Celtic head cult has been described above and it is often difficult to decide which of the many stone heads were intended to represent local deities. The only guiding factor is the recognition of the true *tête coupée*, which must belong to the cult; heads still attached to necks may reasonably be classified as individual deities, but there is, however, little hope of identification, even though they may have been found in a temple or shrine. The difficulty is that there are so many of these deities without names in many forms in stone, metal, bone and pottery, and some of them are most probably clumsy local attempts to portray classical deities. To make a catalogue would be tedious for the reader,[47] and therefore a small selection has been made to illustrate the wide range and the fascination always attached to the unknown. An excellent example of this is the remarkable stone head found in a small shrine by John Ward in 1901, in his excavations at Caerwent. This shrine was found in Insula XI between houses VIII

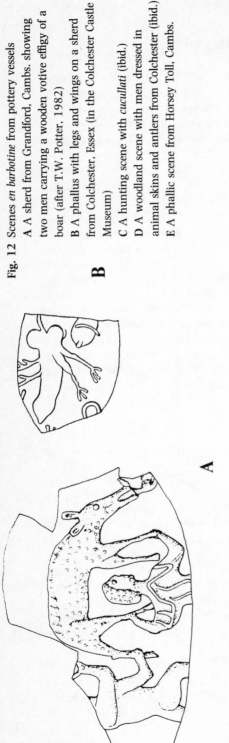

Fig. 12 Scenes *en barbotine* from pottery vessels

A A sherd from Grandford, Cambs. showing two men carrying a wooden votive effigy of a boar (after T.W. Potter, 1982)

B A phallus with legs and wings on a sherd from Colchester, Essex (in the Colchester Castle Museum)

C A hunting scene with *cucullati* (ibid.)

D A woodland scene with men dressed in animal skins and antlers from Colchester (ibid.)

E A phallic scene from Horsey Toll, Cambs.

A

B

C

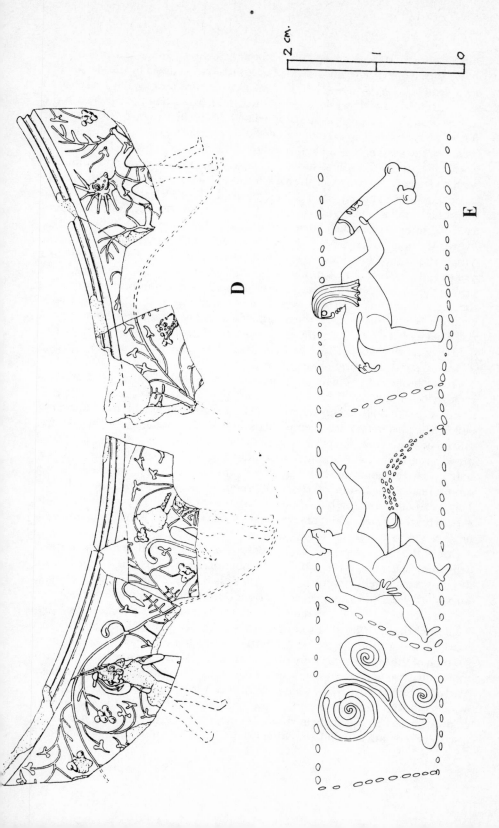

2 cm.

D

E

and XV, and it can be deduced from his report[48] that it belongs to a period when house VIII, which originally extended over the area occupied by the shrine, had been demolished. This area then became a large yard presumably attached to house XII in the north-west corner of the insula. The stone head has been the subject of study[49] by George Boon, who dated this change to c.AD 300; thus, the shrine would have been an independent structure facing the street. Inside, in a corner of the shrine, was a platform with three shallow steps, a circular stone block, c.41cm (16in) in diameter, and a head carved from a local sandstone. The head had deeply cut circles for the eyes, a rectangular nose, small mouth, deeply carved ears and an indication of hair on the head. The neck is extremely thick and the whole is overwhelmingly expressive, exuding power (Pl. 19), and far removed from the images from the classical world (see discussion above p. 43).

A very much cruder piece of carving in a local soft limestone was found on the temple site at Ivy Chimneys, Essex.[50] It appears to be a male deity standing in a niche (Fig. 13). It is only 120mm (4¾in) high and is carved on both sides with similar figures, one of which has a more pointed head and a shorter tunic than the other. They may perhaps represent the same deity in male and female versions. What is of interest is the way in which the eyes have been hollowed out and filled with a white paste. However crude and small it seems to us, in the dim light of the shrine it could have had a profound effect, giving the impression of an all-seeing spirit guarding one's interests.

The technique of hollowing out the eyes was probably copied from classical craftsmen, since it had been the practice to give special treatments to the eyes from the fourth millennium and may have been connected with the ancient eye cult.[51] The idea must have been to focus attention on the divine all-seeing eye, and it became a common practice with Celtic craftsmen in stone. A female head in red sandstone was found at Viroconium in the nineteenth-century excavations, with eye-holes filled with a vitreous paste.[52] An unusual example of a bronze head comes from Silkstead, Otterbourne, near Compton, Hampshire.[53] This is a small (5cm [2in] high) hollow-cast head of a young girl with large round eyes of black pebbles, and it may be a poor, but praiseworthy, effort to imitate a head of Venus.

One of the finest pieces of Celtic sculpture in Britain is the head of a youthful deity from Gloucester[54] (Pl. 20). The protuberant lentoid eyes and wedge-shaped face are typical Celtic features, but the hair is a very stylised copy of an early Roman model. There is, however, a serious dispute over the date of this head. Dr Kevin Greene has pointed out some close Romanesque parallels, and has suggested that the head is from a corbel of this period.[55] If this is a correct ascription, it demonstrates the strength of the Celtic survival of this art form.

Some of the figures bear symbols of authority, like the tin mask found in the main culvert at Bath.[56] The features are very heavily stylised, but on the head is a kind of crown. The eyes have been carefully cut out of the sheet, and round pieces attached to the back, so it would have been possible to fill in the void with a coloured paste, as was done in stone and metal. What is interesting here is the discovery of a native male deity, either as part of a shrine or as a votive offering, in

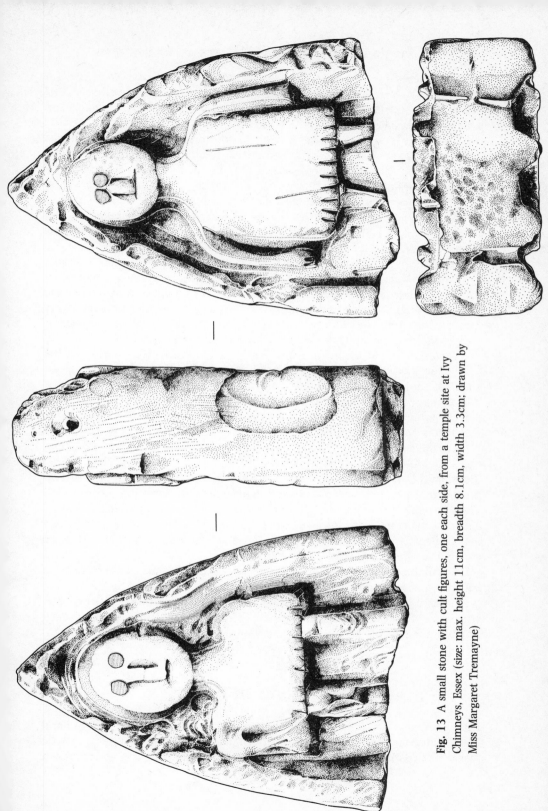

Fig. 13 A small stone with cult figures, one each side, from a temple site at Ivy Chimneys, Essex (size: max. height 11cm, breadth 8.1cm, width 3.3cm; drawn by Miss Margaret Tremayne)

the area sacred to Sulis-Minerva. This seems to indicate that there was no exclusiveness at these holy places, and that one could introduce one's own trusted deity. Another example of a similar intrusion is a small bronze male head with a large beard and bald pate, found in Coventina's Well.[57]

A local deity is possibly represented by a small stone relief, 30cm (12in) high, found at Wilsford, near Grantham, and published by Professor Frere.[58] It is of a figure wearing a kind of double-pleated skirt and with very bushy hair. The figure is suggested as a male hunter, but the hairstyle and skirt could indicate that it is a local copy of Diana or Attis.

A small bone plaque found on the site of a Romano-British villa at Great Casterton, Rutland (Fig. 9C), could represent a Celtic version of a goddess.[59] This consists of the bust of a figure, incised in the bone, wearing a high, elaborate crown, and behind and round the neck a necklace, or possibly a collar, indicated by five dots. Her arms are across her chest, and lines at the waist may show stitching or decoration. The head-dress, as Professor Toynbee stated, may have Roman or oriental origins, but the figure is of a religious nature. It probably decorated the toilet box of a lady of the villa, but it also acted as a protection charm and may not have been intended to be an actual goddess.

A remarkable Celtic head from Corbridge[60] has a sunken dish on the top of the head to act as the *focus*, clearly indicating that the head was intended to be an altar and that the base has been broken and lost. Like the Gloucester head, it is wedge-shaped with large lentoid eyes, a moustache and short beard. Although only 18cm (7in) high, it is an impressive, but almost malevolent, face (Pl. 17) which has been identified as Maponus.

Two small sculptured stone votives were found in the settlement at Wycomb, Gloucestershire, in the 1863–4 excavations by W.L. Lawrence.[61] The better of the two (Fig. 14) depicts an impressive looking square figure in flat relief with two much smaller figures under his hands. A particularly interesting feature is the marking on the back and sides of the stone, which, according to Jocelyn Toynbee, appear to indicate wickerwork.[62] The carving seems to be a crude representation of a Celtic shrine, perhaps even a portable one. Basketry or wickerwork were widely used in Celtic lands[63] and chairs made in this manner are depicted on stone sculptures[64] and pipe-clay figurines[65] and also baskets thought to have been used in wine and cider making, as seen on a stone from Sens.[66]

Similar decoration is on the smaller and cruder stone from the same site, which has the outline of a figure pecked out on one side, and lines cut on the back and top, which may also be a representation of wickerwork.

Cult figures in pottery

It may seem surprising that, with all these cult figures rendered in stone and metal, there are so few made from pottery, which is a highly suitable, plastic medium. The answer probably lies in the missing element of wood, which is even

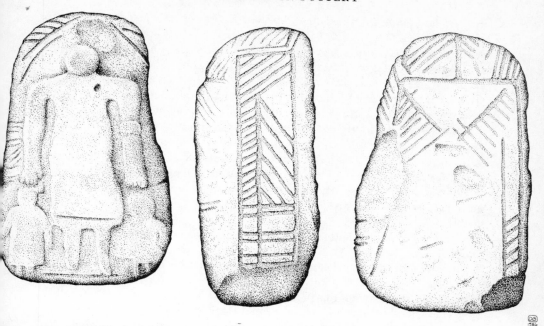

Fig. 14 Three views, front, side and back, of a relief of a sculptured stone from Wycomb, Glos., with a large figure and two small ones under each hand, standing in a shrine with markings which may represent basketry (10.7cm × 6.5cm × 4.5cm)

simpler and cheaper than pottery, and the vast majority of the figures would have been carved in this material, but have since perished. The only consolation to this loss is that when a cache of such figures is found in waterlogged conditions, as described elsewhere, they rarely include many recognisable deities, but are very crude representations of humans without attributes of any kind.

There are at least two figures in pottery which are worthy of attention. The first is from a large Romano-British site at Westbury, Wiltshire, which was destroyed in the digging for iron ore for the Westbury iron works from 1877 to 1882. Unfortunately, very little record was made of any structure, but it is evident from the large collection of finds deposited in the Devizes Museum[67] that it included a religious site of some size and importance.[68] No. 644 in the published list is also illustrated (Cat. Pl. xxxvii, 9),[69] and is described as:

Bust of a woman, rudely modelled in light grey pottery; broken off below the neck and bust. The hair is represented twisted and coiled round the head. The ears are little coils of clay, her eyes round dabs. The face is outlined by little bands of clay across the forehead and down each cheek. Nose and chin beak-like; the whole face grotesque. Diam. of head roughly 2¼in [6cm].

105

This is a fair, but uninformed, description which hardly does justice to the great interest of this cult figure (Pl. 21). It is not the hair which is twisted but a crown, with cross-straps on the top of the head terminating at the back with a rosette. The centre of the latter feature is broken, and this could have been an upright extension like a plume. The bands of clay round the face are attached to the crown, suggesting straps which continued under the chin. It is evident that the nose was applied as a strip, swelling at the bottom, which was then cut to form the mouth and the lower lip. There is some uncertainty as to whether it was originally a bust or a full figure. It was made in the fashion of a flagon, with the neck luted onto the body, and then burnished vertically, a technique peculiar to the potters of the south west in the Roman period. The sex is indeterminate and identification impossible. The crown must indicate a deity with power and authority, and this figure is a fascinating glimpse of a Celtic image of one of their deities.

A much finer pottery cult figure with more detail comes from Carlisle (Pl. 22), found in Castle Street in 1902.[70] It has always been described as part of a bottle or flagon, but any cursory examination shows that the top of the head was completed,[71] although at a later time a small hole (12mm [$\frac{1}{2}$in] in diam.) was made in it, perhaps to mount a plume or even pour offerings. It is a well-modelled head of an elderly male with beard and moustache and side-whiskers. The eyes are large and enclosed with markings, intended probably for eyelashes; the eyebrows are also clearly delineated but extend from the full width of the brow. He wears a crown with a projecting rim and is decorated with inscribed pellets. The back is partially broken, as if it may originally have been incorporated in a plaque or possibly into the neck of a vessel which would have provided a base. It is a small head, the total surviving height only 147mm (6in), but it is nevertheless impressive.

CHAPTER FIVE

CELTIC SANCTUARIES, TEMPLES AND SHRINES

The sacred places favoured by the Celts were woodland groves for which the Roman name was *luci*,[1] and the Celtic *nemeton*, a word which survived into Roman times in many place names.[2] In Ireland and Gaul there were individual trees which were thought to have special sanctity. The early Christians in Gaul had difficulty in combating this practice, and eventually accepted it by building a chapel near the tree or setting up a Virgin in the branches.[3]

The evidence for the existence of Celtic sanctuaries in Britain is surprisingly scant, since, as the literary sources suggest, the sites of seasonal festivals were places of special sanctity, often associated with natural features such as rivers, lakes, pools and springs. Water was a vital factor in primitive life, especially with desert and nomadic peoples. One of the human instincts not entirely obliterated by so-called civilisation is the ability to find water – a matter of life or death to desert nomads, as Moses demonstrated, thus becoming one of the earliest recorded water diviners. Water was always seen as a vital life-force and given the sanctity it deserves, having also a universal role in purification and lustral practices.[4] The places where water gushed from the ground were held in special reverence and seen as the abode of powerful spirits.[5] Even more sacred were the hot and healing waters, their mineral content giving them special properties by which they came to be widely recognised, and some of these places, like Bath and Buxton in Britain, developed under the Romans into large health spas.

Deities also had their abodes in rivers and streams and their sources had a peculiar significance, as that of the Seine has shown from the remarkable discovery of a large collection of wood effigies, obviously votive gifts at the temple there.[6] One might expect to find similar sanctuaries in Britain, especially at the source of the Thames, but the finest water deposit so far recovered has been that of the sacred pool at Llyn Cerrig Bach, in Anglesey.[7] This consists of a large collection of Celtic metalwork, mainly war-gear. In the sacred grove described by Lucan with such poetic fantasy, there were felled tree-trunks crudely hewn in the shapes of gods, and altars heaped with hideous offerings.[8] No standing shrines are mentioned in the Irish sagas, but the Celto-Ligurian sanctuaries in southern Gaul at Roquepertuse[9] and Entremont[10] were stone structures with monumental *propylaea*, decorated with sculptured relief and polychrome paint, in which the *tête coupées* feature prominently. From the shrines at Roquepertuse, a number of statues were recovered[11] including figures in the Buddha position.[12] This development on the south coast of Gaul must be considered exceptional and due to the influence of the Greek colonies such as Massilia (Marseilles).

Elsewhere in the Celtic lands of the north-west Empire, the building of shrines or houses for the cult statues was probably very late and may have been inspired by the Roman temples in Provence. There is a serious difficulty in identifying Celtic remains as shrines, since they have all the characteristics of the circular houses, and normally the only evidence is the close proximity to a later temple or shrine. This problem arose at Winchester, where a large circular area, 10.6m (35ft) in diameter and defined by a gully, was claimed as a shrine by its exavator, Martin Biddle.[13] This suggestion was based on the absence of any posts except those of a four-post structure in an off-centre position. Unfortunately, there was no stratigraphical relationship between the gully and this later structure, so they could have belonged to different periods and the gully merely represent an enclosure.

The later construction of the Romano-British temples, with large stone foundations and pits dug for ritual deposits, has had the effect of destroying much of the evidence of any slighter, earlier structures. Celtic shrines preceding later temples have been claimed at Frilford[14] and Maiden Castle,[15] but there is some doubt over their identification since they could have been priests' houses or store-huts; the practice of erecting timber circular buildings in rural areas continued long after the Roman conquest.

The only late Celtic temple to survive without any later structure covering it is that at Thetford, Norfolk, which has been completely excavated by Tony Gregory.[16] All the timbers had been thoroughly stripped by the Roman army after the Boudican Revolt of AD 60, and when a Romanised temple was built later, it occupied an adjacent site. This remarkable site consisted of three large circular structures, each c.30m (98ft) in diameter, the centre of which was approached by a ceremonial avenue. The most fascinating aspect of this site is the elaborate system of timber enclosures round the sacred area, consisting of seven rows of close-set palisades set out in straight lines and meeting at right angles.[17] The exact nature of these palisades, or fences, is difficult to determine, but it seems evident that it was designed to make the central area exclusive and free from impious eyes. The Roman deity who presided at a later date was the woodland spirit Faunus, not otherwise known in Britain and presumably, therefore, an import.[18] This choice may, however, indicate that the Celtic deity was a similar woodland spirit, and the palisades may perhaps have been meant to represent a kind of artificial grove. However, no artefacts were found to prove the religious nature of this site, and it has quite seriously been identified as the palace of Boudica.[19] The discovery of late Iron Age pottery and artefacts has been used as evidence of pre-Roman predecessors to later shrines at Worth, Kent,[20] Brigstock,[21] Hayling Island,[22] and Thistleton.[23]

More recently, structures with a totally different plan have been postulated as Celtic temples. These are square, some with a portico, and resemble the so-called Romano-Celtic temple which is very commonly found in the north-west provinces. At one time there was only one of this type, the result of a wartime rescue excavation in advance of the great airbase at Heathrow. Professor W.F. Grimes, the excavator, had some difficulty in accounting for this building[24] found on the edge of a small Iron Age settlement, and advanced the idea that it was a crude copy of a Greek prototype; this has not been widely accepted, though it is supported by M.J.T. Lewis.[25] It has been the brilliant excavation and interpretation of the hill-fort at Danebury, Hampshire, by Professor Barry Cunliffe which has led to a reconsideration of Heathrow, which had until then, been unique. At Danebury there were three square structures and an enclosure all in the same alignment.[26] The method of construction appears to be by vertical planks placed in the slots cut into the chalk. Another factor which separate these structures from the remainder of the buildings on the hill-fort, is that they appear to have continued in use after the site had been destroyed. The evidence considered as a whole would seem to indicate the probability of their religious nature.[27] This is strengthened when a comparison is made with similar sites at Lancing[28] and Cadbury.[29] The date of the Cadbury shrine is the ultimate period of the site, just prior to AD 43, and its function was confirmed by the burial of a complete ox and weapons in association; later votive offerings indicate the continuity of a religious nature, but it is assumed that all trace of any structure had been robbed to the rock-top.[30] With these discoveries, the Heathrow temple seems to fall into place, although it is much larger than Danebury and there was one piece of Roman pottery from a ditch, so some doubt still lingers.

The obvious similarity between the circular plan and the Celtic house has led to the concept of the shrine as a house for the god in the image of the cult figure. An alternative suggestion has been made by S.J. de Laet – that the model for this shrine was not the house but the tomb.[31] This theory is based on the urn cemeteries in Flanders, with circular areas for each burial, corresponding to the circular shrine. He also postulated that the later La Tène square enclosures, which have become known as *viereckschanzen* (four-cornered)[32] could be the origin of the Romano-Celtic temple plan. This is an attractive suggestion, since the great respect paid to the dead could be seen as a kind of ancestor worship, and the monuments in southern Gaul have numerous carvings of the *tête coupée* which provide another link. A serious flaw in the argument is that, in appearance, neither the tombs nor the La Tène cemeteries bear any likeness to the temple. Also, the introduction of the square burial enclosures would appear to be directly connected with the cart-burials which occupied such a space. In Britain, the late Celtic square shrines are all in southern Britain, whereas the only *viereckschanzen* cemeteries are in East Yorkshire.[33]

Votive shafts, pits and wells

There are other archaeological features which have been considered to have had religious functions of pre-Celtic ancestry, and they include what we know as 'votive' or 'ritual' shafts, which are deep holes penetrating the earth, some to a considerable depth of over 30.5m (100ft). What is of particular significance is the way in which these shafts were filled. In examples from Bavaria there were large timbers and even whole tree trunks, and one can readily appreciate the obvious symbolism in terms of fertility; but in some cases the timbers appear to have been carefully placed in position at the base of the shaft.[34] The filling of most of the shafts includes bones, animal skulls and traces of blood, which has led to the conclusion that they were related to sacrificial ritual.

The problem with these shafts is to deduce if they had a ritual function, or if they are merely disused wells, for, whilst well-sinking had become commonplace by the Roman period, there must always have been an element of magic attached to springs. Since wells are for repeated, and often long-term use, they normally had a timber or stone surround built at the top. During their use, objects fell in and could not be recovered, and one often finds complete vessels which had been lowered to draw water. When a well had for some reason ceased to be of use, it was usually deliberately filled in with domestic rubbish, which may have included large quantities of animal bones, and this could be interpreted as a ritual act. This applies also to large pits and one has to study the material of the filling, and how exactly it was placed, before being certain that it was not merely a disposal of rubbish and other unwanted material. Positive acts of vandalism can occasionally be postulated, especially in the destruction of pagan monuments.

The sacred Celtic sites under Roman influence

One of the most remarkable changes effected by the Roman Conquest was on the religious life of the Britons. Although seasonal ritual continued to be community events, those Britons who saw an improved fortune for themselves through manufacture and trading soon discovered that the newcomers were accustomed to making personal approaches to the deities and even to making contracts by means of vows made in the presence of a priest at a sacred place. This introduced not only the freedom of an individual to seek help from the unseen world, but also the element of commercialism.

Religion could be made profitable and there were landowners and other agents only too anxious to exploit the sanctity of places and the potency of resident spirits. It was in the interests of a landowner to develop a famous shrine to attract more people seeking cures, pregnancy, protection or some good fortune in their lives. The exploitation of man's deepest fears, and greed for wealth and power, has been the main business of organised religion in the more sophisticated societies for millennia. It was eventually perfected by the Christian Church, with its brilliant plan to create the fear of damnation and the promise of eternal bliss; the latter priceless benefit found multitudes of willing benefactors.

The Romanised businessmen had not advanced as far as that, but sacred sites could be made profitable, especially if there were springs producing an abundant supply of holy water, with a known or presumed efficacy, which could be bottled and sold commercially.[35] Health spas were an excellent investment, although the capital outlay in buildings could have been considerable. Some cults became self-supporting and could undertake the development work themselves, especially with the help of wealthy benefactors. Nor must it be forgotten that temples were used as banks since deposits were protected by the sanctity of the place; and no doubt astute temple management could arrange loans at suitably high rates of interest. The pagan temples were wealthy enough to attract the cupidity of the early Christian emperors such as Constantine;[36] by making Christianity the official Imperial cult, he gained control of the temple treasures.

This change in attitudes towards religion may have affected only a small minority of Britons engaged in commerce. The bulk of the rural peasantry and urban poor continued their traditional practices, many of which were later taken over by the Church and preserved into present times. The exploitation and commercialism seem not to have caused the Britons any doubts over their belief in an unseen world, and may even have been seen as confirmation and natural recognition of those forces by the newcomers. Despite this, however, impecunious peasants could still seek the aid of the gods in time of need as individuals and family groups.

The temples and shrines

One effect of the development of religious sites in Britain, as in Gaul and elsewhere, was that the old sacred Celtic shrines continued to be venerated. In the process, however, larger and more elaborate shrines were erected, usually in stone or with stone foundations, and this obliterated most of the traces of the earlier timber work. Many of the later Romano-British temples have produced evidence of this in the form of earlier artefacts and slight structural features.

The Romano-Celtic temple
By far the most common form of temple has come to be known as the Romano-Celtic, and one of the first to recognise it as a type, and to describe its main elements and draw a distribution map, was Sir Mortimer Wheeler.[37] The main structure is a square *cella* in which stood the cult statue, and, surrounding it, a low wall to carry the rows of columns of the ambulatory. The whole structure stood on a raised podium with a flight of steps approaching the central door to the shrine. The *cella* rose above the ambulatory roof and was provided with clerestory lighting. The temple stood in the sacred *temenos* area, which was usually rectangular in plan and walled, but it did not often occupy a central position, being sited at one end of the long axis. An altar would have stood in front of the temple, where people could offer their sacrificial victims to the priest and the *victimarius* who performed the ritual slaughter. Within the *temenos* area would have been buildings of various kinds, which could include the priest's

111

house and stores; if there had been a cult with its *collegium*, meeting and changing rooms would have been provided, and possibly a dining room and kitchen, and bath-house for purification. Other buildings could have been the temple shop where votives and sacrificial creatures could be bought. On festival days many people would come, and booths were erected to provide food and trinkets. In those temples on the site of a sacred pool or spring, this would have been the focus of attention and subject to architectural treatment.

In the past, excavations were concentrated on the temple itself, and only in recent years has attention been paid to the *temenos* area. Only when a number have been carefully excavated and published will it be possible to study all these other features important to the ritual of the place and its cult. These temples would have varied greatly in size and splendour according to their popularity and beneficiaries, and there would doubtless also have been many small shrines everywhere, most probably of timber, just as today there are the ubiquitous wayside crosses and shrines.

The healing spas

In a quite different category were the healing spas, where those needing to be cured could hold ritual commune with the resident deity. This would have been a lengthy process of preparation which could have included purification, the ritual meal and also contact with the deity – perhaps, as suggested below at Lydney, even in the temple itself – followed by the holy sleep. These activities required elaborate buildings within the sacred enclosure, thus creating what the Germans have conveniently termed a *Tempelbezirk*.

In Britain the finest and most prestigious was the hot springs at Bath. It is unfortunate that it was fated to become the site of an important abbey and later developed as a splendid Georgian spa, all due to the powerful magnet of the hot springs, whose curative qualities have always been widely recognised. This has meant that the Roman remains have suffered destruction or been built over by fine buildings which are equally worthy of preservation. It is remarkable just how much of the earlier period has been recovered by ingenious and expensive excavation and underpinning, especially by Professor Barry Cunliffe.[38] In spite of all this prodigious work and the earlier clearance, only part of the central area of this large temple complex has been uncovered. Of the great classical type temple, its podium and enclosure walls, only fragments are known. The other main structures are the sacred spring itself, the Great Bath, and a small normal bath-house at its east end. Of all the other buildings, essential to the operation of the spa, nothing is known, as they remain buried under medieval and Georgian buildings.

The sheer size and magnificence of the remains mark this spa out as the only one comparable to similar places in the Roman world. There is little doubt that there was a Celtic shrine to Sulis and that Rome recognised its great potential at an early date, as the earliest monumental inscription, although from a small shrine, is to Vespasian and dated to AD 79 (*RIB* 172). From the large number of dedications by soldiers and officers of the army, it would seem that there was a strong military association with its early development, and lavish Imperial patronage was also possibly the reason for the scale of the planning, although this has yet to be established by inscriptions.[39] One of the most remarkable features of the site has been the large number of votive objects recovered from the lower deposits of the pool, which include a fine collection of curses on pieces of lead.[40] These objects clearly indicate that by the fourth century this practice was open to all and sundry, but special facilities for the wealthy must also have existed in separate establishments, possibly on the north or west side of the temple.

A healing spa of a more selective kind has been more fully explored at Lydney Park by Wheeler in 1928–9.[41] It was built on the southern part of a large Iron Age hill-fort, where presumably there had been an earlier Celtic shrine, all traces of which had been eradicated by the monumental structures of the later temple and its accompanying buildings. The temple itself is extremely large and of a basilican plan, unusual in the north-west provinces. Even more strange is the temple shrine, and the four side-chapels formed by symmetrical external projections, three of which were screened from the rest of the temple. Wheeler suggested that these side-chapels may have been connected with a secret cult, devotees of which gathered here for special rituals. A simple and more probable explanation which he also offered, is that they were places where a small number of privileged people could partake of their 'holy sleep'. A large narrow building with about twelve cubicles standing to the north west of the temple was identified by Wheeler as the 'abaton', on the basis of a comparison with the great healing temple of Asklepios at Epidaurus, where a similar building produced inscriptions recording cures. This implies that there were two grades of patients: those who could afford the higher fee could sleep inside the temple, but the rest had to be content with the nearby abaton.

A very large courtyard building to the north east of the temple was identified as the guest-house. This had two ranges of rooms on the north-west side of the courtyard; on the south-west side a long hall with large piers to carry columns to support a substantial roof was entered from the courtyard by a massive arch. The south-east range was more fragmentary but thought to have been the servants' and kitchen quarters. This building was the hostelry where the pilgrims stayed during treatment, and the large basilican hall was probably the dining-hall. On the north-east range, one of the central rooms in the plan of the normal triclinium is much larger than the others and this could be a small, more private dining-room, or one used as a kind of commonroom for social occasions or, perhaps, group rituals associated with the cult.

The final building is a large and well-appointed bath-house, about the size of the town baths at Silchester. The spaciousness was not designed for large crowds but to offer a sense of magnificence, like the rest of the building. Nor is there any doubt as to its function: temple baths were an essential part of the cure and contain also the element of purification prior to any significant rituals. Lydney is an excellent example of a healing temple, but its scale and sumptuous character must indicate that it was only for those who could afford it – the wealthy landowners, merchants and high-ranking officials and army officers.

Another site on an even larger scale, although little is known about it, is Chedworth, dedicated to Lenus-Mars and probably based on the large and magnificent temple near Trier.[42] The pilgrim's hostel of the former has always been considered to have been a villa, but the absence of a house makes this identification very doubtful. The presence of a nearby temple and a number of votive reliefs is eloquent of its real function.[43]

A more difficult site to interpret is Nettleton Shrubb, in Wiltshire, excavated during the years 1938 to 1970 by various hands. The buildings were crowded into a very narrow valley, across the mouth of which ran a small stream fed by a spring. The stream was canalised and some buildings constructed over it. This seems to indicate that there was a water cult, and an altar is dedicated to Apollo-Cunomaglos, a Celtic deity not otherwise known and whose name means 'the hound-prince' (see p. 82 above). Many of the buildings on this site are difficult to identify, since they were savagely wrecked, presumably by Christians (c.AD 360).[44] Also there were considerable alterations due to a later use of some of the buildings, including a pewter factory which was established in the old temple workshop. The whole site was divided into walled areas, and it is probable that some of these were to restrict public access, as the plan suggests. This helps to a limited extent to postulate functions, some of which had been previously suggested by the excavators. The main problem is the absence of the bath-house. There is, however, a large area to the north of the stream where a spring has been indicated. It was in this area that sculptures were found in 1911, and where the original excavator, W.C. Priestley, started his excavation in 1938; after his death in 1956 no further work was undertaken here. Thus there remains an unexplored area immediately to the north of the temple and the structures over the river, and it seems a suitable place for a large bath-house.

Temple regalia

Some of the temples had bands of devotees who were dedicated to particular cults. They would gather together at festivals and carry out cult practices as a body. This was particularly attractive to the guilds (collegia), which favoured deities associated with their trade or crafts. A temple at Silchester in Insula XXXV produced fragments of statuary and three inscriptions (RIB 69, 70, 71) all from statue-bases dedicated by members of a collegium peregrinorum constistentium Callevae, a guild of non-citizens resident in Calleva[45], who may have been merchants. This temple is a Romano-Celtic type and appears to stand in isolation. Guilds and other bodies who formed the cult observances often had special facilities at the temples, such as a meeting hall, dining-room and perhaps a bath-house. There are indications of such provisions in city temples at Wroxeter[46] and Caerwent. The Silchester temple, however, has no such buildings near it. House 1 was also in the insula, but there is no evidence from the excavation[47] of any obvious religious associations. There is an altar base to the west of the temple, but no indications found of the temenos enclosure, so the extent of the sacred area in the insula remains unsolved.

The ceremonies performed by cult and guild members required special costumes and regalia. In addition most temples, and certainly the more wealthy, would have internal fittings, including elaborate candelabra and standards for processions. The priests too would have been suitably garbed, according to the type of ceremony. Most of this equipment would have been stripped from the buildings when the temples were thoroughly desecrated and vandalised by the Christians. The Emperors Constans and Constantius II permitted such activity, which was more violent in some provinces than others, and depended on the bitterness of local feeling and the memories of the sufferings of the Christians in earlier times.[48] Britain was also badly affected by the zeal of the Imperial agent Paulus, sent to root out all the supporters of Magnentius, as recorded by Ammianus (XIV, 5, 6–9).

The British metalwork one can positively identify as temple regalia equipment or furnishing is extremely poor, both in quantity and quality. There are no standards to match the remarkable example from Flobecq in Belgium,[49] but fragments may lie unrecognised in museums and undetected in excavation reports. For example, Wheeler published bronze chains from Lydney which he thought could have been part of a ceremonial head-dress.[50] They could, however, equally well have been hung from a standard, and could not readily have formed part of a head-dress such as that from Cavenham. The pieces of elaborate bronze sheets from Lydney could also have been attached to standards rather than having decorated boxes – in particular, the flat piece in the form of a diadem,[51] which would hardly have been suitable for a head-dress. Wheeler made the further suggestion that it was part of a round tray or bowl, but it could equally have fitted a standard of the Flobecq type. It depicts in relief the healing god Apollo in his chariot, accompanied by *putti* and sea creatures. Ritual crowns and other temple paraphernalia have been fully described by Dr Martin Henig.[52]

Burial customs

Another important subject to consider is changes in burial customs in Britain with the advent of Rome. The strong primitive belief that after death there was a spirit form of continued existence underlies the great respect paid to the dead in elaborate traditional burial rites, to avoid any inimical action by the departed spirit.[53] The Celts too, like many other societies, had a form of ancestor worship, for according to Caesar (*BG* VI, 18), the Gauls believed they were descended from a common ancestor, Dispater,[54] who was associated with the Underworld, the abode of the spirits. The burial customs in Celtic Britain varied considerably from tribe to tribe, according to their origins in Gaul and elsewhere, and, like all traditional practices, any changes took place over long periods of time. When a different practice suddenly appears in any area, it is usually evidence of a group which had arrived there and settled by right of conquest or superior power.

Knowledge of the burial rites of the Celtic Britons is unfortunately scarce, with a few notable exceptions,[55] and this may be due to the hierarchical structure of Celtic society, with the wealth being concentrated in the hands of the ruling groups. This could have led to a small number of wealthy burials, while the rest of the community were committed to graves without any artefacts which would help to date them. It must be assumed that everyone received due rites and a proper internment, and that a scatter of dismembered remains was due to the execution of enemies or criminals, whose bodies were often thrown away to be picked clean by scavengers, like any other rubbish.[56]

The best evidence from Britain to date comes from the large-scale meticulous excavation by Barry Cunliffe of the Iron Age hill-fort of Danebury in Hampshire.[57] Ten years of excavation produced seventy human skeletons and most of these were presumably due to natural death. A notable exception, however, was a large pit under the reconstructed north rampart; this contained three skeletons of men in their prime (i.e. 25–40)[58] deposited with reasonable care, suggesting some kind of sacrificial rite.[59] A feature of many of the other burials was their discovery in storage pits with domestic rubbish, which seems an easy but casual way of disposing of the dead; whether anything symbolic was intended is impossible to prove.

The war cemetery at Maiden Castle, excavated by Wheeler,[60] showed that thirty-eight skeletons were found, many with evidence of fatal wounds received in battle. Although the burials had been carried out in a hasty manner, they still had some of their war-gear, armlets and rings, including three bronze toe-rings. But more significant were the joints of meat, bowls and mugs which doubtless held sustenance, including the local brew, for the journey to join their ancestral shades. Wheeler found other burials of the period, but laid out under peaceful conditions, in all cases in the crouched position, and in most cases also with food and drink. Thus the Durotriges preserved the more ancient burial traditions.

With the more recent arrivals from Gaul, one might expect different practices. The major change which had gradually been spreading to the west from central Europe was that from inhumation to cremation. This had not, however, reached the most interesting groups of people in East Yorkshire, where an earlier La Tène culture persisted and with it burials of warrior chiefs with all their martial gear and chariots. They provided rich evidence in their cart and sword burials of their way of life[61] and equipment representing two distinct cultural groups. These burials have been found in small mounds, or in square enclosures (*vierecken*). Unfortunately, many were excavated in the last century, when methods were much less refined than today, and many of the details of particular interest that were not recovered are the details of the cart fittings and harness. Jewellery has been found, however, and even mirrors, but they seem poor when compared with the rich burials of similar type on the Continent. Not all the graves have produced goods – about a quarter seem to have been totally without them. These groups, probably herdsmen and farmers, had been settled in East Yorkshire for at least two centuries before the invasion and were presumably part of the large client kingdom of Cartimandua. There is no evidence so far discovered to indicate that these burial customs extended into the period of Roman occupation, but why this change should have occurred with a community which appeared to have no quarrel with Rome is difficult to understand.

In the south east was the latest group of settlers, who may have migrated to Britain in the mid-first century BC as a result of Caesar's invasion of Gaul. They came from areas where the cremation rite had been established. There are several different examples of such burials of this period, the best known of which are the Aylesford-Swarling group in the Medway Valley in Kent[62] and those at Welwyn.[63] The rich array of grave-goods must indicate that these are the burials of wealthy people anxious to take the visible remains of their status with them to the Underworld. The most interesting objects are the wooden buckets with their decorative bronze mounts and strips[64] in which the ashes had been placed. This may have been an association with Rosmerta, the Celtic goddess of plenty and good fortune. The Welwyn group of burials is even richer, and distinguished by the wine *amphorae*. That in Welwyn Garden City, investigated by Dr Stead, also contained other vessels of pottery and bronze including a wine strainer and a silver drinking cup. There was also a gambling board with a set of pieces. These displays of wealth also demonstrate the close links by then established with Roman traders in wine and fine drinking vessels.

In the south east there are examples of Gallo-Belgic type burial mounds, so common in Gaul and Belgica.[65] The most famous of these in Britain is undoubtedly the Lexden Tumulus at Camulodunum.[66] It was a large barrow, 24m (80ft) in diameter, but it has had a sad history of early robbing and general despoliation. When it was examined by the two Laver brothers in 1924, they found in the centre a large hole 6m (20ft) across, 'full of black soil'. The finds they made show how extensive had been the early robbing, and thus emphasise what must have been the astonishing richness of this burial. A fine bronze gryphon was probably a mount for a large wine crater. There were also pieces of a mail cuirass, and small marble *tesserae* which may represent the inlay of a table top. Another remarkable find is a silver medallion of Augustus, which is actually a *denarius* of 17 BC, cut and set into a small mount.

The remarkable survivals from the extensive robbing are worthy of detailed study. The man buried at Camulodunum was obviously a person of great distinction with connections with the Roman world, and it may even have been Cunobelinus. The rather slight gift of the medallion may have been given to him when he was a youth, possibly by a member of a royal embassy. This problem of interpretation needs much fuller and more detailed consideration, but it is an example of the importance of Celtic practices before the Conquest, which became an accepted pattern thereafter.[67] For the people of the south east, by AD 43, well accustomed to Romanised ways and gods, there was little dramatic change; but for the north and the west the picture is blurred, and the present lack of evidence inhibits any satisfactory conclusion.

Personal offerings to the gods: votive objects and amulets

Whereas the gods and goddesses may represent the hopes and fears of tribal or cultural groups, it is the amulets and votive offerings which reflect the desires and needs of individuals. By studying their forms and symbolism, one moves closer to the hearts and minds of Britons and Romans, and of men and women of other origins who settled in or were sent to Britain.

The amulet which anthropologists call the fetish was to be worn or carried to give protection against evil spirits and ward off accidents and disasters. It could take many forms and be incorporated into jewellery – especially rings, ear-rings and necklaces. Primitive people often made amulets of bone, ivory, horn or shell, as these materials do not corrode, thus giving them an extra potency, whilst jet and amber, with their electrostatic properties, were especially magical. This is usually true of gold, which in a pure state never tarnishes, and even today, many people wear gold jewellery as an apotropaic charm, or, more likely, by tradition. To the Celts the most effective amulet was the boar's tusk, as that animal was most widely revered for its savage power.[68] Boars' tusks and bulls' horns were attached to Celtic helmets, according to Posidonius,[69] and examples can be seen on the Gundestrup cauldron.[70] Small pendants are also found on Iron Age sites in Britain and two of these took the form of the axe, which later became a popular votive offering. These early axes[71] are quite different from the later forms, in having a bronze splayed blade somewhat like the medieval battle-axe. This particular type could have had a variety of functions in sacrifice or warfare – where it would have been particularly useful in severing heads – or in hunting or even agriculture. Apart from this, it has always been a symbol of power and an attribute of the sky-gods, so there is little doubt of its apotropaic value.

Men and women of the royal household wore rich colourful clothes, heavy with jewellery in gold and silver, according to the Irish sagas. Whilst some poetic licence must be allowed for here, one must bear in mind that these stories were not written down until the tenth century, by which time there would have been Viking influences, especially in metalwork and use of silver and some of the coloured stones. The description of Étaín at the well is a good example.[72]

> She had a bright silver comb with gold ornamentation on it, and she was washing from a silver vessel with four gold birds on it and bright tiny gems of crimson carbuncle on its rims. There was a crimson cloak of beautiful curly fleece round her, fastened with a silver brooch coiled with lovely gold; her long-hooded tunic was of stiff, smooth, green silk embroidered with red gold, and there were wondrous animal brooches of gold and silver at her breast and on her shoulders . . . .

Celtic workmanship in all metals was remarkably fine and heavily ornamented, and the scrolls derived from vegetation are a wondrously exciting art form. Often incorporated into the design are human and animal heads. Perhaps the intricate scroll work, like the maze, was thought to hold its own magic, but these other features added their own potency. Many examples have been illustrated by Paul Jacobsthal in his classic study.[73]

One can reasonably assume that these decorated features with their animal and bird motifs were thought to have a protective influence, whether worn as ornaments or as a status symbol, or carried and used as war-gear. Rome introduced her own protective symbols through the army, especially the eagle, heads of which often adorned cart-fittings.[74] Soldiers invariably had strings of melon beads hanging from their equipment, as the great number of these objects found on military sites demonstrates.[75] These blue glass beads were probably manufactured in Alexandria and were thought to reflect the blue waters of the sacred Nile and the sky, and thus to contain the essence of both the waters of life and the powerful sun for protection against being wounded or killed in combat. Another common amulet was the phallus, found in the form of pendants on many military sites, of both simple and elaborate form.[76] While these were obviously believed to give protection, it may be questionable whether decorative features on military equipment would have been considered to have had the same kind of effect. In the early first century, for example, many of the metal parts of the soldiers' armour were highly decorated with black niello inlay on a tinned surface. These designs are basically vine scrolls, but did this vegetation form symbolise the life-force? And was the vine specially selected for its product, the wine itself, with its obvious links with the Bacchic Cult? Similarly, one finds embossed reliefs on belt-plates – they depict the wolf and twins, or a bust of Tiberius flanked by a pair of *cornucopiae*.[77] Likewise, helmet cheek-pieces are often embossed or engraved with deities.[78] One can thus understand similar but more extensive decorations on cavalry parade armour,[79] since this was worn on special ceremonial occasions[80] at the beginning of the year, and therefore was of a religious character. At some stage, there had been a departure from personal choice to general issue on matters of equipment and its decoration, but this is not always an easy point to determine. There is no doubt at all about the jewellery, however, and in particular the finger rings with gem stones and intaglios, which have been the special study of Dr Martin Henig.[81] The bewildering variety of themes must indicate desires of individuals for the special protection they were thought to offer. From their extensive use in the Roman world, it is clear that most people appear to have believed firmly in the potency of such objects, and this would have been understood by the Celts.

In their closely integrated society, the Celts may have had little freedom of action as individuals, unless they belonged to the house of the ruling order. The fine clothes and ornaments, like those of Étaín, were the symbols of authority and power, as they have been until the most recent times;[82] even today there are types of status clothes, indicating social or professional distinctions.

The Celts sought to appease their gods with votive gifts on behalf of each tribal community rather than by individuals, which took the form of war-gear and bullion. Clearly the tribal chiefs were asking for more victories, conquests and wealth in precious metals. The Celts, as has been seen, were obsessed by war; it was part of their way of life and the proving ground of the youths aspiring to manhood.

The seasonal fighting of neighbouring tribes on the boundary territories were for the most part skirmishes, with much shouting, boasting and hurling of abuse, but the honour of the day was settled by hand-to-hand combat between picked champions. (Most young men were more likely to be bloodied by raids for cattle and slaves.) There is growing evidence from southern Britain that in the centuries preceding Caesar there were considerable shifts in the rise and fall of communities, as powerful tribes absorbed weaker neighbours,[83] and with this went the strengthening of the hill-fort defences. The reasons for this are difficult to understand, but it has been suggested that population growth may have been one of the more compelling factors.[84]

From c.200 BC, another factor gradually began to have an effect, and this was the steadily growing trade across the English Channel. This began through the sea-route with the Mediterranean, and the goods were shipped by the Gallic tribes of Armorica, the Veneti, Coriosolites and Venelli.[85] The British ports of entry for this trade along the south coast were Mount Batten, Hengistbury and Hamworthy in Poole Harbour. It is evident from the distribution of amphora fragments of this date that the trade was mainly in wine, for which the Celts soon acquired a great taste. The problem for the kings and chiefs of the British tribes was how to pay for these expensive imports. Without a currency it could only be done by barter, and the return goods had to be of a satisfactory nature to the Gallic traders. In transportation and profit return, precious metal and slaves may have been an immediate answer, but to maintain the supply, the rulers were obliged to increase their raids and conquests. It also seems likely that there was a large expansion of agriculture to produce grain surplus to local requirements. The effect of these changes on Celtic society is discussed elsewhere; what this brief reference is intended to convey is the growing need of the tribal rulers, either to ask the gods for success in their raid wars, or for the weaker to seek protection. Growing contacts with Gallic and later Roman traders may have led to craftsmen and other individuals, as well as the traders, offering gifts on their own behalf. This process would explain the number of pre-Conquest coins as votives found on the Hayling Island temple site.[86]

The votive offerings of the Celts

Caesar has a curious passage concerning the spoils of war, when he describes Gallic religion (VI, 17). He states that they vow to Mars (presumably his Celtic equivalent) that whatever they take after a victory, they will sacrifice the captured animals (*animalia capta immolant*); the remaining things they collect together in one place. Some tribes make heaps at sacred places and individual members of the tribe rarely conceal anything they have taken, nor do they venture to steal anything from the heaps for fear of death and torture, as was the punishment for such crime. Such a heap was found in Switzerland in the mid-nineteenth century.[87] The Romans continued this practice in the form of the trophy (*tropaeum*), and an example of this is at Idisiaviso, marking the victory of

120

Tiberius over the Germans.[88] A trophy is also seen on the monumental arch at Carpentras in Vaucluse[89] and forms the basis of the reliefs on the famous Arc d'Orange. It was also the Celts' practice to cast their offerings into sacred lakes and pools, as Posidonius records through Strabo's copy (IV, I, 13). In a temple enclosure at Tolosa (Toulouse), the Roman consul Q. Servilius Caepio found a great treasure of gold and silver bullion estimated at 15,000 talents, part of it in sacred lakes and the rest in the temple store; some of it may have derived from the famous Gallic raid on Delphi.[90] Posidonius also informs us that the Celts deposited great treasure in many other sacred lakes and that, when the Romans conquered Celtic lands, they sold off the lakes by public auction, and among the finds made by the lucky purchasers were complete mill-stones of silver.

Apart from these rich accumulations there were offerings in wood which only survived in special conditions, such as lakes and bogs where waterlogged conditions excluded oxygen, thus preventing the normal process of organic decay. Several votive deposits of this nature have been found in Gaul and Germania. One of these places is the Temple de la Forêt d'Halatte near Senlis, from which has come a remarkable collection of wood in addition to stone carvings, mainly of human heads, figures and parts of the body, but also of animals, though only domesticated varieties such as oxen, horses and pigs, and all in stone.[91] Excavations in 1963 at the source of the Seine produced over 200 figures carved in wood, but again mainly human[92] (Fig. 11), and parts of the anatomy obviously indicating diseased organs for which a cure was being sought. Whether they are images of deities it is not possible to determine, although one is of a little hooded man who could be a *cucullatus*.[93] These discoveries of large wood carvings of votive animals call to mind scenes which could help to explain a scene on the Gundestrup cauldron where a bearded deity, identified by J-J Hatt as Taranis,[94] with his arms aloft, is holding in each hand a human figure, which in turn is holding an animal. From the stiff positions of the human and animal figures it seems they must have been votive offerings hewn from wood.

Votive caches in Britain

During the last war, when the RAF station at Valley was under construction, the nearest bog was emptied by a drag-line and the peat scattered over the runways. Mixed up in it was a large quantity of iron-work, of which one chain was actually used for hauling lorries out of the marshy ground. Thanks to the quick action of the engineers in reporting the discovery to the National Museum of Wales, and Sir Cyril Fox, who hastened to the site, most of the metalwork was recovered, conserved, studied and published with great promptitude in wartime conditions.[95] It was soon recognised that this was an exceptional collection of Celtic war-gear and that it must have been deposited in a sacred lake. Analysis showed that the objects had widespread origins and had been deposited as contributions from many of the tribes of southern Britain. The dramatic description by Tacitus (*Ann.* XIV, 30) of the Druids and their followers facing the army of Paullinus on the Menai Straits adds significance to this discovery.

On Anglesey, there must have been an ancient sanctuary to which the Druids had eventually fled from Camulodunum and other tribal centres at the time of the Roman invasion.[96] Among the masses of war-gear there were some currency bars, but no sign of any bullion, which may still be buried in one of the other lakes, unless the Romans emptied them all, which is more than likely. Another aspect of the hoard is that a large number of the objects had been deliberately bent or broken as an act of ritual killing, to make them acceptable as sacrifices. One important element in the study of the material was that Fox, with his typical skill and imagination, was able to reconstruct the Celtic chariot from the many pieces recovered,[97] although it was calculated from the metalwork that there were remains of at least ten vehicles.[98] Similar finds, but on a much smaller scale, have been made at Hayling Island[99] and Uley.[100]

The *pax Romana* put an immediate stop to these warlike offerings, and the tribal chiefs were obliged to recognise the Roman state religion as part of their loyalty to the Emperor, and offer the appropriate sacrifices, which at first must have caused much resentment. Tacitus cites this bitterness at being forced to make large donations to State worship as a cause of the great revolt of AD 60. The British notables would have been 'honoured' by being appointed *flamines*, which gave them the responsibility of paying for the religious ceremonies laid down by the Roman *fasti*, and the attendant games. Some were singled out for an even higher honour, that of attending to the worship of the deified Claudius at his altar at Camulodunum. These *sacerdotes* were forced to pour out their fortunes in this service.[101] While Rome was totally unconcerned at how individuals worshipped their gods, providing it was within the law, in matters of State there was a rigid line to be followed.

Gradually, with the breakdown in Celtic society, individuals began to appreciate the freedom they had to make their own approaches to the gods; and as seen elsewhere, the first would probably have been the craftsmen and traders, who had to come to terms with the new economy. It has been found in recent years that many of the Romano-British[102] temples and shrines had earlier origins, although with few exceptions, there is little evidence of the presence of what could be defined as personal offerings, unless they were all of materials which have completely decayed. Another possibility is that the sacred springs, pools and other deposits were continually emptied throughout the Roman period for the recycling of the metal, with the subsequent loss of any of the earlier offerings. This problem can only be resolved by meticulous excavation of the entire *temenos* areas on religious sites. But, even then, it will only be possible to detect the clearance of wells and pools; any deposits inside the shrine itself, or any ancillary structures, would have been removed when the site became disused and the buildings demolished. It is noticeable that most of the published material belongs to the late period, and the chances of ever obtaining a sequence of votive offerings in a lake or pool seems to be remote. This is most unfortunate, since there will always be a serious gap in knowledge, and in particular of the period of change when the Britons began to adopt the classical practices.

Types of votive offerings

There are four categories of votive objects: coins; small symbolic models; personal jewellery and objects of personal use, and curse tablets, known as *defixiones* (see p. 135 below).

Coins were the easiest and most direct way of seeking a favour of the gods, and the practice survives today in those who cast a coin into a well or fountain and make a wish. But what is desired remains locked in the heart and mind of the donor. Most religious sites produce large numbers of small coins, but the spring at Bath has produced silver and even gold coins. There is a special kind of coin peculiar to temple sites, a very small copy of a contemporary coin. They have become known as minims, and Wheeler, describing a hoard of thin tiny coins at the temple at Lydney Park,[103] made sub-divisions into *minimi* and *minimissimi*. He divided the coins into six classes, A to F. A were normal Constantinian issues; B, small fragments or clippings, the largest being 1.15cm ($\frac{7}{16}$in) in diameter; C, an average diameter of 7.5mm ($\frac{5}{16}$in); D, an average diameter of 6mm ($\frac{1}{4}$in); E, an average diameter of 3.5mm ($\frac{1}{8}$in), and F, an average diameter of 2.75mm ($\frac{3}{32}$in). Wheeler suggested that these tiny coins belonged to the darkness of sub-Roman Britain,[104] but, as Dr John Kent has since pointed out, are copies of issues which belong to the middle of the fourth century, and it is illogical to suppose that anyone would choose to imitate coins of a past generation[105] rather than contemporary coins. There is also an interesting section on the method of manufacture by J.A. Casey, who shows that the blanks had been cut from rods of metal, for which some degree of technical competence would have been required. The character of the hoard, with the inclusion of fragments of scrap metal, would tend to suggest that this work was being carried out on the temple site. This raises the question of the function of these coins, which were too small to be usable in the normal way. It could be seen as a kind of token money specially made as gifts for seeking favours. It may seem to us inconceivable that the deities would welcome such miserable scraps, but the donors obviously thought otherwise. A similar practice is seen in the Far East to this day, where token prayer money is burnt at the shrines with the same purpose in mind. If these tiny coins were merely votive, then one would tend to find them only on temple sites, but fourth-century copies of sizes A-D are found on most Roman sites, and their common appearance and situation suggests a continuing commercial use. When, however, the coins are as small as at Lydney Park, Class E of 3.5mm ($\frac{1}{8}$in) and less, one might begin to question any commercial value. These *minimissimi* must surely be votive tokens, and, if so, their provenance could indicate the presence of a religious site.[106]

There is certainly evidence from other temple sites in Britain of metal workshops[107] and one presumes that a suppliant could have bought the votive objects required at the temple shop, including token money, as well as 'souvenirs' and amulets with the added potency of being from a sacred site. By merely being inside the *temenos*, the visitor would have felt the divine presence and gained something by it, just as today some people consider occasional church-going to be beneficial, although they may take very little part in the ritual. The key events in human life, baptism, marriage and burial, are required by most people to be conducted in a church to give sanctity to the proceedings. Contact with the spirits, however slight, appears always to have been a basic human need.

Votives as symbols

Votive symbolism can easily be defined in anatomical terms – the model demonstrating to the spirit the part of the body needing attention – and it is a practice which still continues in Catholic Europe, although it is also evident that some of the gifts are thanksgivings. Problems arise with other types of votives, which are obviously symbolic, but precisely what they represent in the minds of their donors can never be known. In the case of token coins, one could feel confident in thinking that it was an appeal for more of the same but of full value, and similarly a single gold coin might be an investment to secure many more. On the other hand, when people today cast coins into wells and pools, they are traditionally asking for the fulfilment of a wish, and in this sense, the coin may originally have been seen as a payment for the granting of favours addressed to the spirit. In suggesting the symbolism of other objects, one is obliged to exercise imagination, and this can easily become excessive, a factor to be borne in mind when reading the suggestions on the following pages. There is no way of establishing the truth, although it is possible to gain some insight from the continuity of such practices into living memory and recorded by folk-lore specialists.

Votive offerings take a variety of forms, but they are invariably symbolic of the request being made. The most obvious are those associated with healing, since they take the form of a small model of the afflicted part of the anatomy. They were made in baked clay or metal in the solid, or merely cut from sheets, and no doubt the temple shop could provide for all requirements and purses. The temples of the healing cults were, however, in the minority and were in two main classes. First there was the healing spa, where the sufferers stayed for the cure, which would have included careful preparation, ritual eating and purification by bathing and finally a night in the sacred area, when suitable hallucinogenic drugs induced the 'holy sleep' in the *abaton*, a special dormitory adjacent to the temple. This was probably an expensive experience and beyond the reach of peasants and labourers. The best examples of healing temple spas in Britain are at Bath (of which only a part of the large establishment has so far been investigated),[108] Lydney Park,[109] Nettleton,[110] Chedworth,[111] and probably Gadebridge Park.[112] There are much larger and more splendid spa temples in Gaul and the Rhineland, like the famous one to Apollo-Grannus at Aachen,[113] and to Lenus-Mars near Trier.[114] The former was the special preserve of the Rhine army and it seems probable that there was much the same arrangement here as at Bath, judging from the large number of tombstones and dedications by soldiers.

For those who could not afford the full spa treatment, there were local shrines where one could visit and make offerings, but these tended to be specialised and not all of them related to healing. For fertility one turned to the *Deae Matres*, the three mother goddesses who probably had many small local shrines, to judge from the large number of dedications and sculptured reliefs. For ease in childbirth, it would seem that every household had its own little shrine with its pipe-clay figure of Venus, to which small offerings would be made by women in labour. There is, however, little indication of any temples in Britain devoted to these vital aspects. In Italy, one of the most famous centres was the temple of Diana Nemorensis, on the shores of Lake Nemi.[115] Excavations in the nineteenth century produced a large quantity of votive objects associated with childbirth.[116] The only objects from Britain which could have such an interpretation are a small bone plaque from Lydney of a woman holding her stomach,[117] but this could equally be a case of appendicitis, and also a pair of ivory breasts from Bath.[118]

Some of the more specialised shrines were those concerning the eyes. These organs had a great fascination for primitive man, as they gave immediate access to the world around but could be completely closed by blindness. The eye could also be seen as a solar symbol, with all the manifestations that implies.[119] Eye cures were the realm of the oculists, who prepared their own ointments and salves, as we know from the moulds which often survive.[120] The only votive eyes in Britain have been found at Wroxeter and they appear to be concentrated on the basilican *palaestra* of the bath-house,[121] where there may have been a shrine at the east end.

Model objects of everyday use

The axe

A popular votive model was the axe, usually in bronze but occasionally in lead. It is an implement symbolising several different aspects, one of which is power and authority, as in the Roman *fasces*. The double axe was an attribute of the sky-gods, in particular Jupiter-Dolichenus;[122] this strong religious association with the most powerful of the gods would have made the axe a potent amulet to ward off evil spirits. As such, it is usually found as the terminal of pins, both metal and bone.[123]

The axe was often cut in outline on tombstones with the inscription *sub ascia* or *ad asciam dedicatum*, the precise meaning of which has aroused much speculation,[124] though the general opinion appears to be that it secured the protection of the monument from desecration. The *ascia* depicted on the tombstones appears to be a type of stone-mason's hammer,[125] with a hammer at one end and small adze at the other, the end of which is turned down at a considerable angle[126] (Fig. 15). Helene Wuilleumier has suggested that the *ascia* had a deep mystical significance in symbolising eternal life[127] and equates it with the mallet of Sucellos, a view not accepted by J-J Hatt.

These axes are different from those depicted on altars, so it seems unlikely that they were associated with the sacrifice of a pig, which was an essential part of all Roman burials.[128] The axes on the sides of altars appear with the other implements of the sacrifice, the *patera*, jug, incense-box etc., and they exhibit a wide variety of shapes. On some altars there are more than one, as with the axe

Fig. 15 Masons' tool and an inscription: SVB ASCIA DEDICATVM, carved on the side of a tombstone at Chester

and the knife from Ems.[129] This may be because different creatures had to be ritually killed in different ways (birds of all kinds were sacrificed as well as lambs, sheep, pigs, boars, oxen and bulls, even horses) or because different implements were used for the stages of the ceremony which were laid down by law and tradition.[130] When all the preparations had been made and the area cleared of intruders, the hands were ritually washed, and there was a call for silence; the priest covered his head and sprinkled the sacred mixture of salt and flour (*mola salsa*) over the head of the animal and the sacrificial knife. The animal was now stripped of its decorations, and the suppliant spoke out his petition toward the cult statue. The *popa* (the man who felled the animal), on being given the signal, struck the animal's head with his hammer with the required force and direction, so that it was stunned and sank to the ground. Then the *cultrarius*[131] stepped forward, lifted the animal's head and cut its throat for the blood to flow freely.[132] The blood-shedding was an essential element in the sacrifice. Blood was considered by the ancients as the vital life-substance and it was thought that by a ritual transfer from the animal to human or another animal, restoration of life-renewal took place.[133] Whether all the blood was allowed to gush out or only a token amount is not clear, but blood obviously played a significant part of the ritual.

It is clear from the wide range of creatures subjected to sacrifice that a variety of knives and axe-hammers was needed. Votive axes also exhibit a variety of types : those from Woodeaton, Oxfordshire, have a simple axe-blade with a stout handle with a knob terminal;[134] some of them have crosses and other marks on the blade, thought to have some mystical significance (Fig. 16.5). Only one has a projection on the other side of the shaft, which could have indicated a hammer. Other specimens, illustrated by Dr Miranda Green from different sites,[135] are more like the hammer-axe used for sacrifice or the knife, as illustrated from a temple site at Muntham Court, Sussex.[136] It is difficult to understand the significance of axes as votive objects unless they had some symbolical value to the donor, and the most sensible explanation is that they were considered as sacrificial implements and could thus symbolise the sacrifice. For those who could not afford to purchase the animal or bird and pay for the ritual, the gift of a model may have seemed an adequate token, like the tiny scraps of make-believe coins.

Perhaps the most interesting sacrificial implement is the short sword, a dagger with a corrugated bone handle grip from Argentomagus in northern Gaul.[137] It resembles the sword used by Mithras in the bull-slaying (*tauromachia*), the central scene on the sculptured screen or painted rear wall of all *Mithraea*. It was also similar to the implement used in the ritual bull sacrifice when the initiate was bathed in the blood (*taurobolium*).[138] The sword (*ensis hamatus*) is depicted on the sides of two altars from Lyons dedicated to the great mother goddess, Cybele of Mount Ida.[139] The Argentomagus votive sword is in a scabbard which could not have contained an *ensis hamatus*, so it cannot represent this particular sacrificial implement.

Another model to be considered is that of the altar. These are small copies 7–8cm (2¾–3in) high, carved out of stone, often found on temple and other religious sites, like Nettleton[140] and Chedworth.[141] They are sometimes referred to as 'portable' or 'household' altars, but must be regarded as token altars to be placed in the shrine, possibly with the name of the deity painted on one of the sides by suppliants who could not afford the full ritual. Perhaps the most enigmatic of the models is the so-called 'stool': it has the shape of a small square table with four legs, and the panelled sides are decorated with enamels, on the flat top is a circular hole which takes up most of the space, and at each corner are small knobs.[142] The 'stools' are of different sizes and it seems likely that they originally existed in sets of three, each standing on the other. The problem with these objects is determining what exactly they were copying. There are bases to candelabra and statues which are square and have four feet, but there the resemblance ends. The idea that they were miniature candle- or taper-holders has not found general acceptance.[143]

Fire and the flame had a great fascination for primitive people and was regarded as pure magic. It represented light and heat and was directly associated with the sun; as a result, fire-lighting and bonfires were universal seasonal rituals. The sacred hearth was the focus of Roman domestic worship, and the ancient role of the Vestal Virgins was to tend the sacred flame of the State. Torch-carrying and the lighting of candles were widespread customs in many rituals and ceremonies, and a candle was lit to aid childbirth;[144] its bright flame in the shape of the 'mystical almond' or 'divine oval'[145] symbolised the new, innocent life. This practice has continued in the Catholic Church and is still customary. The idea of offering candles or tapers in these model stands to be lit by the sacred flame of the shrine is not one to be lightly dismissed, especially in the absence of any other suggestions. A serious practical objection which must be faced is that the centre holes diminish in size with each 'stool' in the set of three.[146] A miniature candle-holder of a different kind was found at Silchester, crudely cut in a small tapering chalk block, bearing reliefs of Mercury, a cock and a serpent.[147]

Weapons were also used as votive objects, and took the form of model swords and spears.[148] It has even been suggested that pieces of fine mail have been used as votives,[149] though it would, of course, have been very difficult to miniaturise such fine metalwork. All these fragments are in triangular shape and therefore could possibly have come from priestly head-dresses or some other regalia.[150] As with Mars and Minerva, the weapons, especially the shields (Fig. 16.4), should be considered protective, not merely against threats on the person but shielding the suppliant from dangers to property, possessions and status, disease and ill-health.

Model tools

Apart from the axe there are other tools and objects of general use often found in burials as well as temple sites. Dr W.H. Manning, in publishing a group from Sussex said to have been found in a tumulus,[151] has pointed out the repetition of some items such as snakes, frogs and tortoises. The tools are adze-hammers, spades, saws, harrows and ploughs (Fig. 16.3), and other objects including ladders, keys, wheels, bells, yokes (Fig. 16.2), scale beams and pans. Models of

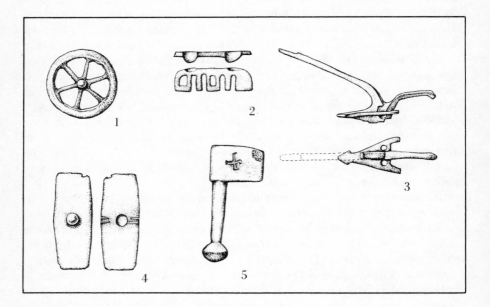

Fig. 16 Votive objects
1 A wheel from London
2 A ploughshare from Sussex
3 A yoke from Sussex
4 A shield from Fairford
5 An axe with a swastika on the blade from Woodeaton

these objects are also found individually as votives, and, in general, could be considered to be offering divine protection for both the living and the spirits of the dead. Such a concept would have been logical to people who totally accepted the reality of the birth-death-regeneration cycle. Some of the objects could be explained as having individual symbolic functions, such as the key, which was the symbol of marriage and the wife's role as the household manager; and bells, which could have been attached to temple regalia. The plough was an important Roman symbol of religious conservatism in the founding of towns, and the defining of *temenos* areas, while the ladder was the ancient Near Eastern symbol of the link with the heavens. This strange assortment of objects and the inclusion of animals and snakes has given these assemblages a religious aspect. As Dr Manning has indicated, the only deity directly associated with snakes, frogs and the tortoise was Sabazius, of Thraco-Phrygian origin. His was a mystery salvation cult, closely linked with Dionysus,[152] and he was considered to have tamed the wild animals into domestication, and invented the plough. This aspect would account for this implement and the yoke being one of his symbols, as well as the hammer. The balance still stands for justice, but in ancient times it was also needed for the weighing of souls.

Sabazius is known in the West for his strange bronze votive hands, one of which is illustrated by Dr Manning (his Pl. XVI). Others are known from the Rhineland and Switzerland.[153] These hands are covered with symbols of all kinds, and invariably include the snake, frog and tortoise. There is, however, little trace of his worship in Britain except for a thumb found at Chedworth.[154] The symbols of Sabazius also appear on pottery, on a handled tazza found in a Mithraeum at Friedburg which has, in *appliqué*, a scorpion, a snake and a ladder.[155] The snake or serpent was a symbol of his powerful life-force, hence its appearance in the Garden of Eden. It was also closely associated with healing, as on the wand of Aesculapius.

Other models

There are a number of other curious models listed by Dr Green which are not so common as those already considered. From Ancaster, Lincolnshire, comes a model cauldron[156] which could symbolise the magic Celtic cauldron of the feasts of the gods which never empties. The classical equivalents would have been the *cornucopia* of Fortuna and the purse of Mercury, but no examples are recorded. Another oddity is a miniature decorated bronze shovel[157] from Cirencester and now in the BM; it could have represented a bakers' peel (*pala*) for putting bread in the oven, although it does not have the usual flat shape, or it could have been meant as a fire shovel (*rutabulum*) and associated with the rituals of tending the sacred domestic hearth, the focus of Roman family life.[158] The model anchor from Woodeaton may be seen as a classical symbol of hope and security,[159] as it has continued to be in Christianity. Whether the small bronze lamp from Corbridge[160] can be considered a votive object is doubtful, as it appears from the drawing probably to have been attached to a base or sceptre. Other types of small objects like bells and pendants were probably pieces of temple regalia. It is difficult, however, to explain a 'miniature bronze column 3cm (2in) high' from Felixstowe in Norwich Museum, unless it was part of a small shrine.[161]

The wheel

One of the most interesting and common objects, both as an amulet and a votive object, is the wheel.[162] This powerful solar symbol and attribute of the sky god Jupiter, and his Celtic equivalent Tanaris, was depicted on altars and reliefs of both deities,[163] and it was also evidently an important Celtic apotropaic symbol.[164] In some examples the spokes of the wheels have been replaced by the swastika, introducing the suggestion of motion, as well as the added potency of this magical symbol of great antiquity.[165] In this form it was seen as the great wheel of the heavenly constellations of the night sky.

Stars have been grouped into figure types from very early times, when priests studied the sky in the deserts, where it is seen in its awesome magnitude. It was from the regular rotation and phases of the moon that the first calendars were constructed from which the priests could forecast the season and the time for sowing and reaping. This annual prediction appeared to give them power over the heavens and a position of unassailed supremacy. But with this developed the art of astrology, linking birth times with the heavenly constellations, which were divided for convenience into the Signs of the Zodiac.[166] This ancient Eastern lore was to have a profound effect on humanity which is still with us to this day.

It is not difficult to appreciate how from the concept of the wheel of the heavenly constellations developed the idea of the Wheel of Fortune, since a turn of the wheel could so dramatically change a person's circumstances. It became an important attribute of the classical goddess Fortuna[167] (*Fortunae rota*), who was also provided with the cornucopia of plenty, the rudder (*gubernaculum*) to steer a course towards one's destiny, and a globe (*orbis*), another form of the wheel.[168] Fortuna was thus an attractive and popular deity, as is her more modern counterpart, Lady Luck; but, just as today, Fortuna was courted mainly by the lower ranks of society, and in classical times such popular beliefs were despised by the Stoic intelligentsia and writers. Hence Tacitus refers to the use of the term *Fortunae rota* by Cicero in the most disparaging terms,[169] but the orator was probably using this image deliberately in his savage, even scurrilous character-assassination of Piso, using a vulgar term, Fortune's Wheel, as befitting the character of the man he was attacking. However, living languages are in a constant state of change and what may be gutter-slang for one generation may be respectable to a later one; and by the end of the fourth century the historian Ammianus Marcellanus found the phrase acceptable[170] for describing the elation of Procopius at the fall of Cyzicus.

Fortuna was often shown on sculptured reliefs and statues with her wheel, globe and rudder in Britain[171] and elsewhere[172] (Fig. 17A and B). Like other deities she suffered mutations in the hands of the Celtic stone masons and it is often impossible to decide whether the figure is that of Fortuna or her Celtic equivalent Rosmerta, or in some cases, a *genius*.[173] As seen above (p. 58), Rosmerta is more often in association with Mercury, but there is one example in Britain where she appears on her own, at Corbridge.[174]

The offering of wheels as votives seems most likely to have been by men and women who had fallen on hard times, or suffered a sudden adversity and needed the turn of the wheel in their favour. They have been found on known religious sites and also towns and settlements where there were probably temples and shrines. Dr Green illustrates a number from civilian sites in Britain.[175] The wheel is also found in jewellery, where it was evidently considered to be a powerful

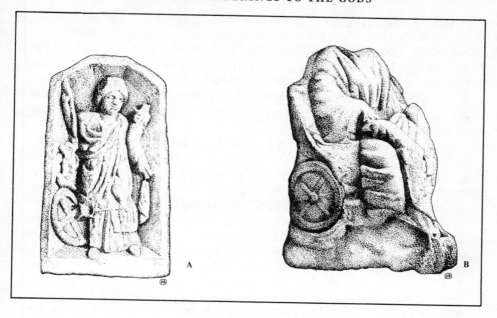

Fig. 17 Stone reliefs of Fortuna and her wheel, rudder and cornucopia from Wiesbaden (Esp. 1931, No. 129) and a seated figure of Fortuna with her wheel from Oehringen (ibid., No. 670)

amulet. These wheels for attachment to pendants on gold chains were in the hoard found *c.*1796 at Dolaucothi, the Roman gold mine in Wales,[176] and considered by Nash-Williams to have been 'a sun symbol and love charm'.[177] Two more with their pendants were part of the Backworth hoard found before 1812, and as some of the other pieces are dedicated to the mother goddesses, the whole hoard was thought to have been a votive deposit.[178] The symbol is quite common as a type of brooch, 'the Wheel Brooch', and Dr Green has illustrated several,[179] but this extends votives into the most numerous group of all these objects, that of personal jewellery.

Personal jewellery as votive offerings
By far the largest class of objects, apart perhaps from coins, are items of personal 'jewellery in use. This springs from the primitive idea known as contact magic. It was firmly believed that objects which are associated with one person only and worn or used only by them become imbued with the *persona* of the owner. This explains the widespread practice of burying women wearing all their jewellery and men with their weapons or objects signifying their posts or status. It was thought that if others gained possession and wore or used them, the spirit of the deceased would be able to extend a malignant power over them through the objects. This still exists in the repugnance occasionally felt about wearing

131

second-hand jewellery. One finds also in burial practice that personal objects have been deliberately broken as an act of sympathetic magic to 'kill' them, since only in that state can they join their owner in the next life. An outstanding case of this was discovered in a burial at Chester which included a small mirror that had been broken into twelve pieces, all of which had then been carefully placed in a small vessel.[180] The mirror was the most personal of all the objects since it was thought to contain the image of its user, and therefore an extension of that personality.[181]

Jewellery consists of brooches, rings, bracelets, ear-rings, hair and dress pins, chatelaines, and decorated toilet and jewel boxes, and all these are found in quantity on temple sites. Unfortunately, very few of these sites have been thoroughly excavated and all the finds fully analysed. One is, therefore, obliged to draw conclusions from such collections which have survived of those items an excavator has considered worth illustrating. Wheeler reported that there were about 270 bronze bracelets in the Lydney Park Museum before he began his excavation,[182] and quoted an earlier excavator who had remarked that the number seemed too large to be attributed to losses by the inhabitants, and 'it may be that they were deposited in the Temple as the votive offerings of the poor'. Wheeler was able to construct a basic type-series of eighteen patterns of decoration (his Fig. 17). It is interesting to note from the published brooches that many of them were of apotropaic significance, such as the two shield type and two wheel brooches (his Fig. 16), and that there are also very fine examples of cross-bow type (his Fig. 13) which have been considered as late fourth-century status symbols.

A factor not so much in evidence at Lydney Park, but certainly present at Nettleton[183] and Ivy Chimneys,[184] is the large quantity of broken fragments of jewellery. Bracelets in particular have been chopped up into small pieces. There is also evidence from some sites of extensive metalworking. The metal work-shop at Nettleton was identified and, after the temple had ceased to operate and was heavily vandalised, presumably by Christians in the late fourth century, a small industry developed for the manufacture of pewter vessels.[185] This evidence strongly indicates that there were temple work-shops for the production of votives for sale at the temple shop, which also sold amulets and other suitable religious souvenirs, much as church shops do today. But what is the meaning of so many broken bracelets?

There are three possible solutions. Firstly, it could be argued that votive gifts had to be deliberately broken or bent to become proper sacrificial offerings. But this would entail a mere twisting of the bracelet and not its dismemberment. Secondly, these small pieces may have been available as token bracelets, like the coins. If this is the case then one can suppose a recycling operation whereby the metal votives, after a reasonable period of deposition either in the sacred pool or in the shrine itself, were collected and reworked or broken up for sale. There is further evidence for this suggestion in the recovery of small rings made by bending pieces of bracelets into circles.[186]

The third possible explanation may be too imaginative, but should not pass unconsidered. Following the principles of sympathetic magic, rings and bracelets have a symbolic meaning in the union of two people, and are still seen as such in engagement and wedding rings. The offering of a complete object belonging to the donor combined the force of contact with sympathetic magic, and could indicate the wish for a satisfactory union, which has always been one of the basic human needs. Conversely, the gift of a broken bracelet or ring may have been seen by the suppliant as a symbol of the need to break an established union which had turned sour. Although there may always be as many men or women wanting to end, as those wishing to form, a partnership, only in a society free from the restraints of a tightly-enforced code of taboo would it be possible to make and break sexual unions. One of the main results of the Roman conquests of Gaul and Britain would have been the dissolution of the highly stratified Celtic society and its codes of conduct, firmly controlled by long-established taboos and traditions. In the freer Roman world there were still the bonds of poverty and class, and the great mass of land-tied peasantry had very little freedom or opportunity for individual action, as the old ways of life would have persisted. New ways of approaching the gods may have penetrated but it is doubtful if the rural workers would have had sufficient money for anything but the cheapest kind of votive gift, and many were probably hand-carved from wood, as the crude figures from a few waterlogged sites demonstrate.[187]

One could pursue the application of sympathetic magic to other types of personal objects. Brooches are exceptionally common on temple sites, but they were widely used by men and women and had the advantage of carrying a decorated shape which could in itself have the powers of an amulet. These include wheels, swastikas, animals and birds and other forms which their wearers imagined had a protective force. The function of the brooch was to hold together pieces of garment, and this could have been thought to symbolise the continuity of a union in danger of breaking. The pin of the brooch had its analogy of sexual penetration, and pins are prolific on religous sites; although some of them are bent, it is not possible to be sure if this was a deliberate act.[188]

Bone pins were used to maintain elaborate hair coiffures, and silver and bronze pins for fastening garments together. Some have carved or moulded heads which may have some apotropaic force; those with the pine cones symbolised everlasting life. Others have small gold balls inserted in the top as the uncorruptible property of the metal was considered to be beneficial to anyone carrying it on their person. Some of the heads are very elaborate with clear religious motifs, as in the case of two from London, one with Fortuna and her cornucopia and what may have been intended for her rudder, and another in silver with Venus.[189] A hand holds a ball or globe which has been identified as an apple or symbol of fertility,[190] and a silver pin from the Walbrook shows a hand holding a pomegranate, a life symbol.[191]

A different class of votive is found in the chatelaine – those small toilet instruments attached in a group to a holder and carried on a belt or chain.[192] These consisted of nail-cleaners, ointment scoops (sometimes described as ear-scoops), nail files, tweezers and tooth-picks. Since these objects are of such a domestic and personal nature, it is difficult to interpret them in symbolic terms. The word is derived from the French *châtelain*[193] and would appear to symbolise the status of a matron. This could be interpreted as a desire on the part of a widow or maiden for marital status, but there appears to be no direct evidence for this suggestion.

Fragments of thin sheet bronze with repoussé decoration are often found on religious sites, and these could be votive offerings showing reliefs of the deity or their attributions. It is sometimes difficult to be certain of their category, although at Lydney Park there seems to be less doubt, since from the character of the reliefs and the shapes it seems that some were probably pieces of temple regalia,[194] though others would appear to have been decorative mounts to jewel boxes.[195] The few fragments from Woodeaton are poorer in quality and more uncertain, but some can be recognised as poor-quality votive leaves,[196] though the long thin strips and rectangular pieces are more likely to have been box-mounts.[197] At Nettleton the pieces are also of poor quality, with the notable exception of the Apollo mask, and all the other fragments of sheet bronze are clearly box-mounts.[198]

Another class of object is that of the solid cast figures of animals and birds, but these also present a problem. One could imagine that a small bronze cock would have been a suitable offering to Mercury or Aesculapius instead of a sacrifice of a real one, which would have included fees to the priest and his assistant, but this is very speculative. Another more possible explanation is that these figures were attached to temple banners or sceptres.[199] The most famous British example is probably the Lydney dog, of which there were more representations; the finest, in solid form (Report Pl. XXV), was thought by Wheeler to be 'a small masterpiece' (his p. 88) which could have been an offering. The others cut from thin bronze sheet have nail holes, showing they were attached to boards (his Pl. XXVI), perhaps with suitable lettering, and these would presumably have been attached to a temple wall. There is also the base of a small stone figure of which only part of the forefeet survive (his Fig. 21, No. 106). The Brigstock shrine produced fragments of horses and riders[200] who appear to be armed and wear crested helmets, similar to a better preserved figure from a cemetery at Westwood Bridge near Peterborough.[201] The Celtic horse-cult was associated with Epona, a fertility goddess, but warrior gods like Mars, as seen above, were considered as protectors against disease and other evils. Mounted warriors have been found at Willington Fen in a hoard of religious objects[202] which includes a club or mace bearing the figure of Tanaris and his wheel; it is, therefore, a Celtic votive object but in a classical form.[203] There seems little doubt from these finds and the common occurence of horses and horse-heads on coins and in decoration, especially on La Tène metalwork, that the horse played a significant part in Celtic religion, and far more so than in the classical world.[204]

The curse tablets: negative magic

These represented the dark side of religion which was identified by the early Christians with sorcery and witchcraft, emanating from demons and devils. The later polarisation into a good-evil axis has obscured the motives behind the earlier practices. In pre-Christian times any deity or spirit could be approached for favours, for good or ill, indiscriminately. The casting of harmful spells has been practised in all societies from the earliest times and it has always been feared and, at times, prohibited by law. Pliny informs us that the original Twelve Tables of Rome included clauses against spell casting and incantation against the crops;[205] he also felt obliged to admit that there was no one unafraid of being bound by an evil spell.[206] Weak-minded emperors like Nero were always fearful of having spells put on them. At times magicians and soothsayers were banned from Rome and prosecutions staged for the removal of persons thought to threaten those in power. The charge of resorting to magicians was frequently made with the help of informers, who were usually well rewarded.[207] There was thus a widespread belief among the credulous of the efficacy of spell-casting and of inflicting harm by invoking the aid of a deity to curse people for some real or imagined wrong.

These curse tablets usually take the form of pieces of lead in either flattened sheets, or even hammered lumps. The donor's wishes were scratched on the surface. The texts are usually in cursive script, and quite often written wholly or partly backwards to make them virtually illegible to any casual or interested third party. It was presumed that the gods, being all-powerful, would have no difficulty in reading them. There may, therefore, have been scribes available at the temples and shrines who made a reasonable living out of this practice. The language they used is a kind of semi-legal jargon, no doubt to impress the credulous donor. The tablets often have nail-holes, showing that they have been fixed to part of the shrine, but those cast into springs or pools are often in the form of folded sheets of lead.

Examples known for some time include the so-called 'London Curse', found near the Bank of England.[208] The interest of this particular curse, which was directed against the men Titus Egnatius Tyranus and Publius Cicereius Felix, is in the wording *defictus est*, i.e. 'is cursed'. From this the tablets have been called *defixiones*, which is erroneously assumed to refer to the tablets being nailed to the shrine.[209] In the note on this curse published in 1930, it is said that 'only three other Roman curses have hitherto been recorded in Britain'. However, the excavations in the hot spring at Bath, the temple at Uley in Gloucestershire and other sites, have in the last few years produced a positive flood. Their publication is, however, often delayed by the sheer difficulty in reading them. It has already become clear that these curse tablets are of great interest in supplying names of people and of deities, and also in revealing more of the vulgar Latin spoken in Britain than has hitherto been possible. They also bring an instant contact with the strong feelings of outrage and loss suffered by individuals, thus making a personal contact with this period that is so sadly lacking in the total absence of literature.

A few examples will demonstrate these points. They are taken from the Bath and Uley series which have been brilliantly deciphered by Dr Roger Tomlin, and published in successive issues of *Britannia*.[210] One from Uley[211] is typical: a woman, Saturnina, petitions Mercury about a linen cloth she has lost. 'Let him who stole it not have rest until he bring the aforesaid item to the aforesaid temple,

135

whether he is man or woman, slave or free'. Some of the phrases have a semi-legal ring, as they are well-used formulae copied by the scribe, especially *si vir si mulier si servus si liber*, which is very common. What is unusual about this tablet is the word *commonitorium*, which is a late legal term word in the *Codex Theodosianus* and signifies an earnest reminder, but with a legal weight behind it. One from Bath[212] reads: 'I have given the goddess Sulis six silver pieces which I have lost. It is for the goddess to extract it from the debtors Senicianus, Saturninus and Anniola', and ends with the words *carta picta perscripta*, a legal phrase meaning 'this document has been copied'. But this curse used a rare word *argentiolos* (although the first four letters have been lost, this seems to be the only plausible restoration). It is probably a popular name for the *argenteus*, a silver coin introduced by Diocletian who doubled its value in a currency reform of AD 300-1.[213] It was later abandoned by Constantine in favour of another new coin, the *siliqua*,[214] which remained in currency through the fourth century. There is another reference to the *argenteus* on a very different curse, also from Bath.[215] It reads: 'Whether pagan or Christian, whosoever man or woman, boy or girl, slave or free has stolen from me, Annianus . . . six *argentei* from my purse, you, lady Goddess are to exact them from him' etc. On the other side of the curse are eighteen names, which may have been a list of suspects drawn up by Annianus for the benefit of the goddess; five of them are not otherwise attested and Alauna is a well-known place-name.

Another of the Bath tablets,[216] an extremely difficult one to decipher, reads 'I curse (him) who has stolen, who has robbed Deomiorix from his house. Whosoever guilty the god find him, let him recover it with blood and his life.' Apart from giving us a unique Celtic name, the interest of this curse is in the use of the word *hospitium* for house, whereas in the classical usage it means an inn or place for temporary lodging. By the late Empire its meaning had been extended to one's domicile, and this continued into medieval Latin.

Most of the British curses are concerned with theft, but one from Old Harlow[217] may be the result of an amatory battle. It is addressed to the god Mercury 'I entrust to you my affair with Eterna and her own self, and may Timotneus feel no jealousy of me at the risk of his life blood'. The word *negotium* is, however, used for business matters, and on the other side of the tablet it starts 'I entrust to you, Mercury, another matter', i.e. *aliam negotium*, but the rest of it has not yet been deciphered. This presumably suggests that business matters are in hand. Some curses are outpourings of sheer rage against another person, like the one found in London in 1934 near Moorgate:[218] 'I curse Tretia (probably a mistake for Tertia) Maria and her life and mind and memory and liver and lungs all mixed up together her words, thoughts and memory, thus may she be unable to speak of things concealed nor able to . . . .', a comprehensive damnation of someone the suppliant felt had done him or her an injury. It is unfortunate that there are no similar methods of venting spleen today, since it could be psychologically beneficial. The curse tablets, whether one believed in their efficacy or not, allowed a transfer of emotion, just as the oppression of deep-seated guilt can be lifted by the Christian confessional; it is much the same kind of transfer to the gods of human feelings when they become unbearable.

CHAPTER SIX

THE IMPERIAL CULT

Rome's attitude towards the provinces was normally one of toleration and an acceptance of local traditions, laws and beliefs. There was only one institution which was rigorously imposed and that was the Imperial Cult. This was considered as providing, in the form of a religious act, an unequivocal acceptance of the supreme will of the Emperor and Senate. This constitutional basis was paramount, but it also incorporated the traditional religious practice which had, from the distant past, been acccepted as an unbreakable ritual to be observed by strict adherence to archaic formulae and gestures. Augustus strengthened this with his policy, following the constitutional pattern and encouraging the belief that Rome had been chosen by the gods to fulfil a destiny in bringing peace and civilisation to the world. In imposing the Imperial Cult on the provincials, Rome was only fulfilling the divine will, to which the Emperor and State were wholly committed. Even so, Augustus introduced the worship of the Imperial Cult into the West with some caution. The altar to Rome and Augustus was erected in Gaul in 12 BC at Lugdunum, where the *Concilium* of the Three Gauls met annually. These provincial *concilia* were appointed by the *municipia* and *civitates* of their provinces, probably on an annual basis.[1] Ostensibly the bodies advised the Emperor and Senate, but in actuality they were powerless to act, and their main function was to identify themselves with Roman law and order and the total acceptance of the authority of the Emperor by their participation in the Cult rituals.

In the Eastern provinces the *concilia* were accepted without difficulty, since they fitted the types of self-government that communities had practised for centuries. Emperor worship was readily adapted, and although this displeased Augustus, he could do little about it. After his death and deification, worship of the Imperial Cult became more acceptable, since the Imperial House could now be regarded as semi-divine, although Claudius firmly resisted efforts to be worshipped as a divine being.[2] In Britain members of the *concilium* acknowledged the Roman gods at the *ara* at Camulodunum. After the death of Claudius, the erection of a great temple was begun[3] and became, according to Tacitus, the focus for anti-Roman sentiment;[4] in his evocative words it was seen as Rome's *arx aeternae dominationis* (a citadel of eternal domination). Furthermore, he added, those chosen to officiate were obliged under the pretence of religion to lavish their fortunes. It is interesting to note that some of the Britons still had large fortunes to offer, especially after the sudden and unexpected withdrawal of loans by Claudius and Seneca – an important factor, recorded by Dio (lxii, 2), but dismissed by Tacitus (Ann. xiii, 42), leading to the great revolt of AD 60. A conclusion which could be drawn from the somewhat conflicting evidence is that the Senate's decision to build this temple soon after the death of Claudius, and the implication that the members of the *concilium* should contribute, showed a lack of sensitivity towards Britain, so recently conquered. The withdrawal of loans came later, but still in the early days of Nero's reign, when the army was engaged in a widespread and destructive war with the unsubdued tribes of Wales, following the death of Scapula.[5] It was at a time when Nero's advisers were probably in favour of withdrawing from Britain altogether.[6] If the wealthier Britons had been so ruthlessly stripped of their capital and then expected to continue to maintain the expenses of the Imperial Cult and the building of the temple, there would indeed have been very serious grounds for complaint, giving substance to the comment of Tacitus. It must also be appreciated that at this time, in the mid-50s AD, the Druids were still attempting to exercise their influence over the British chiefs, and this was another crucial factor in the causes of the catastrophe which was soon to follow.

It would have taken many years for the Britons to settle down after AD 60 and only gradually was normalisation established. The process of urbanisation, which had started so well in the south east, was now arrested and could hardly begin in the rest of the province while much of it was still occupied by troops. Agricola was still trying to encourage the Britons towards urbanisation, if one accepts that Tacitus gives a true account. In his list of desirable projects that Britons were expected to undertake, the building of temples is placed first.[7] But this passage could be no more than a description of what a good governor should be doing, the kind of bland rhetoric to be expected in a eulogy. It also gives Tacitus the opportunity of inserting a bitter epigrammatical epithet at the end of his chapter – 'Such worthy endeavours, graced with the name of civilisation, were merely aspects of enslavement'.[8]

CONCLUSION: THE SUCCESS OR FAILURE OF RELIGIOUS INTEGRATION

There are very serious problems in reaching any positive judgement on the degree of success or failure, since it has to be based entirely on inference. No written statements by Britons or Romans survive to offer comment, except for the famous passage in Tacitus about the temple to the deified Claudius. But one may then ask; success or failure for whom? Tacitus, for the sake of dramatic emphasis, was probably guilty of hyperbole; even so it is obvious that at least some of the British tribal chiefs could not accept the imposition of the Imperial Cult. This attitude was most probably fostered by the Druids, the one body which faced not merely decline but total annihilation. There were Britons like Cogidubnus and Cartimandua who remained loyal to Rome throughout, and were handsomely rewarded. While the tragedy of the great revolt of AD 60 deeply affected many Britons, they were drawn into it by loyalty to their tribe and its ruling family rather than joining a religious crusade. Undoubtedly they were made to believe that their own gods were on their side; but the very scale of the defeat and the savage reprisals must have shaken their beliefs and the beliefs of those who had remained neutral. It may have been experiences like this that convinced individuals of the undoubted power of the gods of Rome; and even if they were not wholly acceptable, these gods had to be treated with great respect.

Success seems to have been achieved in the main area by the Roman acceptance of the Celtic deities, seasonal festivals and ritual practices. As explained elsewhere, all newcomers to an area, whether soldiers or traders, felt the need to come to terms with the local spirits. The Celts were also prepared, although how readily it is impossible to detect, to accept the deities the newcomers brought with them. There may well have been a universal acceptance that people who moved out of their tribal territories carried their own spirits with them for protection and reassurance. The pairing of deities clearly shows this process at work, and deities, both foreign and resident, with the same basic functions, were conflated into a single entity. In other cases a classical deity was given a Celtic epithet, and in this form must have been more acceptable to the Britons. There were new gods, the most important being Mercury, who covered an aspect of life, such as commerce, which was virtually unknown to most Britons.

Another effect which is very difficult to judge would have been the result of a redistribution of the population. It is evident that it was military rather than

139

Imperial policy to remove the natives from their hill-forts to open sites in the valleys where they could be more easily watched and integrated into the Roman provincial system. In the Conquest period the forts would have acted like magnets, drawing Britons to them to provide the troops with fresh vegetables, milk, and other necessary comestibles; also some of the British women would have found it profitable to respond to the sexual demands of the soliders. Celtic potters and metalworkers would also have found good employment. The old shrines on the hill-forts would have been deserted, but never forgotten, as archaeological evidence has shown. There appears not only to be continuity of usage, but some were actually rebuilt to the Roman model. There must also have been many shrines in the countryside near settlements which may have been depopulated. Nonetheless, at festival times people would have flocked to them from considerable distances. The old sacred places would have retained their magic influence, but in the new settlements the Britons soon learnt from the newcomers that shrines and temples could be erected anywhere, and not necessarily on sacred sites. But there appears to have been earlier practice on the hill-forts where the tribal or community spirits were housed in shrines as part of the general layout, as at Danebury. Communities took their deities with them wherever they went. This adherence to familiar gods is also seen with the newcomers to Britain, such as soldiers and traders who often set up altars to the local deities in their homelands.

All this would have taken time, for Roman pragmatism would probably have allowed for gradual development except in the case of the immediate imposition of the Imperial Cult to bind the British chiefs in a continuing act of loyalty to the State. No doubt some rapacious landowners anxious for a rapid profit from this investment would have made speedier changes. There is still a total lack of evidence on these developments, but there is a possibility that large-scale excavation may eventually help to illuminate these changes and their timing. Meanwhile we can only continue to bemoan the great paucity of epigraphic evidence in the civil zones of Britain, when comparisons are made with Gaul. The reasons for this are not immediately obvious except that southern Gaul had a much longer period of Roman rule. It could be argued that much was lost in the extensive stone robbing by Saxon and Norman builders, and one would dearly like to be able to dismantle one of their large buildings on the site of a Roman city! However, they are ancient monuments too, and deserve the same respect as those of an earlier period.

It is possible too, as Dr Henig has pointed out to me, that there was an emergency building of city walls in Gaul in the late third century, due to the sudden barbarian invasions, and Roman monuments were stripped to provide the stone, thus preserving very large numbers of sculptures and inscriptions. Such events did not take place in Britain apart from the walls of Chester and London.

Another great change was to take place in the late second or early third century which was more insidious, and may even have passed unnoticed at the time, yet was in the end to be the most profound. This was the advent of the

Eastern mystery and salvation cults, brought in mainly through traders and the army. They introduced Mithraism and what was to be its greatest rival, Christianity. But this subject is beyond our main concern, which is the initial impact of Rome on the Britons during the Conquest period.

In summary the main emphasis must be placed on the extraordinary conservatism of religious practice, and its continuity. Our public holidays, known as Bank Holidays, are a direct descent from the Celtic seasonal festivals, as indeed are most of the celebrations of the Christian Church, as well as the ritual practices. The more one studies the people of the past the more one comes to realise that human nature has not changed in the slightest. Exactly the same physical needs dictate behaviour as they have always done; but today, with the breakdown of the structure of society, there is greater freedom and licence, only limited by civil law, which itself is largely based on the ancient laws of Rome: conditions can hardly be said to have improved.

REFERENCES

Chapter 1 (pp. 13–22)

1 An erudite summary of the changes in anthropology in the last century is given in the lectures by E.E. Evans-Pritchard, *Theories of Primitive Religion*, 1965
2 Summarised by Johannes Maringer, *The Gods of Prehistoric Man*, 1956, Chap. 1
3 ibid., pp. 108–14
4 J.G. Fraser, *The Magic Art*, 1911, i, 119–34
5 H.J. Mette, *Pytheas von Massalia*, 1952
6 Avieni, *Ora Maritima*, ed. A. Schulten, 1922
7 J.J. Tierney, 'The Celtic Ethnography of Posidonius', *Proc. Roy. Irish Acad.*, 60, Sect. C, No. 5 (1960), pp. 189–275
8 Athenaeus actually stated that he wrote his *Histories* in accordance with his philosophical convictions (IV, 36)
9 This was poetically expressed by Tacitus in his eulogy of Agricola – *Si quis piorum manibus locus, si, ut sapientibus placet, non cum corpore extinguuntur magnae animae, placide quiescas, nosque domum tuam ab infirmo desiderio et muliebribus lamentis ad contemplationem virtutum tuarum voces quas neque lugeri neque plangi fas est* (*Agric.* 46), i.e. 'If there is any place for the shades of the just, if as the wise say, the spirit of the great does not perish with the body, rest in peace and call your household from feeble regrets and womanish tears to contemplate a man of great *virtus* it would be sinful to mourn or lament.'
10 It is difficult to find an English word to do full justice to the Latin *virtus* which means far more than the weakly 'virtuous'. It stood for what the Romans considered to be the essence of manliness. As Sir Ronald Syme has put it: 'The word means courage, the ultimate virtue of a free man with *virtus*, *libertas* and *fides* blending in a grand ideal of character and conduct – constancy in purpose and loyalty'. (The Roman Revolution, 1960, ed. p. 57)
11 *Ann* xii, 36
12 Tacitus showed skilful use of the adjective *incuriosus* (negligent) because when read aloud it produced a sneering or hissing sound, indicating contemptuous distain. He uses it of Tiberius in his neglect in extending the *Imperium*, a favourite theme of the historian: *princeps proferendi imperi incuriosus erat*, i.e. an Emperor negligent of enlarging the Empire (*Ann* iv, 32)

13 This work is mentioned by Tacitus elsewhere (*Ann* i, 69)

14 R. Syme, 1958, p. 46

15 *plusque ibi boni mores valent quam alibi bonae leges*, i.e. 'moreover, good habits are more effective there than good laws elsewhere', *Germ.* 19

16 *Nat. Hist.* XXIX, 54; see also Nora Chadwick, *The Druids*, 1966, pp. 73–4 referring also to Zwicker, *Fontes Religionis Celticae*, i, 1934, p. 57

17 ibid., XXIX, 52; the text is very corrupt and may originally have been *anguinum*, a serpent's egg

18 ibid., XVI, 10, 28–9. Dr Juliet Clutton-Brock has suggested, in correspondence, that these objects may have been bezoars, i.e. dried hair-balls from the guts of animals, which were highly prized as amulets in the Middle Ages (Desmond Morris, *Men and Snakes*, 1965, p. 81). Dr Henry Cleere has advanced another idea, that they were apples which had been in sea water, washed up and dried in hard balls with a much wrinkled skin. Others have suggested dried puff-balls; and so the argument will doubtless continue

19 ibid., XXX, iv, 13; they are here described as *genus vatum medicorumque*, i.e. soothsayers and medicine men

20 Suet. *Claud.* XXV, 4

Chapter 2 (pp. 23–51)

1 T.F. O'Rahilly, *Early Irish History and Mythology*, 1945; M. Dillon, *Early Irish Literature*, 1948; G. Murphy, *Saga and Myth in Ancient Ireland*, 1961; K.H. Jackson, *The Oldest Irish Traditions: A Window on the Iron Age*, 1964; see also A. and B. Rees, *Celtic Heritage*, 1961, for the arrangement of the sagas in cycles (Chap. X)

2 This is discussed with great clarity by that brilliant Celtic scholar Marie-Louise Sjoestedt in her *Gods and Heroes of the Celts*, English ed. 1949

3 *The Druids*, 1968, Penguin ed. 1974

4 J.J. Tierney, pp. 189–275

5 4, iv, 4; this threefold division is seen in the Irish Celts as the *druidh*, the *filidh* and the *baird*, but as Proirsias MacCana has indicated, there are analogous institutions in the ancient Indo-European tradition (Celtic Mythology, 1970, p. 15), and Caesar may have recognised a parallel in the Roman priestly/legal strata

6 Memories of the Druids persisted through into the fourth century, according to Ausonius (*Commemoratio Professorum Burdigalensium* iv, 7; x, 27–8)

7 Caesar, *B.G.* vi, 14

8 *De Divinatione* I, 90

9 The two brothers are fully discussed by Nora Chadwick in *The Druids*, 1966, pp. 103–111

10 *Oratio*, xlix

11 Another source of the connection with Pythagoras was probably the writer of the third century BC, Alexander Polyhistor, who anticipated the encyclopaedists of the schools of philosophy with a compendium, and who had a special interest in Pythagoras

12 xvi, 95, 249, *ita suos appellant magos*; the word *magus* derived from the Greek μάγος was used in an ambivalent manner to mean both a sorcerer and a philosopher or a man of great wisdom

13 M. Sjoestedt, 'Le Siège de Druim Damhgaire' *Rev. Celt.* 43, 1926, quoted by A. Ross, 1967, p. 57

14 Strabo said that the Celtic Galatians assembled at a *drunemeton* (Δρυνέμετον: 'oak sanctuary', xii 5, 1). The oak was associated by the Romans with Jupiter, and the oak leaf crown (*corona civica*) given for saving the life of a citizen was Rome's highest military honour. The acorn, by its very shape, was credited by primitive man with the power of a fertility symbol in the death-regeneration cycle

15 Stuart Piggott has pointed out that tough stems would have needed sharp iron but the metal could have been gilded (*The Druids*, p. 99)

16 Virgil suggests that mistletoe possessed a potency against the power of darkness when describing the journey of Aeneas into the mouth of Avernus, in a beautiful line (*discolor unde auri per ramos aura refulsit*). Aeneas saw among the varied hues of the foliage a glitter of gold and eagerly plucked a reluctant sprig to carry with him (*Aen.* vi, 204–211). Virgil emphasised the golden colour of the berries and even used the word *bractea*, i.e. gold leaf (209). This metal, through its property of resisting corrosion, has always been held to have a high amuletic value. The theme has been thought to be depicted on one of the Frampton mosaics, but it has also been identified as Mars Pacifer (D. Smith, 'Mythological Figures and Scenes in Romano-British Mosaics' in *Roman Art and Life in Roman Britain*, ed. by J. Munby and M. Henig, *BAR*, 1977, No. 37, p. 117)

17 *tanta gentium in rebus frivolis plerumque religio est*

18 The word *lucus*, although normally translated as 'a grove' means no more than a wood sacred to a spirit

19 iii, 399; Nora Chadwick has drawn attention to the similarity of this passage to one in the *Thebais* of Statius (iv, 149ff) haunted by the presence of Latonia (*The Druids* 1966, p. 36)

20 *Ann.* XIV, 30, *nam cruore captivo adolere aras*

21 *Nat Hist.* XXX, iv, describing them as *hoc genus vatum medicorumque* i.e. this sort of soothsayer and medicine men

22 Suet, *Claud.* XXV, 5

23 *Nat. Hist.* XXX, iv

24 S. Dill, *Roman Society from Nero to Marcus Aurelius*, 1904, p. 45 with references to Suet, *Tib.* XIV, 69; *Ann.* xii, 52; Suet. *Vitell*, XIV; see also Tacitus, *Hist.* i, 22

25 *Táin Bó Cúalnge*, ed. Cecile O'Rahilly, Dublin Institute of Advanced Studies, 1970

26 The subject has attracted considerable literature from Fraser's *Taboo and the Perils of the Soul*, 1911, onward

27 *Nat. Hist.* xxviii, 17, 59

28 They are recorded by Aulus Gellius, *Attic Nights*, X and Fabius Pictor; for a summary see F.C. Grant, *Ancient Roman Religion*, 1957, pp. 30–2

29 *The Religious Experience of the Roman People*, 1911, pp. 27–41

30 Polybius (II, 93), referred to the Celtic swords which the warrior had to bend straight with their feet; Professor Walbank thinks this is a tall story or may have originated from the ritual bending of weapons when making sacrificial gifts to the gods (*A Historical Commentary on Polybius*, i, 1957, p. 209)

31 Paul-Marie Duval, *Études Celtiques*, x and xi; fully illustrated by J-J. Hatt, *Celts and Gallo-Romans*, Archaeologia Mundi, 1970, Pls. 126–7

32 E.O. James, *The Ancient Gods*, 1960, pp. 234–7

33 Or Samhain, a word meaning 'a gatherer'

34 Óengus or Angus was one of the sons of the tribal god Dagda

35 *Early Irish Myths and Sagas*, Penguin, 1981, pp. 107–12

36 W. Stokes, *Lives of the Saints from the Book of Lismore*, 1890; Anne Ross, *Pagan Celtic Britain*, 1967, p. 360

37 Bel means 'bright' and was a Celtic sun god and appears in the name of the local Cumbrian deity, Belatucadros, 'the fair and shining one', see p. 74 above; Beli Mawr, in the Mabinogion, was one of the great ancestral spirits of Wales

38 Ovid, *Fasti*, iv, pp. 721–862 (Loeb, ed.) with its purification by fire and offering of milk

39 *The Golden Bough, The Magic Art*, 1911, Chap. XIX

40 Another interesting practice was of naked females processing round the fields which may have survived in the legend of Lady Godiva; see also Pliny, *N.H.*, xxii, 2, who refers to women in Britain parading naked at festivals with their bodies stained with a vegetable dye resembling that of Ethiopians

41 Maíre MacNeill, *The Festival of Lughnasa*, 1962

42 Made from the first sheaf and cut and winnowed for this purpose

43 LVGVDVNVM is an unidentified place in northern Britain (A.L.F. Rivet and C. Smith, *The Place-Names of Roman Britain*, 1979, pp. 401–2) and there is another place near Verulamium, known from a potter's stamp on a mortarium (*Brit.* 6, 1975, p. 258); a name with the same prefix is Luguvalium (Carlisle)

44 *BG* vi, 17; P-M. Duval, *Les Dieux de la Gaule*, 1957, p. 67

45 *Revue Celtique* 12, pp. 52–130; see also *Ancient Irish Tales*, ed. T.P. Cross and C.H. Slover

46 He is also portrayed as a shoemaker (M. MacNeill, 1926, pp. 7 and 665)

47 ibid., pp. 4–5; see also M. Dillon and N. Chadwick, *The Celtic Realms*, 1973, pp. 186–7

48 *Early Irish History and Mythology*, 1946; he distinguishes four successive invasions down to *c*.100 BC

49 This is the conclusion of Maíre MacNeill (p. 409)

50 There is an interesting exception. In one of his letters (Ep., iii, No. 5) Pliny, writing to Baebius Macer, describes the working habits of his industrious uncle, who wrote that in the winter he protected his hand by *manuum tegumenta digitalia*, which means a covering of the hand and fingers, and had this been a common practice, a word would have been coined, although Varro gives us the word *digitabulum*, worn specially for gathering olives (*Res Rusticae*, i, 55, 3)

51 This is self-evident from the surviving document 'The Feriale Duranum' which is a list of official military observances of AD 223–7 (R.O. Fink, *Roman Military Records on Papyrus*, 1971, *Philological Monographs of the American Philogical Ass.*, No. 16, No. 117, pp. 422–9

52 The best contemporary account is the great poem of Ovid, *Fasti*, although it covers only the first half of the year, since he was prevented from completing his great work by his sudden and unexpected despatch into exile by Augustus. The edition includes notes by Sir James Fraser, 1926, but he also produced his own great study in five volumes (1929)

53 T.G.E. Powell, *The Celts*, 1958, p. 152, on the annual wooing of a maiden at Cruachain which has echoes of *The Golden Bough* with its priest-king and successor which started Frazer on his long quest

54 MacNeill, Chap. XVII and Appendix 1

55 T.G.E. Powell, 1958, p. 154

56 Ovid, *Fasti*, V, 621–2, and Fraser's Notes in the Loeb ed., p. 425

57 K. Meyer, *The Voyage of Bran*, 1895; a selection of his verses is given in K.H. Jackson, *A Celtic Miscellany*, Penguin, 1971, No. 144

58 Three groups of nine, numbers of powerful magic

59 The same concept appears in the second epistle of St Peter: 'one day with our Lord is but a thousand years and a thousand years is but as one day' (A. and B. Rees, 1961, p. 344)

60 M. Dillon and N. Chadwick, 1973, p. 186; R. Thurneysen, *Die irische Helden- und Königsage*, 1921

61 K.H. Jackson, 1951, No. 132, pp. 152–9; for the full text see W. Stokes, *Revue Celtique* ix, 452, ix, 50. The men they saw with animal heads resemble a medieval bestiary, but the idea may have been taken from the head-dresses worn at the season festivals and which later survived as the mummers

62 K.H. Jackson, 1951, No. 127, pp. 143–5; J. Pokorny, *Zeitschrift für celtische Philologie* 17, pp. 195–201

63 A. and B. Rees, 1961, p. 325. The thirty-one islands and two wonders (thirty-three is clearly a magic number) are listed (pp. 319–22)

64 W. Stokes, *Revue Celtique*, xiv, 24, ed. ix, 14

65 *Dating the Past*, 1953, pp. 274ff

66 J.M.C. Toynbee, *Death and Burial in the Roman World*, 1971, p. 47; Pliny the Elder, *Nat. Hist.* XXXV, 6

67 Anne Ross, 1967, pp. 61ff

68 Wheeler found a skull with a fatal sword-cut near the entrance at Stanwick, and a sword with scabbard nearby (Sir Mortimer Wheeler, *The Stanwick Fortifications, North Riding of Yorkshire*, Res. Rep. Soc. Ant. No. XVII, 1954, pp. 53–6 and 44–50, Pls. XXVIII B, XXVI and XXVI); similar conclusions were drawn from finds at Bredon Hill, Glos. (*Arch. J.* 95, 1938, pp. 54–7)

69 C. Cichorius, *Die Reliefs der Traianssäule*, 1900, Section XXIV, panel 57

70 W. Warde Fowler, 1911, p. 29

71 It is only in recent years that they are being adequately recorded and much of this has been due to the indefatigable Anne Ross, who has published quite a number in her *Pagan Celtic Britain*, Pls. 22–41

72 *Bristol and Glos. Archaeol. Soc. Trans.* 102 (1984), pp. 212–5

73 C.F.C. Hawkes, 'A Romano-British phallic carving from Broadway, Worcs.', *Ant. J.* 28 (1948), pp. 166–9 and Pl. XXIV, e and f

74 *Ant. J.* 16 (1936), pp. 205–6

75 *Ant. J.* 16 (1936), p. 323 and Pl. LIX, No. 2

76 Anne Ross, 1967, Pl. 26a and p. 93; known as the 'Serpent Stone'

77 ibid., Pl. 26c and p. 93

78 *Fundberichte aus Baden-Württemberg* 1 (1974), pp. 252ff; *Der Keltenfürst von Hochdorf, Katalog zur Ausstellung Stuttgart, Kunstgebäude,* 1985, Nos. 1–7, pp. 46–9

79 Many of these fragments have been collected together by F.C. Grant, *Ancient Roman Religions,* 1957; see also W. Warde Fowler, *The Roman Festivals,* 1899, pp. 46–50 and H.H. Scullard, *Festivals and Ceremonies of the Roman Republic,* 1981

80 J.G. Fraser, *The Fasti of Ovid,* and his abbreviated notes in the Loeb ed. of the *Fasti,* pp. 385–442

81 They had at an earlier date been forced to acknowledge the great appeal and potency of some of the Eastern mystic cults, which later became established in Rome and spread into the western provinces.

82 A. and B. Rees, *Celtic Heritage,* 1961, Chap. IX, for the significance of numbers in Celtic society

83 J.M.C. Toynbee, 1964, p. 179

84 *Classical Art Forms and Celtic Mutations,* New Jersey, 1978; one could add Silvanus, Vulcan and Apollo

85 R. Goodburn, *Nat. Trust Guide to Chedworth,* 1979, p. 10.1 and 10.2

86 JRS 45 (1955), pp. 101–2, Pl. 30, Fig. 1; J.M.C. Toynbee, 1962, No. 124, Fig. 146

87 Frazer's great classic study, *Totemism and Exogamy,* has been superseded by more recent anthropological studies of primitive societies in the field

88 Frazer, *The Golden Bough, Aftermath,* 1936, pp. 247–56

89 For this reason Roman ritual always had to be performed with perfect precision; any wrong word or gesture brought an immediate stop to the proceedings and a new start had to be made from the beginning

90 They have been identified and classified by J.E. Fontenrose (*Orion; The Myth of the Hunter and the Huntress,* Univ. of California, pub. Classical Stud. 23, 1981) following the Levi-Strauss theory (*The Structural Study of Myth,* 1963)

91 E.O. James, 1960, p. 84

92 E.O. James, 1960, pp. 103–4 and Fig. 6

93 M.J. Vermaseren, *Cybele and Attis,* 1977, p. 14

94 On the *stelae* from the graves on the Acropolis at Mycenae (P. Garner, *Sculptured Tombs of Hellas*)

95 e.g. Mrs Arthur Strong, *Apotheosis and After Life,* 1915, p. 128, followed by Jocelyn Toynbee in her comments on the Hinton St Mary pavement (*Animals in Rome – Life and Art,* 1973, p. 285), although here she may have been interpreting this as a paradise scene, rather than the hunt

96 J.M.C. Toynbee, *Animals in Roman Life and Art*, 1973, pp. 284–8

97 This theme is echoed in the Irish myth in the lands of plenty over the western horizon and in the Muslim paradise awaiting the true believer, but restricted, it would seem, to men

98 Virgil in his *Ecologues* 4, 22 and 8, 27 and Horace in his *Epodes*, 16, 33

99 E.O. James, 1960, p. 220

100 J.G. Frazer, *Folk-Lore in the old Testament*, 1923, pp. 29–36

101 J.M.C. Toynbee, 1973, p. 65

102 K. Dunbabin, *The Mosaics of Roman North Africa*, 1978, p. 48

103 ibid., Pl. xvii, Nos. 36 and 37

104 ibid., Pl. X, No.20

105 *De Laudibus Constantini*, 14

106 As early as the first century Martial refers to a fountain in Rome crowned by Orpheus drenched in spray (*Epig* x, 19, 6–8)

107 K. Dunbabin, 1978, p. 61 and fn. 50

108 ibid., p. 63

109 ibid., Pl. XV, No.31

110 I.A. Richmond, *Archaeology and the After-Life in Pagan and Christian Imagery*, 1950

111 *The Song of Songs: Commentary and Homilies* translated and annotated by R.F. Lawson, 1959, p. 226

112 *Proc. Dorset Arch. Soc.* 102 (1980) pp. 43–8

113 fn. 111, p. 226

114 *Greek Myths and Christian Mystery*, translation 1963

115 Ovid, *Metamorphoses*, iii, 232

116 Nilotic scenes were also common and these can be used as images of the beneficence and plentitude of a nature under divine rule

117 The Ark is curiously shown as a chest with feet and a lock which Sister Charles Murray has convincingly shown to have been taken from scenes of the locked chest which contained Danae and her infant son, Perseus, when they were cast into the sea by Akrisios, King of Argos (*Rebirth and After Life*, BAR Int. Ser. 100, 1981, pp. 103–4)

118 This mosaic has been the subject of several studies including J.M.C. Toynbee, *JRS* 54 (1964), pp. 7–14; *Dorset. Arch. Soc.* 85 (1964), pp. 116–21; R.T. Eriksen, ibid., 102 (1982), pp. 43–8; K.S. Painter, *Brit. Mus. Quart.* 32 (1967), pp. 15–31

119 Pliny, *Nat. Hist* xxxvi, 116ff

120 *Ann.* iv 62–3; *Hist.* ii, 21; Suet. *Tib* 40

121 Livy XXXIX, 5–6

122 Dio, lxviii, 15, 1

123 These products were at the time known as Castor ware; *Roman Pottery from the Nene Valley: a Guide*, Peterborough Museum, Occ. Pap. No. 2

124 A typical example was illustrated by J.M.C. Toynbee, 1962, No. 158; see also M.R. Hull, 1963, Fig. 51, No. 8 and Fig. 52

125 They were first published by E.T. Artis in his *Durobrivae of Antoninius*, 1828; see also Roach Smith, *Collectanea Antiqua* IV, 1857, pp. 80–94

126 M.R. Hull, 1963, Fig. 80, p. 145

127 Roach Smith, 1857, Pl. XXII; these garments were worn by gladiators shown on late samian appliqué vessels (J. Dechélette, *Les Vases Céramique Ornés de la Gaule Romaine*, 1904, ii, Nos. 93–97, pp. 220–3). Dechélette describes the garment as a *subligaculum*, a rare word which had changed to *subligar* by the mid-first century AD. It was used by Martial in *BK* iii *Epigram* 87 addressed to Chione 'Rumour has it that you have no lovers and your body is pure – yet you bathe with pudenda exposed, for shame, cover your face with your knickers' (*transfer subligar in faciem*)

128 It is well illustrated by Professor Toynbee, 1962, No. 158, Pls. 176–7

Chapter 3 (pp. 52–82)

1 'Essai sur l'evolution de la religion gauloise' *Revue des Études Anciennes*, 1 (1965), pp. 80–125; see also Garrett S. Olmsted, 'The Gundestrup version of Táin Bó Cúalnge', *Antiquity*, 50 (1976), pp. 95–103

2 *Ant. J.* 43 (1963), p. 119 and developed in an unpublished MA thesis (London University, 1962)

3 *De Bello Civili* (also known as the *Pharsalia*) i, 445–6

4 *Teutates horrensque feris altaribus Esus/Et Taranis Scythicae non mitior ara Dianae*

5 *Recueil Général de Bas-Reliefs, Statues et Bustes de la Gaule Romaine*, 1907ff., Paris, in ten volumes

6 *Recueil Général des Bas-Reliefs, Statues at Bustes de la Germanie Romaine*, 1931, Paris and Brussels

7 One must make exceptions of the valuable studies of Professor J.M.C. Toynbee in her *Art in Roman Britain*, 1962 and *Art in Britain under the Romans*, 1964, and Anne Ross, *Pagan Celtic Britain*, 1967; amends are now being made in the new volumns of the *Corpus Signorum Imperii Romani* series of which fascicules have appeared for Bath and Wessex (1982); Hadrian's Wall, east of Corbridge (1977), York (1983) and Scotland (1984); but even here the description and identification of the Celtic stones occasionally lacks understanding

8 D.R. Dudley and Graham Webster, *The Rebellion of Boudicca*, 1962, fn. 2, p. 151

9 *EE* vii, p. 349, No. 1162; L. Allason-Jones and R. Miket, *Cat. of Small Finds from South Shields Roman Fort*, 1984, No. 3.357, pp. 146 and 8

10 C. Johns and T. Potter, 1983, pp. 46–8

11 This may not be entirely the case since there are three altars from Bath dedicated to Sulis by freedmen of a centurion and an *imaginifer* perhaps in response to gaining their freedom (*RIB* 143, 44 and 145)

12 J.M.C. Toynbee 1962, No. 79 and Pl. 78

13 *RIB* 452, where the name is given as Tanarus; Miranda Green *Chester Arch. Soc.* 65 (1982), pp. 37–44

14 Fr. Le Roux, *Ogam* (1958), p. 39

15 M. Green, The Wheel as a Cult-Symbol in the Romano-Celtic World, *Latomus* 183 (1984)

16 *AA* 3rd ser. 6 (1910), pp. 224–6 and Fig. 6; see also p. 90 above

17 Esp. 1907, No. 3139; J-J. Hatt, 'Les monuments gallo-romains de Paris, et les origines de la sculpture votive en Gaule romaine', *Rev. archéolog*, 39 (1952), pp. 69–83; Paul-Marie Duval, 'Le groupe de bas-reliefs des nautae Parisiaci', *Monuments et mémoires de la foundation Eugène Piot*, 48, 2, 1956, pp. 63–90 and Figs. 1–14; *Les Inscriptions antiques de Paris*, 1961, pp. 17–19. An illustration of a reconstruction of the monument and the surviving sculptured blocks appear in *Lutèce, Paris de César à Clovis*, 1985, pp. 299–307, published by the Musée Carnavalet

18 In the case of Cernunnos, damage has eradicated the first letter; however, George Boon has shown that it must have been present on the stone when it was found in 1711, as an engraving by Baudelot shows; 'A coin with the head of the Cernunnos', Seaby's *Coin Bulletin*, 1982, fn. 2, p. 281

19 *Ant. J.* 43 (1963), pp. 118–9 and Pl. XIX a and b

20 Illustrated in Proinsias MacCana, *Celtic Mythology*, 2nd. ed. 1983, p. 54; also seen on a seal from Mohenjodaro on which a horned god sits in a Buddha position surrounded by animals (R.E.M. Wheeler, *The Indus Civilisation*, 1953, Pl. XXIII)

21 First published in *Arch* 63 (1912), Pl. XLXVI, Fig. 2; also *RCHM Roman London*, 1928, Pl. 51; and in *London In Roman Times*, London Museum Catalogue No. 3; 1930, Pl. XVII B, No. 1 and p. 46, where it is correctly identified

22 J.M.C. Toynbee, 1964, p. 180; illustrated by A. Ross, 1967, Pl. 43a, who has also illustrated a very crude flat relief from Aesica (ibid., Pl. 53a), identified as a horned Mercury, but it has features which could indicate Cernunnos

23 Now in the BM, 1951, Pl. XVIL, No. 16

24 M.R. Hull, 1963, Fig. 53.8

25 Rivet and Smith, 1981, pp. 460–1, in discussing the tribal names SMERTAE and SMERTI

26 *CIL* XIII 4192–5 from Steintafel near Mannheim; 4208 from Wasserbillig; 4237 from Niedaltdorf near Trier, and 4508 from Breumbach. Others are illustrated in S. Reinach, 1917, pp. 93 and 95

27 P-M Duval, 'Le Dieu *Smertrios* et ses Avatars Gallo-Romaines', *Études Celtiques*, 6 from 1953–4, pp. 219–38; his interpretation of the Paris inscription (*CIL* XIII, 3026) and relief is not wholly convincing, and leads him to the conclusion that the god was also a protector against all menaces '*par extermination des monstres qui la menacent*'

28 A list of joint inscriptions is given in *PW* ed. 1129–33 and the relationship of the two deities discussed

29 Esp., 1931, No. 18; the shrine is now in the Bonn Museum

30 ibid., No. 428

31 ibid., No. 350; in the museum at Karlsruhe

32 ibid., No. 4346; in the museum at Metz. A very similar stance is seen with a female figure on a broken stone in the Sarrebourg Museum (ibid., No. 4550)

33 As the finding of altars in bath-houses dedicated to her shows

34 W. Warde Fowler, 1899, p. 100

35 Described by Virgil as the first of the gods (*primamque deorum Tellurem*; *Aen.* vii, 136–7); see also Fraser's note in Ovid's *Fasti*, Loeb ed. pp. 423–4

36 É. Thévenot, *Divinités et Sanctuaires de la Gaule*, 1968, p. 80

37 *CIL* XII 2557, 2570, XIII, 1769, 6018, 6025, 6157, 7532, 7533, 11678b

38 *CIL* XII 2194, 5870, XIII 1748, 4303, 6095, 11064

39 Esp., 1907, III, 5887 shows the panels in their original fragmentary condition and the literature up to 1917; X, 1928, included illustrations of the panels restored with some additions to the literature

40 K. Körber, *Die Juppitersäule in Altertumsmuseum der Stadt Mainz* 1915; A. von Domaszewski, *Abhandlungen zur römischen Religion* 1909; A. Oxé *MZ.* 14 (1919), pp. 28–35

41 Found in 1857 on the site of the Shakespeare Inn, Northgate Street, where remains suggest the existence of a small temple (J.F. Rhodes, 1964, No. 9 and, p. 24; also illustrated by J.M.C. Toynbee, 1964, Pl. XLb p. 157; and A. Ross, 1967, Pl. 70c and p. 210)

42 It is not the double-headed axe, as suggested by Anne Ross (1967, p. 210, Pl. 70c)

43 *CSIR Great Britain*, i, ii, 1982, No. 39, Pl. 11; A. Ross, 1967, Pl. 55a and pp. 159; B. Cunliffe, 1971, Pl. XXXVII

44 *CSIR Great Britain*, i, ii, 1982, No. 116; J.M.C. Toynbee 1964, Pl. XLIIIb and pp. 175–6; BM, 1922, p. 28; ibid., 1951, Pl. XIX 6 and p. 55

45 See on Fig. 6 below

46 *CSIR Great Britain*, I, i, 1977, No. 115 and Pl. 31; *AA* 3rd ser. 8 (1912) pp. 210–2; *Proc. Soc. Ant.* 2nd ser. 24 (1912), p. 269; *Northumberland County Hist.* 10, 1914, pp. 510–1; J.M.C. Toynbee, 1964, p. 204; A. Ross, 1967, Fig. 141 and p. 213

47 *CSIR Great Britain*, I, i, 1977, No. 183 and Pl. 45; *AA* 3rd ser. 8 (1912) Fig. 19 and p. 202

48 A very poor illustration is published in the Nettleton Report (Wedlake 1982) and the over-emphatic lighting fails to show the detail in *CSIR* 1982, No. 117, Pl. 31

49 J.F. Rhodes, 1964, No. 10, pp. 25–6; A. Ross, 1967, Pl. 70b and p. 210

50 *WAM* 45 (1932), p. 197

51 *CSIR* Fasc. 2, 1982, No. 119 and Pl. 31

52 Esp., 1903, VI, No. 4892; H. Schoppa, *Die Kunst der Römerzeit in Gallien Germanien und Britannien* nd. No. 76; J. Scarborough has identified the scene as a soap and salve factory (*Roman Medicine*, 1969, Pl. 32)

53 Esp., 1931, No. 2215. A fragment from another stone in the Epinal Museum (ibid., 4893) is of a wooden tub with a hand over it holding a stirring spoon or stick, which may have come from the same shrine as 2215

54 *Arch.* 52 (1890), p. 317

55 BM, 1953, Pl. XXI, No. 1

56 'The Reconstruction of Iron Age Buckets from Aylesford and Baldock' in BM, 1971, pp. 250–282, and Pls. LXXXCII–XCI

57 É. Thévenot, 1968, p. 142

58 *P-W*, col. 515–6

59 *CIL* XIII 6730, I O M SVCAELO ET GENIO LOCI, the name is a variant. This altar was erected by a *primus pilus* of *Legio* XXII *Primigenia*

60 The evidence is summarised by Dr Miranda Green (*Latomus*, 183 (1984), pp. 207–8)

61 As in the bronze figurine from Prémeaux (É. Thévenot, 1968, p. 135)

62 *P-W* col. 518

63 Illustrated by P-M Duval, *Les Dieux de la Gaule* 1957, Fig. 31, p. 81

64 Esp. 1909, 4566; *CIL* XIII, 4542

65 A. Ross, 1967, p. 244; the prefix 'Nant' is a Celtic word which has survived into Welsh and means a valley or brook

66 S. Reinach, 1, 1917, p. 100

67 A. Ross, 1967, p. 244

68 É. Thévenot, 1968, p. 140

69 Esp. 1909, 4568

70 A. Ross 1967, p. 244

71 ibid., p. 206

72 *NH* x, 60, 121–3

73 An example is an altar from Nîmes (Esp., 1907, 436)

74 Esp., 1909, 4708, unfortunately this stone is only known from a drawing of *c*.1700

75 Esp., 1909, 2034; also S. Reinach, 1917, i, Fig 91

76 Dr Miranda Green seems in no doubt that they are solar symbols, 1984, p. 143

77 One from Prémeaux, Côte-d'Or, now in the Musem of Beaune certainly is, as the god holds the mallet: his tunic is decorated with crosses (S. Reinach, ii, 1921, Fig. 71); one from Cologne, however, has no attributes, is a bearded male and is assumed to be Sucellos (M. Green, 1984, Pl. LXXXIII, Fig. 66)

78 M. Pobé, *The Art of Roman Gaul*, 1961, Pl. 172

79 'Le clou et l'ancre du Dispater de Viège', *La Nouvelle Clio*, 7-9 (1956), pp. 229–46

80 A lynch-pin of similar form is illustrated in the BM, 1922, Fig. 36

81 J.M.C. Toynbee, 1962, No. 79, p. 156 and Pl: 78

82 *Eburacum* RCHM, i 1962, No. 140, p. 133 and Pl. 65

83 *RIB* 919, 920, 1224, 1318, 1989

84 *RIB* 574, 1031, 1032; an altar from Binchester was dedicated to *Matres Ollototae sive Transmarinae* to emphasise the point

85 *RIB* 1988

86 *RIB* 1453 and 1541

87 *RIB* 88

88 *RIB* 653

89 *Brit.* 8 (1977), No. 4, pp. 426–7

90 *RIB* 652, 2025, 2050 and *JRS* 49 (1959), p. 237; *Brit.* 10 (1979), p. 339

91 Ovid, *Fasti* iv, 629–40

92 *RIB* 881 and 951

93 É Thévenot, 1968, Chap. 8

94 As at Dijon, ibid., p. 172

95 É Thévenot, 1968, p. 175

96 *Arch.* 49 (1920), p. 184

97 J.M.C. Toynbee, 1962, No. 72, Pl. 76

98 J.M.C. Toynbee, 1962, No. 73 and Pl. 84

99 They symbolise fertility, the little split rolls of bread are suggestive of the *vulva*. But there are exceptions and in Britain the greatest variety is seen on a relief from Ancaster (S.S. Frere, 'Some Romano-British Sculptures from Ancaster and Wilsford, Lincolnshire', *Ant. J.* 41 (1961), pp. 230–1 and Pl. XLIa). An excellent photograph taken from above clearly shows the differences. The centre goddess holds a large plate of fruits, but those on each side have smaller plates, but what is on them is difficult to identify. Professor Toynbee saw 'a dog, a fish and fruits' (1964, p. 172) and the figure on the left is holding what could be a small animal in her left hand, while in the right hand holds a small flat round object, probably a bun. A triad from Lincoln in the BM appeared to be holding baskets of fruit (?) (*BM Guide* 1922, Pl. II; 1951, Pl. XIX, No. 3). Unfortunately, there is only the lower half of a finely carved triad from Seething Lane, London, but it shows the bases of three large decorated wicker-baskets (*RCHM England Roman London* 1927, Pl. 6)

100 *London and Middlesex Archaeol. Soc. Special Paper*, No. 3, 1980, Pl. 50, pp. 169–71

101 F. Jenkins, 'The Cult of the *Dea Nutrix* in Kent', *Arch. Cant.* 71 (1957) and pp. 39–46

102 Two are illustrated in *London in Roman Times* 1930, Pl. XXI, Nos. 5 and 6

103 J.M.C. Toynbee, 1964, Pl. XLIIIa and p. 172

104 J.M.C. Toynbee, 1964, pp. 101–4

105 J.M.C. Toynbee, 1962, No. 74, Pl. 81 and p. 155

106 *CSIR Great Britain* I fasc. 1, 1977, Nos. 62 and 63, Pl. 19 and p. 24

107 ibid., No. 236, Pl. 63 and p. 85; J.M.C. Toynbee 1964, p. 173

108 Similar arched niches are on a stone from Carlisle found in 1888 (*Proc. Soc. Ant. Lond.* 2nd s. 12 (1889), p. 168; *Tullie House Cat.* 1922, No. 108)

109 *Bull. of Board of Celtic Studies*, 15 (1954), pp. 88–9, Pl. 6; also Cefni Barnett, *The Handbook of the Roman Caerwent Collection*, 1954, p. 10 and pl. unnumbered

110 I.A. Richmond and J.P. Gillam, 'The Temple of Mithras at Carrawburgh', *AA* 4th ser. 29 (1951), p. 30 and Pl. XA

111 Pliny, *Nat. Hist.* XXII, 2

112 This larger garment was also called the *barbocucullus*; Martial xiv, *Ep.*, 128

113 J.P. Wild, 'Clothing in the North-West Provinces of the Roman Empire', *BJ* 168 (1968), p. 225

114 There is a passage in Juvenal (vi, 117–8) about Messalina, the notorious wife of Claudius, leaving her palatinate bed to prowl the streets of Rome as a prostitute with a blond wig over her hair and wrapped in her nocturnal *cucullus* (*ausa Palatino tegetem praeferre cubili sumere nocturnos meretrix Augusta cucullos*); in another satire (VIII, 148) he refers to the nocturnal adulterer who conceals his face beneath his Santonian *cucullus* (*quo, si nocturnus adulter tempora Santonico velas adoperta cucullo?*). The Santones were a tribe of Aquitania between the Loire and the Garonne

115 Martial, in writing about Flaccus, who must have told all his friends that all the girls were chasing him, said 'Nothing will stop them from kissing you, even if your head is covered with a *cucullus* (*non te cucullis adsertet caput tectum*, xi, 98, 10)

116 1, viii, 9, in his advice to farmers, he advises them to take care of their slaves and protect them against wind, cold and rain with *pellibus manicatis, centonibus confectis vel sagis cucullis*, i.e. long-sleeved leather tunics, patchwork garments, large cloaks and *cuculli*; there is a slight gloss in the text which could be corrected with the addition of *cum* between *sagis* and *cucullis*

117 *Codex Theo.* XIV, 10, 1

118 R. Egger, *Wiener praehistorische Zeitschrift*, 19 (1932), pp. 311–23

119 *AA* 4th ser. 12 (1935), pp. 191–2

120 'De Télesphore au 'moine bourru'. Dieux, génies et démons encapuchonnés', *Latomus*, 21 (1955); review by Professor Toynbee, *JRS* 46 (1956), pp. 180–1

121 *Latomus*, 28 (1957), pp. 456–69

122 *RIB* 110 and Pl. IV

123 E.M. Wightman, *Roman Trier and the Treviri*, 1970, Pl. 6b

124 H. Menzel, *Die römischen Bronzen aus Deutschland Trier II* 1966, No. 86, Taf. 40 and p. 41

125 'The Piercebridge Plough Group' in Sieveking, G. de, ed., 1971, pp. 125–36

126 1957, pp. 456–7

127 J.M.C. Toynbee, 1957, No. 1, pp. 458–9 and Pl. LXIII, Fig. 1; J.C. Bruce, *Lapidarium Septentrionale*, IV 1874, p. 403, No. 786; *AA* 2nd ser. 15 (1892), p. 337, No. 47, Fig. 1; ibid., 4th ser. 12 (1935), p. 188, No. 3

128 *JRS* 24 (1934), p. 190, Pl. 7, Fig. 1; *AA* 4th ser. 11 (1934), p. 190–1; and Pl. XXVI; J.M.C. Toynbee, 1957, No. 3, p. 460 and Pl. LXIII, Fig. No. 2; 1962, No. 77 and Pl. 83

129 *AA* 4th ser. 12 (1935), p. 187

130 Now in the Netherhall Coll. at Maryport; *Trans. Cumb. & West Antiq. Arch. Soc.* 2nd ser. 15 (1915), p. 140, No. 7; *AA* 2nd ser. 15 (1892), p. 337, No. 47; J.M.C Toynbee, 1957, No. 2 and Pl. LXII, Fig. 2

131 See fn. 127, II, 1871, No. 419, p. 209

132 J.M.C. Toynbee, 1957, No. 5 and Pl. LXIV, Fig 1; 1962, No. 76 and Pl. 82

133 ibid., No. 6 and Pl. LXVI, Fig. 1, Acc. No. B2048

134 *Brit.* 4 (1973), p. 307, No. 3 and Pl. XXXVIB

135 J.M.C. Toynbee, 1957, No. 7 and Pl. LXIV, Figs. 3 and 4

136 *JRS* 41 (1951), p. 140, No. 1; 42 (1952), p. 98 and Pl. XIII, No. 1; J.M.C. Toynbee, 1957, Nos. 8 and 9 and Pl. LXV, Figs. 1 and 2 RCHM *Iron Age and Romano-British Monuments in the Gloucestershire Cotswolds* 1976, p. 41

137 M.J.T. Lewis, *Temples in Roman Britain* 1966, p. 126

138 J.M.C. Toynbee, 1957, No. 9 and Pl. LXV, Fig. 2

139 RCHM *Cotswolds* 1976, pp. 78–80 and Pl. 53; Helen O'Neil, 'Some Features of Building Construction in a Rural Area of Roman Britain' in *Studies and Building History* ed. by E.M. Jope, 1961, Chap. 2, pp. 28–37

140 Helen O'Neil and J.M.C. Toynbee, 'Sculptures from a Romano-British Well in Gloucestershire' *JRS* 48 (1958), pp. 49–55 and Pls. VIII and IX

141 J.F. Rhodes, 1964, No. 131 – vii, with a plaque of Minerva found in 1769

142 RCHM *Cotswolds* pp. 125–6 and plan

143 J.M.C. Toynbee, 1957, No. 10 and Pl. LXV, Fig. 3

144 J.M.C. Toynbee, 1957, No. 11 and Pl. LXV, No. 4

145 *CSIR* 1, ii, 1982, No. 39, Pl. 11; A. Ross, 1967, p. 155 and Pl. 55a; B. Cunliffe, 1971, Pl. XXXVII

146 *CSIR* I, ii, 1982, No. 12 and Pl. LXVI, Fig. 2; BM 1951, p. 55 and Fig. 25, No. 5

147 J.M.C. Toynbee, 1957, No. 14 and Pl. LXIII, Fig. 4; *Arch. Cant.* 66 (1953), pp. 81ff and Fig. 1

148 H. Vertet and G. Vuillemot, *Figurines Gallo-Romaines en Argile d'Autun*, Coll. du Musée Rolin, nd. Pl. 15

149 'Genius Cucullatus', *Wiener praehistoriche Zeitschrift* 19 (1932), pp. 311–23

150 'Telephoros', *Egyetemeses Philologiai Koezloeny* 57 (1933), pp. 7–11

151 *AA* 4th ser. 12 (1935), p. 194

152 The name is derived from the Celtic *epo* 'a horse'; see also S. Reinach, *Epona*, 1895; R. Magnen and É Thévenot, *Epona, Déesse gauloise* 1953

153 É Thévenot, *Antiquité*, 18 (1949), p. 400

154 *The Mabinogion*, the Tale of Pwyll, Lord of Dyved, Penguin ed. pp. 52–65

155 Mack, *The Coinage of Ancient Britain*, 1953, Pls. VI–VIII

156 ibid., Pls. VII–VIII

157 ibid., Pls. XXIII–XXIV

158 C. Fox, *Pattern and Purpose – A Survey of Early Celtic Art in Britain*, 1958, Pl. 52b

159 ibid., Pl. 33a; also I. M. Stead, 'The Reconstruction of Iron Age Buckets from Aylesford and Baldock', in Sieveking, G. de, ed., 1971, Fig. 6, p. 267

160 C. Fox, 1958, Pls. 34–36

161 F. Jenkins, 'The Horse Deity of Roman Canterbury' *Arch. Cant.* 77 (1962), pp. 142–7; there must be many more finds since this paper and it must also be appreciated that small fragments often escape identification, like a small piece in the Newport Museum from Caerwent (House VII, Room 8) which was noticed by Dr Jenkins on a visit (personal communication)

162 See distribution map in J. de Vries, *La Religion des Celtes*, 1963, Map 10, p. 133

163 E. Birley, 'Marcus Cocceius Firmus: An Epigraphic Study', *Proc. Soc. Ant. Scot.* 70 (1936), pp. 363–77, also in his collected papers *Roman Britain and the Roman Army*, 1953, pp, 87–103

164 *Ant. J.* 55 (1975), pp. 299 and 335–6 and Pl. LVIII

165 *Juvenal* xi, 191

166 Suet. *Nero*, 22

167 In the case of Janus it symbolised the opening of the New Year

168 Lemprière, *Classical Dictionary*; it was also carried by Janus, the god of doors (Ovid, *Fasti*, i, 228, *clavigerum verbis adloquor ipse deum*, i.e. 'I address the god who carries the key'

169 I.A. Richmond, 1950; this basic concept has been developed by Lambrechts, 'Divinités equestres Celtique ou defunts Héroïses?', *L'Antiquité Classique* 20 (1951), fasc. 1, pp. 107–128

170 É. Thévenot, 'Sur les traces des Mars Celtiques' in the *Diss arch. Gandenses* 3, 1955, pp. 170ff; 'Le cheval Saare dans la Gaule dell'Est' *Revue archéologique del'Est* (1951), pp. 129–41; for examples in Britain see M.V. Taylor, 'Statuettes of horsemen and horses and other votive objects from Brigstock, Northants', *Ant. J.* 43 (1963), pp. 264–8

171 There were also some five boars, a stag and a bull as well as sacrificial bowls and a 5ft trumpet. It has been suggested that these remarkable pieces came from an important Druidic sanctuary known to have existed near Orleans (P. Mackendrick, *Roman France*, 1971, p. 208; and figs. 7.14 and 7.15); the stag is illustrated by Olwen Brogan in her *Roman Gaul* 1953, Fig. 43b; see also her pp. 178, 183 and 193

172 The same name appears on inscriptions linking the deity with Mars (*CIL* xii, 1566, 2204)

173 *English River Names*, 1968, p. lii

174 Rivet and Smith, 1979, map on p. 336

175 ibid., pp. 243–246 and fig. 27

176 *AA* 2nd ser. 6 (1862–5), pp. 153–5 and 169–71

177 By I.A. Richmond, *AA* 4th ser. 19 (1941), pp. 37–9

178 First published in Collingwood and Myres, *Roman Britain and the English Settlements* 1937, p. 265

179 *RIB* 733, 772–7, 809, 887–9, 914, 918, 948, 970, 1521, 1775–6, 1784, 1976–7, 2038–9, 2044, 2056; *JRS* 49 (1969), p. 237, No. 7; *Brit.* 9 (1978), p. 474, Nos. 7 and 8

180 1967, p. 371 and Pls. 49 and 50

181 E. Birley, *Research on Hadrian's Wall*, 1961, p. 233

182 *RIB* 966, 985–9, 993, 1017

183 *C. and W. Trans.* 38 (1938), p. 208 and Fig. 14; *JRS* 28 (1938), pp. 175–6, 203 and Pl. XXXIV, 2; see also Ross 1967, pp. 169–171 and Pl. 51 b and c

184 *RIB* 1207; I.A. Richmond and S. McIntyre, *AA* 4th ser. 14 (1937), pp. 103–9 and Pl. X

185 E. Birley, *Research on Hadrian's Wall*, 1961, p. 240; quoting Sir Walter Scott 'a sulky churlish boor has destroyed the ancient statue, or rather relief'

186 According to J. Hodgson who saw the figure when it was still complete in 1810 (*Hist. of Northumberland*, 1827, Pt. ii, Vol i, p. 166)

187 *Britannia Romana*, 1732, pp. 239–40 and p. 192, No. 30, XCIV; reproduced by Richmond, Fig. 4

188 *Brit.* 14 (1983), pp. 143–53 and Pl. XIV A

189 ibid., p. 151 and Pl. XV B

190 *RIB* 993 (Bewcastle), 602 (Lancaster), 1017, 2015 and 2024 (probably from milecastles)
191 The stone is now in private hands; *Brit.* 16 (1985), p. 331
192 Rivet and Smith, 1979, pp. 395–6
193 *Trans. Dumfriesshire and Galloway Nat. Hist. and Archaeol. Soc.*, 1954, pp. 35ff
194 W.S. Watson, *The History of the Celtic Place Names of Scotland*, 1926, p. 181
195 I.A. Richmond, *Roman Britain*, 2nd ed. 1963, pp. 138–9
196 *JRS* 58 (1968), p. 209, No. 28 and Pl. XIX, 2; see also Anne S. Robertson, *Birrens (Blatobulgium)* 1975, pp. 95–7 and Fig. 25, No. 3
197 Ian Richmond, 'Roman legionaries at Corbridge, their supply-base, temples and religious cults', *AA* 5th ser. 21 (1943), pp. 206–10
198 *Iter Boreale* 1776, p. 63; E.J. Phillips, 1977, No. 60, pp. 23–4 and Pl. 18
199 *JRS* 35 (1945), pp. 15–29 and Pl. 1
200 *Brit.* 2 (1971), No. 12, p. 291; *AA* 5th ser. 1 (1973), pp. 113–4 and Fig. 1
201 *AA* 5th ser. 1 (1973), pp. 114–5 and Pl. XV
202 *Dark-Age Britain*, ed. D.B. Harden, 1956, pp. 11–15 and Pl. 111
203 A point also made by Dr Ross, 1967, p. 369
204 Trans. in the Penguin Classics, 1976, pp. 158–9, 164–9, 174, 190
205 *AA* 2nd ser. 8 (1880) pp. 1ff.; L. Allason-Jones and B. McKay, *Coventina's Well: A shrine on Hadrian's Wall*, 1985
206 Some of the objects are illustrated by Dr Ross, 1967, Pl. 5 and the altars Pls. 7–9
207 At Birdoswold (*RIB* 1897) and Burgh-by-Sands, *RIB* 2043
208 A. Birley, *The People of Roman Britain*, 1979, pp. 107–8
209 A German origin was first proposed by Haverfield, who listed 40 altars, *AA* 3rd ser. 15 (1918), pp. 33–43, *EE* ix, 1122
210 *RIB* 1145, illustrated in E.J. Phillips, 1977, Pl. 20, No. 65, p. 25
211 *RIB* 973; E. Birley, *CW* 53 (1953), pp. 37–8 and Pl. II, Fig. 6
212 *RIB* 1335; E.J. Phillips, 1977 No. 245 and Pl. 67; see also *AA* 3rd ser. 15 (1918), No. 1, p. 39
213 *RIB* 1805; see also *AA* 3rd ser. 15 (1918), No. 13, p. 39; this creature is identified in *RIB* as a dolphin
214 On another from Lancaster (*RIB* 1088) the dedicator has been identified as a *princeps* but the stone is damaged and this seems a very doubtful reading. Professor A. Birley has suggested the name is Unthaus which is clearly Germanic, not surprising as there was a detachment of Suebians there in the third century
215 These names are discussed by Professor A. Birley, 1979, p. 107
216 *JRS* 52 (1962), No. 6, p. 192
217 *The Roman Riverside Wall and Monumental Arch in London*, London and Middlesex Arch. Soc. Spec. Pap. No. 3, 1980
218 ibid., No. 34, pp. 169–171 and Pl. 50
219 In *Roman Life and Art in Britain*, ed. by J.T. Manby and M. Henig, BAR. 41 1977, pp. 383–6 and Pl. 17. 111a
220 *Current Archaeol.* 58 (1977), p. 350

221 A. Holder, *Alt-celtischer Sprachschatz* ii, 1896–1907, Col. 1663

222 Haverfield drew attention to this unusual name and suggested he may have been called after the Suleviae (*Arch.* 69 (1920), p. 182 and fn. 1), but it is more likely that he was born at Bath where his father Brucetus may have worked, probably also as a sculptor, in which case he may have been named after Sulis

223 The idea advanced by Fr le Roux that it was derived from Sulis = Sol (*Ogam* No. 19 (1952), p. 213; see also J. de Vries, 1963, p. 87)

224 Rivet and Smith, 1979, p. 291

225 G. Boon, Silchester: *The Roman Town of Calleva*, 1974, p. 154

226 Rivet and Smith, 1979, p. 454, under the name of the British tribe Segontiaci listed by Caesar (*BG.* V, 21), an expansion is suggested as: Saegontio

227 *Bull. Board Celtic Stud.* 15, pt i (1952), pp. 10–17; unfortunately the 1908 excavation was typical of its period and is wanting in detail (*Arch.* 62 (1910), pp. 4ff)

228 *Second Report on the Excavations on the Site of the Roman Town at Wroxeter*, Res. Rep. Soc. Ant., No. 2, 1914

229 *Brit.* 14 (1983), p. 336, No. 3(a)

230 B. Cunliffe and M. Fulford, *Bath and the Rest of Wessex*, Pl. 11, No. 38 and p. 11

231 ibid., No. 39 and p. 11

232 A. Ross, 1967, p. 174

233 *Trans. Bristol and Glos. Arch. Soc.* 101 (1984), pp. 5–20

234 R.E.M. and T.V. Wheeler, 1932

235 W.J. Wedlake, 1982

236 Listed by M.J.T. Lewis in his *Temples in Roman Britain*, 1966, which includes a brief section on dedications (pp. 45–6); to this must be added two important sites at Uley, Glos. (*Brit* 9 (1978), p. 457; 10 (1979), p. 323; 12 (1981), p. 370); and Hayling Island (T. Ely, *Roman Hayling, a contribution to the history of Roman Britain 1904*; *Brit.* 8 (1977), p. 418; 9 (1978), p. 464; 10 (1979), p. 329–31; 12 (1981), p. 363; 13 (1982), p. 389; 15 (1984), p. 324

237 *Arch.* 19 (1821), p. 410; *Ant. J.* 8 (1928), p. 300; *JRS* 27 (1937), p. 241; *VCH Essex* iii (1963), pp. 139ff; *Brit.* 4 (1973), p. 304; 12 (1981), p. 350; 13 (1982), pp. 371–2; N.E. France and B.M. Gobel, *The Romano-British Temple at Harlow*, 1985

238 *Oxon.* 14 (1949), pp. 1ff; 19 (1954), pp. 15ff

239 This appears to be a small *Tempelbezirk*, but it has produced no evidence of the deities venerated there. The results of the excavations over a long period have been summarised by Alec Detsicas, *The Cantiaci*, 1983, pp. 60–76

Chapter 4 (pp. 83–106)

1 S. Loeschcke, 'Applikenform einer Planetenvase im Prov-Mus. zu Trier, *Römische-germanisches Korrespondenzblatt* 8 (1915), No. 1; another important centre of the production of these vessels and others of some religious significance was Bavai; for a definitive study see Marcel Amand, *Vases à bustes, vases à décor zoomorphe et vases cultuels aux serpents dans les anciennes provinces de Belgique et de Germanie*, Mémoires de la Classe des Beaux-Arts Coll. in 8°–2ᵉ série T XV: fasc. 2, 1984

2 E. Krüger, 'Die Trierer Göttervase', *Trier Zeitschrift* 1 (1926), pp. 1–17

3 A Trier vessel is illustrated in *Trier: Kaiserresidenz und Bischofssitz*, 1984, p. 263 (Kat 173c); behind the helmeted bust of Minerva is a staff with a knobbed end and a double-bladed axe, unusual attributes of the classical goddess, while the *petasus* of Mercury has become a pair of wings barely attached to the hair

4 M. Bös, 'Aufschiften aus Rheinischen Trinkgefässen der Römerzeit', *Kölner J. für vor-und Frühgeschichte* 3 (1958), pp. 20–5

5 *Ant. J.* 39 (1959), p. 92 and Pl. XXIV, F

6 BM Guide, 1951, p. 36 and Pl. V, No. 24

7 G. Braithwaite, 'Romano-British Face Pots and Head Pots', *Brit.* 15 (1984), Figs. 11–13; some of these were published with others by Dom Perrin in his 'Aspects of art in Romano-British pottery', with J. Munby and M. Henig 1977, pp. 253–75, but whether any of these can be considered as 'art forms' is a matter of debate

8 J.P. Bushe-Fox, 1932, p. 185 and Pl. XLIII

9 Thought to be based on the ORIEN AVG reverse of coins of Aurelian (*RIC* 230) and Gallienus (*RIC* 494); but there is little comparison between the two full-face figures on this pot and Sol on the coins

10 Lucian, *Hercules*, 1-3

11 *Arch. Cant.* 72 (1958), pp. 211–2 and Fig. 4. I am most grateful to Alec Detsicas for finding these sherds in the Maidstone Museum and arranging for me to study them

12 C. Going, 'Some Nene Valley Folded Beakers with Anthropomorphic Decoration' in *Roman Pottery Research in Britain and North West Europe* ed. A.C. and A.S. Anderson, BAR Int. Ser. 123, 1981, pp. 313–9

13 *Collectanea Antiqua* IV, 1857, pp. 91–2

14 I am most grateful to David Brown for drawing my attention to these sherds and providing facilities for their study; *The Ashmolean* No. 5 (1984), p. 3

15 H.B. Walters, 1908, M 2483, pp. 397–8 and Fig. 243

16 J. Déchelette, *Les Vases Céramique ornés de la Gaule Romaine*, 1904

17 *AA* 3rd ser. 6 (1910), pp. 224–6 and fig. 6; J.M.C. Toynbee, 1962, Nos. 164–5; Cat. No. 161, p. 191

18 J.M.C. Toynbee (1962) No. 256; *AA* 4th ser. 40 (1962), pp. 35–6 No. 1 and Pl. 4, Fig. 1; *JRS* 49 (1959), p. 106

19 *AA* 4th ser. 21 (1943), pp. 192–3 and Pl. X G, No. 1

20 *Ant. J.* 39 (1959), Pl. XXIV, F

21 *VCH Hunts.* i. Pl. V; *Ant. J.* 39 (1959), p. 92 and Pl. XXIII; J.M.C. Toynbee, 1964, p. 414

22 Xenophon, *Anabasis* ii, 1, 6ff; the barbotine and slip appear to indicate rather more than the heavily protected arm guard of the *retiarius*

23 I am grateful to David Gurney of the Norfolk Archaeological Unit for drawing my attention to it

24 M.R. Hull, 1963

25 I.M. Stead, 'Celtic Dragons from the River Thames', *Ant. J.* 64 (1984), pp. 269–79

26 Dr Anne Ross has suggested to me that the figure may be holding a banner or effigy on a pole, but the upside-down position is more difficult to explain

27 H.B. Walters, 1908, No. 2480

28 T.W. and C.F. Potter, *A Romano-British Village at Grandford, March, Cambs.* BM Occ. Pap. No. 35, 1982, Fig. 38, No. 289 and p. 77

29 D. Planck, *Germania* 60 (1982), pp. 105ff; *Der Keltenfürst von Hochdorf,* Katalog zur Ausstellung, Stuttgart 1985, pp. 341–53

30 ibid., D. Planck, 1985, Abb. 527

31 Simone Deyts, 1983

32 J-J. Hatt, 1970, Pl. 50

33 M.R. Hull, 1963, Fig. 53

34 ibid., No. 13

35 ibid., No. 11

36 Illustrated on an intaglio from South Shields (M. Henig, 1974, No. 184), this figure has been identified as Silvanus Cocidius (M. Henig, 1984, Pl. 86). A similar stick is being held by a figure on a pottery mould found at Kettering in 1983. The figure is unclothed and is also holding two large balls which may have been used for bowling swiftly along the ground to knock over hares; Professor Hawkes offers an alternative explanation – that of someone playing a kind of early Celtic hurley (*Ant. J.* 20 (1940), pp. 497–90)

37 M.R. Hull, 1963, Fig. 53, No. 8; this has also been described by Professor Toynbee in *Latomus* 28 (1957), pp. 468–9

38 The conclusion also of J.M.C. Toynbee, 1964, pp. 412–3

39 *Ant. J.* 46 (1966), pp. 338–9 and Pl. LXVII; *JRS* 56 (1966), pp. 206–7 and Pl. ix, 3

40 J.M.C. Toynbee, 1962, No. 191 and pp. 191–2, with a brief list

41 *Brit.* 10 (1979), p. 285 and Pl. XV, No. 6; also G. Braithwaite, 1984, p. 115 and Fig. 10, No. 6

42 *Ant. J.* 39 (1959), p. 93 and Fig. 2

43 M.R. Hull, 1963, Fig. 54, Nos. 2, 6, 8 and 10

44 A vessel in Wisbech Museum is covered with *phalli*

45 This shows a winged *phallus* pulling a cart full of *phalli*, G. Webster, *The Cornovii,* 1975, Fig. 41

46 *Roman Pottery from the Nene Valley: A Guide,* Peterborough City Museum, Occ. Pap. No. 2, No. 28, Fig. 3

47 Professor Toynbee recognised this problem and included a list of seventeen in a footnote in her *Art in Britain under the Romans,* 1964, p. 110, fn. 2; most of these items are, however, small busts which were originally attached to various objects possibly of a religious use, and cannot be regarded as cult figures. They are of great interest as an aspect of Celtic decorated art which E.T. Leeds dismissed as 'crude and puerile', 'the acme of *naïveté*' (1933, p. 89)

48 *Arch.* 58 (1902), pp. 148–50

49 'The Shrine of the Head, Caerwent', in *Welsh Antiquity*, 1971, ed. G. Boon and John Lewis, pp. 163–175

50 Report forthcoming in *E. Anglian Arch*; the figure was published on the cover of an Interim Report by Robin Turner in 1982 by the Essex County Council and *Brit.* 1 (1970), p. 267 and Pl. XXIX

51 E.O. James, *The Ancient Gods*, 1960, Pl. 9 and p. 48; for figures of eye goddesses from Tell Brak, Mesopotamia *c.*3000 BC and O.G.S. Crawford, *The Eye Goddess*, 1957, Pl. 2 of figures from Jokha (ancient Umma)

52 *Arch. J.* 21 (1864), p. 131

53 *JRS* 28 (1938), pl. 26, No. 1 and p. 196; J.M.C. Toynbee, 1962, No. 8, Pl. 9 and p. 126

54 Found on the Bon Marché site in Northgate St. *Trans. Bristol & Glos. Arch. Soc.* 56 (1934), pp. 78–9 and Pl. 8; J.M.C. Toynbee, 1962, No. 8, pp. 125–6 and Pl. 8

55 K. Greene, *Ant. J.* 55 (1975), pp. 338–45

56 B. Cunliffe and M. Fulford, 1982, No. 40; B.W. Cunliffe, *Roman Bath*, 1969, Pl. XI

57 L. Allason-Jones and B. McKay, *Coventina's Well*, 1985, No. 35 and pp. 21–22; but it could have been a decorative mount symbolising the head-cult

58 *Ant. J.* 41 (1961), pp. 229–30 and Pl. XL a, the figure was at this time preserved in Wilsford Church

59 *The Roman Town and Villa at Great Casterton, Rutland*, 1951, p. 21 and Pl. IIb; also illustrated is J.M.C. Toynbee 1964, Pl. LXXXIII b and p. 362

60 *CSIR* I fasc. 1, E.J. Phillips, *Corbridge, Hadrian's Wall East of the North Tyne*, 1977, No. 122, Pl. 33 and p. 44; J.M.C. Toynbee, 1962, No. 42, Pl. 49 and p. 146

61 Summarised with a full bibliography in RCHM *Iron Age and Romano-British Monuments in the Gloucestershire Cotswolds*, 1976, pp. 125–6

62 In her contribution to *Essays in Bristol and Gloucestershire History*, 1976, pp. 85–7

63 Bobart, *Basketry through the Ages*, 1936

64 J. Liversidge, *Furniture in Roman Britain*, 1955, Pl. 28; also in a relief from Köln of a toilet scene (Esp. VI 5142, and *Römer am Rhein* 1967, A 176, Taf. 51, and pp. 188–9)

65 H. Vertet et G. Vuillemot, *Figurines Gallo-Romaines en Argile d'Autun* nd., Pl. 1 b and c

66 Esp. IV, 2852

67 *Catalogue of the Antiquities in the Museum of the Wiltshire Archaeological and Natural History Society at Devizes*, pt. ii, 1911, Nos. 600–732, pp. 70–86

68 Colt Hoare, *The History of Ancient Wiltshire, 1810, South*, p. 53

69 It was also published in *WAM* 36 (1889), Pl. vi, Fig. 9

70 *CW Trans.* 3 (1903), p. 408; T. May and L.E. Hope, 'Catalogue of Roman Pottery in the Museum, Tullie House, Carlisle', ibid., 17 (1917), No. 182, p. 58 and Pl. XIV

71 I am most grateful to the Curator of the Museum and Keeper of Archaeology, Colin Richardson, for his careful examination of the figure, his comments and supplying the photographs

Chapter 5 (pp. 107–36)

1 *Ann* xiv, 30. *luci saevis superstitionibus sacri*: of the sacred groves on Anglesey destroyed by the Roman army; Virgil refers to a sacred grove in the middle of Carthage, *Lucus in urbe fuit media Aen* i, 441; Lucan used the word *lucus* twice (*de Bello Civili* i, 453–4) *nemora alta remotis incolitis lucis* and *lucus erat longo numquam violatus ab aevo*, iii, 399

2 In Britain there is Vernemeton, on the Fosse Way, the prefix *Ver* gave an added importance to the sacred grove of Aquae Arnemetiae, the Roman spa at Buxton (Rivet and Smith, 1979, pp. 254–5); Medionemeton, a place near the Antonine Wall (ibid. pp. 416–7); Nemeto Statio, North Tawton, Devon, the names may originally have been Nemeto-totatio (ibid. p. 424). There are also river names like Nymet or Nemet which preserve the name (Ekwall, 1928, p. 304; see also A. Ross, 1967, pp. 53–7)

3 Émile Male, *La Fin du Paganisme en Gaul*

4 E.O. James, 1962, pp. 149–160

5 Joan P. Alcock, 'Celtic Water Cults in Roman Britain', *Arch. J.* 122 (1966), pp. 1–12; J.M. Blasquez, 'Le Culte des Eaux dans la Peninsule Iberique', *Ogam* (1957), pp. 209–33

6 Simone Deyts, 1983

7 Sir Cyril Fox, 1946

8 *de Bello Civili* iii, 404: *structae diris altaribus arae*; 412–3 *simulacraque maesta deorum arte carent caesisque extant informia truncis*

9 F. Benoit, *L'Art Primitif Mediterranéen de la Vallée du Rhône*, 1955; Henri-Paul Eydoux, *Monuments et trésors de la Gaule*, 1958, Chap. 2

10 F. Benoit, *Entremont capitale Celto-ligure des Salyens de Provence la Gaule méridionale*, 1956

11 J-J. Hatt, 1970, Pls. 41–3

12 M. Pobé, 1961, Nos. 35 and 36

13 *Ant. J.* 45 (1965), pp. 234–5 and Pl. LXVIII

14 J.S.P. Bradford and R.G. Goodchild, 'Excavations at Frilford, Berks', *Oxon.* 4 (1939), pp. 1–70; see also D.W. Harding, 1972, pp. 61ff, Fig. 8 and Pls. 33 and 34

15 R.E.M. Wheeler, 1943, Pl. XX

16 Publication forthcoming; for a brief account of the early stages of the excavation see: *Current Archaeology* No. 81 (1981), pp. 294–7

17 The excavator has calculated that there may have been as much as 70 miles of timbering altogether, well worth the army taking as the *spolia* of victory for their military stock-yards. Dr Henig has drawn my attention to the colonnaded grove not entirely dissimilar to the *Templum Pacis* near the Forum of Peace

18 Dr Henig has suggested that the collection of silver spoons which bears this name and those of his devotees may have belonged to a *collegium* of the god (*Religion in Roman Britain*, 1984, p. 222)

19 *Current Arch.* No. 81 (1981), p. 294

20 *Ant. J.* 8 (1928), pp. 76ff; 17 (1937), p. 310; 20 (1941), p. 115

21 *Ant. J.* 37 (1957), p. 71; 43 (1963), pp. 228; *JRS* 52 (1962), pp. 173

22 *Brit.* 8 (1977), p. 418; 9 (1978), p. 464; 10 (1979), pp. 329–331; 12 (1981), p. 362; 13 (1982), p. 389; 15 (1984), p. 324; although this remained a circular tower-type

23 *JRS* 48 (1958), p. 137; 51 (1961), p. 175; 52 (1962), pp. 172 and 192

24 *Archaeology* 1 (1) 1948, HMSO, pp. 74–8. A brief summary was given in *Problems of the Iron Age in Southern Britain*, ed. S.S. Frere, Inst. London Occ. Pap. No. 11, p. 25 and Fig. 7; *Ant. J.* 28 (1948), p. 29

25 1966, p. 11

26 B. Cunliffe, *Danebury*: 1983, pp. 113–117 and Fig. 60; 1984, i, pp. 81–7

27 ibid., 1984, p. 189

28 O. Bedwin, *Sussex Arch. Coll.* 119 (1981), pp. 37–55

29 L. Alcock, *By South Cadbury is that Camelot*, 1972, pp. 163–4, Pls. 46–50, Figs. 10 and 27

30 ibid., p. 173

31 'Van Grafmonument tot Heiligdom', *Mededelingen van de Koninklijke, vlaamse Academie voor Wetenschappen, Letteren en schone kunsten van België* 28 (1966), No. 2, pp. 17–73

32 H. Brisson – J-J. Hatt, 'Cimetières gaulois et gallo-romains à enclose en Champagne', *Revue Arch. de l'Est et du Centre-Est II* (1960), pp. 7–23

33 I.M. Stead, 1965

34 K. Schwarz, *Jahresber. Bayerisch – Bodendenkmalpflege* 1 (1960)

35 A scene in relief on the inside of a silver cup from Flaviobriga in N. Spain illustrates the process (M. Rostovtzeff, 1947, Pl. XXXV, No. 2)

36 A.H.M. Jones, 1964, p. 92 and III, p. 13, fn. 33

37 *Ant. J.* 8 (1928), pp. 311–26 and Pl. XLVII

38 Who produced a brilliant summary: *Roman Bath Discovered, 1971*; excavations up to 1968 were published in *Roman Bath*, Rep. Soc. Ant. No. 24, 1969

39 Only one fragment of inscribed architrave of the temple has so far been found and it consists of two letters ..]VM, 10.5cm high (*RIB* 177: B. Cunliffe, 1971, Fig. 6)

40 To be published in a forthcoming report; some have already appeared in the annual summaries of Romano-British discoveries in *Brit*. Most of the objects found in the earlier excavations have been dispersed and lost

41 R.E.M. and T.V. Wheeler, 1932

42 E.M. Wightman, 1970, pp. 211–4

43 *Bristol and Glos. Arch. Soc. Trans.* 101 (1983), pp. 5–20

44 'The possible effects on Britain of the fall of Magnentius' in *Rome and her Northern Provinces*, ed. B. Hartley and J. Wacher, 1983, p. 250

45 G.C. Boon, *Silchester: The Roman Town of Calleva*, 1974, p. 154

46 *The Cornovii*, 1975, p. 62; V. E. Nash-Williams, 1952, *Bull. Board Celtic Stud.* 15, pt.i, pp. 13–17

47 *Arch.* 61 (1907), pp. 203–4 and Pl. XXIII

48 A.H.M. Jones, 1964, p. 113

49 M.E. Mariën, 1980, Pl. 135

50 1932 Report, Pl. XXX and p. 91

51 ibid., Pl. XXIX and p. 90

52 1984, pp. 136–42; Pl. XXVII and p. 90

53 This idea still persists in the ghosts causing these spirits to haunt the places where they were so unseemly despatched

54 *Dis* is an early form of *Deus*, but it became linked with the shades of the departed, hence the tombstone formula *Dis Manibus* (to the shades of the departed)

55 D.W. Harding, 1974, p. 113

56 This is, however, disputed by Professor Cunliffe (1974, p. 292). His argument is that the bodies were placed on raised platforms in special enclosures and left to scavengers and the forces of decay. The skull may have been first removed and kept in the family, since the head was the most revered part of the body and was fully representative of the person

57 B. Cunliffe, 1983

58 B. Cunliffe, 1984, Table 43 and Fig. 8.2a

59 B. Cunliffe, 1983, p. 156

60 R.E.M. Wheeler, 1943, pp. 63–4, 351–6 and Pls. LII–LXIII

61 I.M. Stead, 1965, *Excavations of the Late Celtic Urn-field at Swarling*, Rep. Res. Soc. Ant. No. 5

62 A.J. Evans, 'On a Late Celtic Urn field at Aylesford, Kent', *Arch.* 52 (1890), pp. 369–74; J.P. Bushe-Fox, 1925

63 I.M. Stead, 'A La Tène III burial at Welwyn Garden City', *Arch.* 101 (1967), pp. 1–62

64 I.M. Stead, 'The Reconstruction of Iron Age Buckets from Aylesford and Baldock' in Sieveking, G. de, ed. 1971

65 G.C. Dunning and R.F. Jessup, *Antiquity* 10 (1936) pp. 37–53

66 *Arch.* 76 (1927), pp. 241–54; J. Foster, *Bronze Boar figurines in Iron Age and Roman Britain*, Bar 39 (1977), pp. 7–10

67 R. F. Jessup, 'Roman Barrows in Britain', *Latomus* 57 (1962), pp. 855–67; 'Barrows and Walled Cemeteries in Roman Britain', *J. Arch. Ass.* 3rd ser. 22 (1958), pp. 1–32; see also J. Collis, 'Pro-Roman burial rites in N. W. Europe' in *Burial in the Roman World*, ed. R. Reece, CBA Res. Rep. No. 22, 1977, pp. 10–11

68 There is a great display of boar standards on the Arc d'Orange ('L' Arc Orange', XVe Supplement à *Gallia* 1962, Pl. 44)

69 As quoted by Diodorus Siculus (30, 2-3): 'horns are attached to the helmet so as to form a single piece, in other cases images of the fore-parts of birds or four-footed-animals' (Loeb ed. translation)

70 O. Klind-Jensen, 1961

71 From Long Wittenham, Berks, *Oxon.* 2 (1937), Fig. 1, No. 2; from Arras, E. Yorks, *Arch.* 60 (1906), p. 303, Fig. 7

72 It is in 'The Destruction of Da Derga's Hostel' (quoted by Jeffrey Gantz in *Early Irish Myths and Sagas*, Penguin 1981, pp. 61–2)

73 *Early Celtic Art*, Oxford 1944; human heads appear on torcs from Waldalgesheim (No. 55, Pl. 45) from a burial at Rodenbach (No. 59, Pl. 47); *têtes coupées* on decorated discs from near Brescia (No. 84, Pl. 53); also on war-gear as seen on the anthropoid sword and dagger handles (*Proc. Prehist. Soc.* 21. (1955), pp. 198–227); on helmets from Umbria (Jacobstal No. 144, Pl. 85); chariot fittings from Waldalgesheim (ibid., No. 156(d), Pl. 98); a linch pin from Grabenstetten (ibid., No. 160, Pl. 101); on brooches, as one from near Butzbach (ibid., No. 296, Pl. 155), etc.; animals and birds abound as on a large brooch from Czechoslovakia (ibid., No. 318, Pl. 161); on a magnificent vessel in the BM (ibid., No. 381, Pl. 179); etc

74 *Arch. J.* 115 (1960), No. 37, pp. 74–5; see also Nos. 51, 68, 136, 232, 237

75 N. Crummy, *Colchester Archaeological Report 2: The Roman Small Finds from excavations in Colchester, 1971–9*, 1981, Nos. 520–4, Fig. 32 and p. 30

76 For the simple forms: *MZ* xii–xiii (1917–18) Abb. 10, Nos. 1 and 4; *Novaesium*, Taf. XXXIV, Nos. 49 and 50; etc. For more elaborate forms: *Hod Hill*, i, Fig. 3, A 44–45; *Novaesium*, Taf. XXXIV, No. 48; *MZ*. xii, xiii (1917–18) Abb. 10, Nos. 2, 5 and 6; etc.

77 G. Ulbert, 'Das römische Donau-Kastell Risstissen' Teil I, *Urkunden zur Frühgeschichte aus Südwürttemberg-Hohenzollern*, Heft. 4, 1970

78 Russell Robinson, *The Armour of Imperial Rome*, 1975, Pls. 286–7; etc.

79 Jochen Garbsch, *Römische Paraderüstungen*, 1978

80 H. von Petrikovits, 'Trojaritt und Geranostanz', *Egger Festschrift* Band 1, 1952, pp. 126ff

81 *A Corpus of Roman Engraved Gemstones from British Sites*, BAR 8, 2nd. ed. 1978

82 One has only to study the portraits of the Elizabethan Court to realise this. Sir Roy Strong has called them 'Icons', as in the title of his book, *The English Icon*, 1969

83 B. Cunliffe, 1984

84 B. Cunliffe, 'Settlement and Population in the British Iron Age: Some facts, figures and fantasies' in *Lowland Iron Age Communities in Europe*, ed. B. Cunliffe and T. Rowley, *BAR* Int. Ser. 48, 1978, pp. 21–24

85 *Cross-Channel Trade between Gaul and Britain in the Pre-Roman Iron Age*, ed. Sarah Macready and F.H. Thompson, Soc. of Antiqs. 1984. Strabo stated that the Veneti were prepared to stop Caesar's invasion of Britain because they traded extensively with the Britons and doubtless thought Caesar would interfere with their monopoly (IV, 4, 1)

86 W. Rodwell, ed. 1980, p. 301; with a 'high proportion' of plated coins

87 At Tiefenau near Berne: De Bonstetten, *Notice sur les Armes et Chariots de Guerre decouverte à Tiefenau*, 1852

88 Tacitus, *Annals* ii, 18, *struxitque aggerem et in modum tropaeorum arma*; i.e. (the soldiers) built a mound and piled arms on it in the fashion of a trophy

89 This shows two manacled prisoners on each side of a tree-trunk, M. Pobé, 1961, Pl. 103

90 The treasure disappeared on its way to Massilia and a special court of enquiry was set up to investigate. Although Caepio may have escaped from this, he was arraigned in 104 for his disastrous defeat at Arausio, when 80,000 were estimated to havè been lost. He was imprisoned, but later exiled to Smyrna and his daughter forced into prostitution, according to Timagenes (H.H. Scullard, *From the Gracchi to Nero* 1959, pp. 54–57)

91 Esp. 3875–3884

92 Simone Deyts, 1983

93 A. Ross, *Everyday Life of the Pagan Celts*, 1970, Fig. 43

94 J-J. Hatt, 1970, Pl. 48

95 C. Fox, 1946

96 Pliny the Elder tells us that the Druids in Gaul were under threat from Tiberius and expelled by Claudius, most of them coming to Britain (*Nat. Hist.* XXX, 13; see also Suet. *Claud.* XXV, 4). There must have been, in consequence, a large complement of Druids in Britain

97 *Ant. J.* 27 (1947), pp. 117–119 and Pls. XVII and XVIII

98 ibid., p. 117

99 W. Rodwell 1980, see fn. 86 above

100 ibid., p. 308

101 *Ann.* XIV, 31, . . . *delectique sacerdotes specie religionis omnis fortunas effundebant*

102 As noted above in fn. 86 at Hayling Island; of the 92 Celtic coins, 22 are from Gaul and could hàve been offerings by traders; a large number of the British are either plated or of very thin silver, either on the presumption that the gods could be easily deceived or as tokens of real silver or gold

103 R.E.M. and T.V. Wheeler, 1952, pp. 116–131

104 ibid., p. 129

105 'Barbarous Copies of Roman Coins: their significance for the British historian and archaeologist' in *Limes-Studien* ed. R. Laur-Belart, 1959, p. 85

106 An example could be a site near Bourton-on-the Water, Glos., known as The Chessels, an Anglo-Saxon name meaning 'pebbles', but sometimes indicating the presence of a gravelled area and even a tessellated pavement. A hoard of *minissimi* was found here before 1881, and 23 came to Cheltenham Museum and were published by Bryan O'Neil (*Bristol and Glos. Archaeol. Trans.* 56 (1934), pp. 133–139), their average diam. is 3.7mm, the smallest being 3mm. O'Neil also pointed out that they had been made by a similar process as those from Lydney Park

107 As at Nettleton, Wilts, W.J. Wedlake, 1982; at Woodeaton, *Oxon.* 14 (1949), and probably Chedworth (*Bristol and Glos. Arch. Soc. Trans.* 101 (1984), p. 10)

108 B. Cunliffe, 1969; and 'The Excavation of the Roman Spring at Bath', *Ant. J.* 60 (1930), pp. 187–206; B. Cunliffe and P. Davenport, 1985

109 See fn. 103

110 See fn. 107

111 *Bristol and Glos. Archaeol. Soc. Trans.* 101 (1984), pp. 5–20

D.S. Neal, 1974. The features of the site which suggest a religious function are the large pool, elaborate bathhouse and its ante-room with architectural pretensions, large dining-room and range of rooms on the west side, individually heated, as in a hostel. Also a larger number of brooches than usual on a villa have been found

113 *BJ* 167 (1967), pp. 268–79

114 E. Wightman, 1970, pp. 211–15

115 This was where Fraser began his great quest — *The Golden Bough*, 1911

116 *Mysteries of Diana: the Antiquities from Nemi in Nottingham Museums*, 1983

117 *Lydney Park*, 1932, Pl. XXVI, No. 122

118 M. Henig, 1984, Pl. 74; another possible example is a baked clay model of a human leg from a temple site at Muntham Court, Sussex, and now in Worthing Museum, listed by Dr Miranda Green, 1976, p. 220

119 This subject has been explored with perhaps greater enthusiasm than prudence by O.G.S. Crawford, 1957

120 H. Nielsen, *Ancient Opthalmological Agents*, Odense U.P. 1974

121 The finds include a pair of eyes in thin gold plate (*Ant. J.* 51 (1971), pp. 329–31 and Pl. LXVIIc) and many more have been found crudely cut out of wall-plaster (P. A. Barker, 'The Latest Occupation of the Bath Basilica at Wroxeter' in *The End of Roman Britain*, ed. P.J. Casey, BAR 1979, p. 178)

122 As on the silver plaque from Heddernheim where the god is standing on the back of a bull holding the double axe high in his right hand, and the thunder-bolt (*fulmen*) in his left (Esp., 1931, No. 92)

123 A silver pin with military type axe-hoe has been found at Corbridge (*Arch Ael.* 3rd ser. 5 (1909), Fig. 33); two bone pins with axe heads came from Richborough (J.P. Bushe-Fox, 1949, Pl. LIII, Nos. 195 and 196); the bronze pins from Lydney Park (1932, Fig. 18 Nos. 61 and 62) could be votive objects

124 J-J. Hatt, 1951, Chap. vi; F. de Visscher, *Le droit des tombeaux romains*, 1963, pp. 277–94

125 There are two examples from Bordeaux (F. Braemer, *Les Stèles Funéraires à Personnages de Bordeaux* 1959, Pl. XXV, Nos. 59 and 67)

126 Examples have been found in Gaul (*La Quincaillerie Antique* Notice Technique No. 14, published by the Touring Club de France i, Pl. XI, No. 7 from Vindonissa, No. 8 from Trêves, No. 9 from Vaucluse and No. 25 from Vaison-la-Romaine; those on the tombstones at Chester are crudely carved but appear to be the same type (R.P. Wright and I.A. Richmond, 1955, Fig. 3, No. 110)

127 *Revue d'Histoire des Religions* 1944 ii, pp. 62–3. Her conclusions are that *l'ascia est l'instrument que les mortels mettent das la main des dieux de la mort, afin qu'il devienne, par eux, un agent de salut, de force et de vie*

128 J.M.C. Toynbee, 1971, p. 50, quoting Cicero (*De Leg.* ii 22, 57). The pig is slaughtered today with a sticking knife with a long thin blade of the French Sabatier type

129 Esp. 1907, 6a

130 R.M. Ogilvie, 1969, pp. 47–52

131 Derived from the word *culter*, originally a plough-share but later came to mean a knife; thus the word meant literally 'the knife-man'

132 It was considered a bad omen if the flow was poor (Virgil, *Georgics* iii, 492), 'The knife beneath the throat was hardly wet, the sand scarce darkened by the meagre gore' (Folio Soc. 1969, K.R. Mackenzie's translation)

133 E.O. James, 1962, Chap. III; this manifests itself in Christ's death on the Cross, in the Rabbinical tradition of the sacrifice of the Lamb of God and the mystique of the transubstantiation of the wine in the Holy Communion and, of course, in many other similar rituals in other cultures the world over

134 Joan Kirk, 'Bronzes from Woodeaton, Oxon: *Oxon* 14 (1949), Fig. 8

135 M. Green, 1976, Pl. XXVIII and M. Green, 1978; over 30 are listed mainly from religious sites, although there are a few from villas and burials where their powers must have been thought to extend to 'The Shades'

136 ibid., 1976, Pl. XXV g and p. 220

137 Isabelle Fauduet, 'Minature 'Ex-Votos' from Argentomagus (Indre)' *Brit.* 14 (1983), p. 97, Fig. 4 and Pl. XIII B

138 The animal was sacrificed on a grating over a pit in which the initiate lay, thus receiving baptism and regeneration from the vital life substance. This barbaric custom had been practised in the Near East from ancient times, was adopted by the followers of Mithras and spread in the western empire in the third and fourth centuries with the rapid growth of Mithraism mainly in the frontier armies (F. Cumont, 1910, pp. 180–2)

139 Esp. III, 1913, No. 1737; *CIL* XIII 1751 and 1753. This particular sacrifice was not Mithraic but to the Great Mother Goddess Cybele and dedicated to the health and welfare of Antoninus Pius by a *sevir augustalis*. Originally this awesome ritual was to the Earth Mother and continued to be part of the sacrifice to her (J. Vermaseren, *Cybele and Attis*, 1977, pp. 101–7 and 134–8)

140 W.J. Wedlake, 1982, Fig. 80, Nos. 68 and 9; there is also one from Piercebridge (M. Green, 1978, Pl. 124) and one of bronze from Colchester (ibid., 1976, Pl. XXVIII f)

141 Roger Goodburn, *Nat. Trust Guide*, 1972, Pl. 12, Nos. 8 and 9

142 Dr Miranda Green illustrates several (1976, Pl. XXVIII e and i; 1978, Pl. 126 a & b, 127, 128, 129 and 130)

143 BM, 1922, p. 44

144 Tertullian *ad Nat.* 2,11

145 The shape with its dark oval centre, that of the *vulva*, 'the gateway to life'

146 As shown in *London & Roman Times*, 1930, p. 111, see also Fig. 36, No. 3

147 G. Boon, *Silchester* 1974, p. 168 and Fig. 26

148 Dr Miranda Green has illustrated a spear from Owmby on the Roman road north from Lincoln (1976, Pl. XXVIII, h); six are recorded from Woodeaton, three of them bent double (*Oxon.* 14 (1949), p. 40 and Pl. III D); Dr Ross illustrates four from the temple at Worth, Kent (1967, Fig. 15); the temple site at Frilford has produced an oval shield and sword with a hand-grip like the Roman *gladius* (*Oxon.* 4 (1939), p. 14 and Pl. V B)

149 Martyn Jope has drawn attention to a fragment from Woodeaton (*Oxon.* 22 (1957), pp. 106–7) as similar to pieces from Lydney Park (1932, p. 91 and Pl. XXX b); and also fragments from a site near Stony Stratford (M. Green, 1976, p. 179); Silchester (Boon, 1979, p. 196, No. 9)

150 As Wheeler has observed (1943, Fig. 45, No. 6 and p. 284)

151 *Ant J.* 46 (1966), pp. 50–59

152 Diodorus Siculus iii, 64, 2; iv, 4, 1

153 A complete one from Avranches has on it a tiny bell as well as the usual snake and frog; *Römer am Rhein*, Köln 1967, Taf. 93

154 *Trans. Bristol and Glos. Archaeol. Soc.* 101 (1983), No. 19, pp. 19–20. Those in the BM have been published by H.B. Walters (*Catalogue of Bronzes in the British Museum* 1897, Nos. 874 and 5)

155 F. Cumont *Textes et Monuments figures relatifs aux mystères de Mithra* ii, 1894–1900, p. 358, Fig. 240

156 *Lincs. Archit. & Archaeol. Soc.* for 1967–68, 7, pp. 99–101

157 BM, 1951, Fig. 37, No. 2

158 W. Warde Fowler, 1911, pp. 73–4

159 As used by Ovid in a moving appeal to his wife in *Tristia* V, ii, 43 (*ancora iam nostram non tenet ulla ratem* 'no anchor holds my craft')

160 R.H. Forster and W.H. Knowles, 'Corstopitum; Rep. on the Excavations in 1910' *AA* 3rd ser. 7 (1911), Fig. 32 and p. 188

161 Dr M. Green, 1976, p. 218. The ancient Egyptians had as a fetish the *djed* Column which they regarded as a cosmic pillar or sky support; R.T. Rundle Clark, *Myth and Symbol in Ancient Egypt*, 1978, p. 236

162 This has been a special study of Dr Miranda Green (1984)

163 Esp., 1907, 303, 428, 429, 513, 517, 524, 832 etc.: the wheel is on the famous Corbridge pottery mould of Tanaris (A. Ross, 1967), Fig. 65a)

164 A horned god holds a wheel on the Gundestrup cauldron (Klindt-Jensen, *Gundestrup Kedelen*, 1961) and helmets with pairs of horns with a wheel balanced between them appear on the Arch at Orange (XVᵉ Supplément à *Gallia* 1962, Pl. 43 Trophées VI, casques IIa–IIe)

165 It was the primary life symbol of the Jains of India, the four limbs represented the four conditions of future life, which included rebirth in human and animal form

166 This development was part of the primitive magical practices and beliefs of Mazdaism and Semitic star worship (astrolatry) which, absorbed into Persian mysteries, was to be the basis of Mithraism, a salvation cult which spread across the Roman Empire to become the main opposition to Christianity in the fourth century AD

167 Her original name was Vortumna and derived from the verb *vertere* or *vortere* 'to turn', and her Greek equivalent was Tyche

168 In this sense it was used by the poets, by Virgil *Georgics* iii, 361, *undaque iam fero tergo ferratos sustinet orbis* on the effects of a hard winter freezing the river so that waters once welcome to ships 'now carry iron-shod wheels on its waters' and Ovid who used the same image twice with a direct link with Fortuna in *Tristia* V, 8, 7, *nec metuis dubio Fortunae stantis in orbe numen*, i.e. 'nor do you fear the divine will of Fortuna, balanced on her wheel on its wavering course' and *Ex Ponto* II, 3, 55–6 in his letter to Maximus, *scilicet indignum, iuvenis carissime, ducis te fieri comitem stantis in orbe deae*, i.e. 'it would be unworthy, dear youth, for you to become a friend of the goddess who stands on the globe'. Whether one translates *orbis* as a sphere or a wheel is debatable, especially as Fortuna is never shown, like Victory, in this position. The turn of the wheel in directing one path seems to be a more satisfactory image than the revolving sphere, but the matter must remain open

169 Tacitus, *De Oratoribus* 233; Cicero's *L. Calpurnium Pisonem, Oratio* x, 22, *ne tum quidem Fortunae rotam pertimescebat* 'nor did he fear Fortuna's wheel'. For personal abuse in oratory in the late Republic see Ronald Syme, 1939, Chap. XI

170 XXVI, 8, 13, *versa rota Fortunae*

171 From Binchester (F.J. Haverfield, 1899, No. XXI, p. 19)

172 Esp. 1913, No. 2146; sometimes with a cake in the form of a wheel as Nos. 1528, 2142, etc.; ibid., 1931, Nos. 129, 214, 375, 670, 673, etc.

173 Two examples from Netherby, identified as Fortuna, one showing a seated female with cornucopia and a large wheel over an altar (A. Ross, 1967, Pl. 65b), and the other a standing figure with wheel and cornucopia with an animal, possibly a boar (ibid., Pl. 65c)

174 E.J. Phillips, No. 115 from Corbridge with her tub but also two large wheels like rosettes, and No. 183 from Newcastle-upon-Tyne with her tub and cornucopia, but here identified as Fortuna

175 M. Green, 1976, Pl. IX, e, f, g and h from Verulamium, Kettering, Ickingham and Felmingham Hall and one from Houndslow (p. 221, TQ 17, No. 2)

176 V.F. Nash-Williams, *Bull. Board Celtic Stud.* 14 (1950), pp. 81–84

177 There were strange rituals associated with Fortuna Virilis, on 1st April (Ovid, *Fasti* IV, 133ff) when women propitate the goddess so that their blemishes are hidden from the eyes of men. It seems clear that the main purpose of these rites was for women to regain the loss of the waning affection and the desire of men for their wives or mistresses. Fortuna's wheel may, therefore, have been thought a protection against such a change of heart (H.H. Scullard, 1981, pp. 96–7)

178 D. Charlesworth, 'Roman Jewellery in Northumberland and Durham', *AA* 4th ser. 39 (1961), p. 3 and Pl. VII

179 M. Green, 1978, Figs. 46–48 and from Gateshead comes a stone mould for casting them (ibid., Pl. 49)

180 R. Newstead, 'The Roman Cemetery in the Infirmary Field, Chester', *Annals of Archaeol. and Anthrop.* Liverpool 6, No. 4 (1912), p. 141 and Pl. XXXIV, Fig. 2

181 There is a great fear of mirrors among primitive people and in some societies they are subject to taboos. In Madagascar uncircumcised children are not allowed to look into a mirror for fear of losing their soul (Jorgen Ruud, *Taboo: A Study of Malagasy Customs and Beliefs*, 1960, pp. 256–7)

182 R.E.M. and T.W. Wheeler, 1932, p. 82

183 W.J. Wedlake, 1982

184 Report forthcoming. A statistical analysis showed that 26.2% of the finds were objects of personal use, but 61.2% consisted of scrap metal

185 See fn. 183, pp. 106–8

186 From Woodeaton, J. Kirk, 1949, Fig. 4, Nos. 9 and 11, Fig. 5, No. 14; from Nettleton, Fig. 91, No. 29, Fig. 96, Nos. 9 and 10

187 About 200 were found embedded in thick mud at the source of the Seine in 1963, mainly of parts of the body (R. Martin, 'Sculptures en bois découvertes aux sources de la Seine', *Revue archélogique de l'est et centre-est* 14 (1963), 1–19; a brief note P. Mackendrick, *Roman France* 1971, pp. 179–80

188 Maidens up to recent times have been known to cast pins into springs and wells when they wish for a partner. This was a practice at St. Madron's Well, Cornwall, where two pieces of straw were tied to the pin (no doubt on an early Christian instruction to depaganise the site), the maidens looked eagerly as bubbles rose to the surface, telling them of the number of weeks (or years?) they might have to wait (this piece of information was passed on to me by Ralph Merrifield). At St Aldhelms Chapel on the Isle of Purbeck, maidens used to push pins though a small crevice in a column in the Spring Festival, a fair imitation of their desire (*Proc. Dorset Archaeol. Proc.*), 14 (1893); 52 (1930), p. lxvi; I am grateful to Mr Jack Parsons for drawing my attention to this practice

189 BM, 1951, Fig. 14, Nos. 11 and 10 respectively

190 *Der Obergermanisch-Raetische Limes*, Zugmantel, Taf XI, No. 49; *London in Roman Times*, 1930, Fig. 32, No. 5

191 BM, 1951, Fig. 14, No. 12

192 *London in Roman Times*, 1930, Pl. XXXIX, shows a complete set

193 *Châtelain* means the lord or lady of the manor

194 R.E.M. and T.W. Wheeler, Pl. XXVII is part of a head-dress; Pl. XXVIII Nos. 125–127 are probably votive plaques; there is also a small lead plaque with a very crude figure of Apollo and his lyre, Fig. 21, No. 108

195 ibid., Pl. XXIX, Nos. 134–139, except No. 137, a crude votive leaf

196 Joan Kirk, 1949, Pl. VIA, Nos. 1, 2, 3 and 6 and Fig. 9, Nos. 3 and 4

197 ibid., Pl. VI, Nos. 8 and 10

198 W. J. Wedlake, 1982, Fig. 85, No. 5; Fig. 87, No. 32; Fig. 88, No. 37; Fig. 89, No. 60

199 This is the explanation offered by Dr Anne Ross for the small hawks from Woodeaton (Joan Kirk, 1949, Pl. V, who points out that the feet are missing and presumably broken from a base, p. 30 and they are identified here as eagles)

200 E. Greenfield and M.V. Taylor, 'The Romano-British Shrines at Brigstock, Northants', *Ant. J.* 43 (1963), pp. 228–268; see also ibid., 37 (1957), pp. 71–2 and Pl. XVIII

201 ibid., Pl. XLI

202 *JRS* 13 (1923), p. 94 and Pl. IV; this included small figures of an owl and an eagle as well as the two horsemen

203 As Professor A. Alföldi has shown (*JRS* 39 (1949), pp. 19–22 and Pls. 1–14) and disproving the earlier suggestion of M. Rostovtzeff that it represented Commodus-Hercules

204 Summarised by Dr Anne Ross (1967, pp. 321–334); another aspect has been considered by P. Lambrechts in his paper 'Divinités Equestres Celtiques ou Défuncts Héroïsés', *L'Antiquité Classique* 20 (1951), fasc. 1, pp. 107–128

205 *Nat. Hist.* 28 IV. 18 *qui fruges excantassit, et alibi: qui malum carmen incantassit* (i.e. 'whoever shall have cast a spell on the crops and in another place: whoever has cast an evil spell')

206 ibid., 28, IV, 19

207 *Annals* xii, 22: xvi, 8, 2

208 *London in Roman Times*, 1930, pp. 51–3, *RIB* 6

209 *defictio* or *defixio* are glosses on the verb '*defigo*' normally meaning 'to fasten down', or 'fix', but it also has a religious connotation in meaning to 'bewitch or curse' which was derived from the wax image of the person involved, because it was often enforced by piercing the image with a needle

210 In the inscriptions section of Roman Britain in 1980 (*Brit.* 12 (1981) p. 369ff) continuing

211 *Brit.* 10 (1979), No. 3, p. 343

212 *Brit.* 12 (1981) No. 6, pp. 370–2 and Fig. 19

213 *JRS* 61 (1971), pp. 176–7

214 *RIC* VII (1966), p. 7

215 *Brit.* 13 (1982), p. 406, No. 7 and Figs. 32 and 3

216 *Brit.* 14 (1983), p. 336, No. 5 and Fig. 36

217 *Brit.* 4 (1973), p. 325 and Figs. 17 and 18

218 *RIB* 7

Chapter 6 (pp. 137–8)

1 *CAH* XI, 1936, pp. 472–5; G.H. Stevenson, 1939, pp. 112–13

2 In a letter to the people of Alexandria declining this honour, he wrote 'I judge that temples and the like have been attributed by all ages to the gods alone'; E.M. Smallwood, *Documents illustrating the Principates of Gaius, Claudius and Nero*, 1967, No. 370

3 Duncan Fishwick, 'Templum Divo Claudio Constitutum', *Brit* 3 (1972), pp. 164–88

4 *Ann* XIV, 31

5 Graham Webster, *Rome against Caratacus*, 1981, pp. 86–8

6 Suet. *Nero*, 18

7 *Agricola* 21, *ut templa fora domos extruerent*

8 *idque apud imperitos humanitas vocabatur, cum pars servitutis esset*

ABBREVIATIONS

AA	*Archaeologia Aeliana*
Ant. J.	*Antiquaries Journal*
Arch.	*Archaeologia*
Arch. Cant.	*Archaeologia Cantiana*
BAR	*British Archaeological Reports*
BJ	*Bonner Jahrbuch*
BM	British Museum
Brit.	*Britannia*
Brit. Acad.	British Academy
CAH	*Cambridge Ancient History*
CIL	*Corpus Inscriptionum Latinarum*
Coll. Ant.	*Collectanea Antiqua*
CSIR	*Corpus Signorum Imperii Romani*
CW Trans.	*Transactions of the Cumberland and Westmorland Antiquarian Society*
Esp.	Espérandieu, É.
JBAA	*Journal of the British Archaeological Association*
JRS	*Journal of Roman Studies*
MZ	*Mainzer Zeitschrift*
nd.	not dated
Occ. Pap.	Occasional Paper
Oxon.	*Oxoniensia.*
Proc.	*Proceedings*
Proc. Soc. Ant. Scot.	*Proceedings of the Society of Antiquaries Scotland*
P-W	Pauly-Wissowa-Kroll, *Realencyclopädie der Klassichen Altertumswissenschaft*
RCHM	Royal Commission on Historical Monuments
Res. Rep. Soc. Ant.	Research Report of the Society of Antiquaries
RIB	*Roman Inscriptions of Britain*
RIC	*Roman Imperial Coinage*
VCH	*Victoria County History*
WAM	*Wiltshire Archaeological Magazine*

CLASSICAL SOURCES

Caesar	*De Bello Gallico*
Cato	*De Agricultura*
Cicero	*De legibus*; *Pisonem Oratio*
Codex Theodosianus	
(Cassius) Dio	*Roman History*
Columella	*De re rustica*
Diodorus Siculus	*A World History*
Eusebius	*De Laudibus Constantini*
Gellius	*Noctes Atticae*
Horace	*Epodi*
Juvenae	*Saturae*
Livy	*Ab urbe condita libri*
Lucan	*De Bello Civili* (also known as the *Pharsalia*)
Lucian	*Heracles*
Martial	*Epigrammaton libri*
Origin	*Songs of Songs: Commentary and Homilies*
Ovid	*Fasti*; *Metamorphoses*; *Tristia*; *Ex Ponto*
Pliny the Elder	*Historiae Naturalis*
Pliny the Younger	*Epistulae*
Polybius	*The Histories*
Statius	*Thebais*
Strabo	*Geography*
Suetonius	*Divus Julius*; *Tiberius*; *Claudius*; *Nero*
Tacitus	*Annales*; *Agricola*; *Germania*
Tertullian	*Ad Nationes*
Varro	*Res Rusticae*
Virgil	*Aeneid*; *Eclogues*; *Georgics*
Xenophon	*Anabasis*

SELECTED BIBLIOGRAPHY

Alcock, J.P., 1966, 'Celtic Water Cults in Roman Britain', *Arch. J.* 122, pp. 1–12

Alcock, L., 1972, *By South Cadbury is that Camelot*

Allason-Jones, L. and McKay, B., 1985, *Coventina's Well, a Shrine on Hadrian's Wall* (Chesters Museum)

Amand, M., 1984, *Vases à bustes, vases à décor zoomorphe et vases cultuels aux serpents dans les anciennes provinces de Belgique et de Germanie, Mém. de la Classe des Beaux-Arts* 8º–2ᵉ ser. T. VX. Fasc. 2

Angus, S., 1966, *The Mystery Religions*

Benoit, F., 1955, *L'Art Primitif Mederranéen de la Vallés du Rhône*

Benoit, F., 1956, *Entremont capital Celto-Ligure des Salyens de Provence de la Gaule*

Birley, A., 1979, *The People of Roman Britain*

Birley, E., 1961, *Research on Hadrian's Wall*

Blagg, T.F.C., 1983, *Mysteries of Diana: The Antiquities from Nemi in Nottingham Museum*

BM, 1922, *Guide to Romano-British Antiquities of Roman Britain*

BM, 1951, *Guide to the Antiquities of Roman Britain*

BM, 1953, *Guide to the Late Prehistoric Antiquities of the British Isles*

Boon, G., 1957, *Roman Silchester*

Boon, G., 1974, *Silchester: The Roman Town of Calleva*

Braithwaite, G., 1984, 'Romano-British Face and Head Pots', *Brit.* 15, pp. 99–131

Brogan, O., 1954, *Roman Gaul*

Bruce, J.C., 1874, *Lapidarium Septentrionale*

Burris, E.E., 1931, *Taboo, Magic, Spirits: A study of primitive elements*

Bushe-Fox, J.P., 1925, *Excavations of the Late Celtic Urn-field at Swarling*, Res. Rep. Soc. Ant. No. 5

Bushe-Fox, J.P., 1932, *Third Report of the Excavations of the Roman Fort at Richborough, Kent*, Res. Rep. Soc. Ant. No. 10

Bushe-Fox, J.P., 1949, *Fourth Report of the Excavations of the Roman Fort at Richborough, Kent*, Res. Rep. Soc. Ant. No. 16

Chadwick, N.K., 1966, *The Druids*

Clarke, R. T. Rundle, 1978, *Myth and Symbol in Ancient Egypt*

Crawford, O.G.S., 1957, *The Eye Goddess*

Cumont, F., 1910, *The Mysteries of Mithras*

Cunliffe, B., 1969, *Roman Bath*, Res. Rep. Soc. Ant. No. 24

Cunliffe, B., 1971, *Roman Bath Discovered*

Cunliffe, B., 1974, *Iron Age Communities in Britain*

Cunliffe, B., 1983, *Danebury: Anatomy of an Iron Age Hill-Fort*

Cunliffe, B., 1984, *Danebury: An Iron Age Hill-Fort in Hampshire*, CBA Research Report, No. 52

Cunliffe, B. and Davenport, P., 1985, *The Temple of Sulis Minerva at Bath*, Oxford Monograph No. 7

Cunliffe, B. and Fulford, M., 1982, *CSIR. i Fasc. 2, Bath and the West*

Cunliffe, B. and Rowley, R.T., 1984, *Lowland Iron Age Communities in Europe*, BAR Int. Ser. 48

Déchelette, J., 1904, *Les Vases Céramique ornés de la Gaule Romaine*

Deyts, S., 1983, *Les Bois Sculptés des Sources de la Seine* XLIIᵉ Supplément à *Gallia*

Dillon, M., 1948, *Early Irish Literature*

Dillon, M., 1954, *Early Irish Society*

Dillon, M. and Chadwick, N., 1973, *The Celtic Realms*, (Cardinal)

Domaszewski, A. von., 1909, *Abhandlungen zur römischen Religion*

Dudley, D., 1975, *Roman Society* (Penguin ed. 1975)

Dunbabin, K., 1978, *The Mosaics of Roman North Africa*

Duval, P.M., 1957, *Les Dieux de la Gaule*

Duval, P.M., 1959, 'Teutates, Esus, Taranis', *Études Celtiques*, 8, pp. 41–58

Duval, P.M., 1961, *'Paris Antique'*

Ekwall, E., 1968, *English River Names*

Esp., 1907, ff, É. Espérandieu, *Recueil général des Bas-Relief, Statues et Bustes de la Gaule Romaine*, Vols. 1–10

Esp., 1931, É. Espérandieu, *Recueil général des Bas-Relief, Statues et Bustes de la Germaine Romaine*

Evans-Pritchard, E.E., 1965, *Theories of Primitive Religion*

Eydoux, H-P., 1958, *Monuments et trésors de la Gaule*

Filip, J., 1962, *Celtic Civilisation and its Heritage*

Fontenrose, J., 1903, *Orion: The Myth of the Hunter and the Huntress*. Univ. California, *Class. Stud. 23*

Foster, J., 1977, *Bronze Boar and other figurines in Iron Age and Roman Britain*, BAR 39

Fowler, W. Warde, 1899, *The Roman Festivals*

Fowler, W. Warde, 1911, *The Religious Experience of the Roman People*

Fox, C., 1946, *A Find of the Early Iron Age from Llyn Cerrig Bach, Anglesey*

Fox, C., 1958, *Pattern and Purpose: a Survey of Celtic Art in Britain*

Fraser, J.G., 1911, *The Golden Bough; The Magic Art and the Evolution of Kings*

Fraser, J.G., 1911, *Taboo and the Perils of the Soul*

Fraser, J.G., 1923, *Folk-lore in the Old Testament*

Fraser, J.G., 1936, *The Golden Bough, Aftermath*

Frere, S.S., *Problems of the Iron Age in Southern Britain*, Inst. Arch. London Occ. Pap. No. 11

Gantz, J., 1976, *The Mabinogion* (Penguin)

Gantz, J., 1981, *Early Irish Myths and Sagas* (Penguin)

Garbsch, J., 1978, *Römische Paraderüstungen*

Grant, P.C., 1957, *Ancient Roman Religion*

Green, M., 1976, *A Corpus of Religious Material from the Civilian Areas of Roman Britain*, BAR 24

Green, M., 1978, *Small Cult-objects from the Military areas of Roman Britain*, BAR 52

Green, M., 1984, 'The Wheel as a Cult-Symbol in the Romano-British World', *Latomus*, 183

Grenier, A., 1934, *Manuel d'Arch. gallo-romaine*

Harding, D.W., 1972, *The Iron Age in the Upper Thames Basin*

Harding, D.W., 1974, *The Iron Age in Lowland Britain*

Hatt, J-J., 1951, *La Tombe Gallo-Romaine*

Hatt, J-J., 1970, *Celts and Gallo-Romans*, (Archaeologia Mundi)

Haverfield, F.J., 1899, *A Catalogue of the Sculptured and Inscribed Stones in the Cathedral Library*, Durham

Henig, M., 1974, *A Corpus of Roman Engraved Gemstones from the British Sites*, BAR 8

Henig, M., 1984, *Religion in Roman Britain*

Holder, A., 1896, *Alt-celtischer Sprachatz*

Hull, M.R., 1963, *The Roman Potters Kilns at Colchester*, Res. Rep. Soc. Ant. No. 21

Jackson, K.H., 1964, *The oldest Irish Tradition; A Window on the Iron Age*

Jackson, K.H., 1971, *A Celtic Miscellany* (Penguin ed. 1971)

Jacobsthal, P., 1941, *Imagery in Early Celtic Art* (Brit. Acad.)

Jacobsthal, P., 1944, *Early Celtic Art*

James, E.O., 1933A, *Christian Myth and Ritual*

James, E.O., 1933B, *Origins of Sacrifice*

James, E.O., 1960, *The Ancient Gods*

James, E.O., 1962, *Sacrifice and Sacrament*

Jessup, R.F., 1962, 'Roman Barrows in Britain', *Latomus* 57, pp. 855–67

Johns, C., 1982, *Sex or Symbol: Erotic Images of Greece and Rome* (BM)

Johns, G., and Potter, T., 1983, *The Thetford Treasure* (BM)

Jones, A.H.M., 1964, *The Later Roman Empire 284–602*. 2nd. ed.

Kirk, J., 1949, 'The Bronzes from Woodeaton', *Oxon*. 14, pp. 1–45

Klind-Jensen, O., 1961, *Gundestrupkeldren*

Lambrechts, P., 1942, *Contributions á l'Études des Divinitiés Celtiques*

Lambrechts, P., 1951, 'Divinités Equestres Celtique ou Défuncts Héroïses', *L'Antiquité Classique* 20 (1951)

Leeds, E.T., 1933, *Celtic Ornament in the British Isles to AD 700*

Lempriére, J., 1879, *Classical Dictionary of Proper Names mentioned by Ancient Authors*

Levi-Strauss, C., 1963, *The Structual Study of Myth*

Levi-Strauss, C., 1978, *Myth and Meaning* (1971 Massey Lectures)

Lewis, M.J.T., 1966, *Temples in Roman Britain*

Lindgren, C., 1978, *Classical Art Forms and Celtic Mutations*, New Jersey

Liveridge, J., 1955, *Furniture in Roman Britain*

Lutrèce, 1985, *Lutrèce: Paris de César à Clovis*

MacCana, P., 1968, *Celtic Mythology*, revised ed. 1983

MacNeill, M., 1962, *The Festival of Lughnasa*

Macready, S. and Thompson, F.H., 1984, *Cross-Channel Trade between Gaul and Britain in the Pre-Roman Iron Age*

Male, E., 1950, *La Fin du Paganism en Gaule, et les plus anciennes basiliques chrétiennes*, Paris

Mariën, M.E., 1980, *L'Empreinte de Rome*

Maringer, J., 1956, *The Gods of Prehistoric Man*

Munby, J. and Henig, M. ed., 1977, *Roman Life and Art in Britain* BAR 41

Murphy, G., 1961, *Saga and Myth in Ancient Ireland*

Murray Sister, C., 1981, *Rebirth and After-Life: A Study of the Transmutation of some pagan imagery in Early Christian funerary Art*, BAR, S 100

Neal, D.S., 1974, *The Excavations of the Roman Villa in Gadebridge Park, Hemel Hempstead, 1963–8*, Res. Rep. Soc. Ant. No. 31

Nielsen, H. 1974, *Ancient Ophthalmological Agents*, Odense UP

Novaesium, 1904, H. Lehner, *BJ* 111–112

Ogilvie, R.M., 1969, *The Romans and their Gods*

O'Rahilly, C., 1970, *Táin Bó Cúalnge, from the Book of Leinster*

O'Railly, T.F., 1946, *Early Irish History and Mythology*

Phillips, E.J., 1977, *CSIR* i, Fac. i, *Corbridge, Hadrian's Wall East of the North Tyne*

Piggott, S., 1968, *The Druids* (Penguin ed. 1974)

Pobé, M., 1961, *The Art of Roman Gaul*

Potter, T.W. and C.F., 1982, *A Romano-British Village at Grandford, March, Cambs.* BM Occ. Pap. No. 35

Powell, T.G.E., 1958, *The Celts*

RCHM *Cotswolds*, 1976, *Iron Age and Romano-British Monuments in the Gloucestershire Cotswolds*

Reece, R. ed., 1977, *Burial in the Roman World*, CBA Res. Rep. No. 22

Rees, A. and B., 1961, *Celtic Heritage*

Reinach, S., 1895, *Epona*

Reinach, S., 1917, *Catalogue Illustré du Musée des Antiquités Nationales au Château de Saint-Germaine-en-Laye*, i

Reinach, S., 1921, *Catalogue Illustré de Musée des Antiquités Nationales au Château de Saint-Germaine-en-Laye*, ii

Rhodes, J.F., 1964, *Catalogue of the Romano-British Sculptures in the Gloucester Museum*

Richmond, I.A., 1950, *Archaeology and the After-Life in Pagan and Christian Imagery*

Richmond, I.A., 1963, *Roman Britain* (2nd. ed. Pelican)

Richmond, I.A. and Wright, R.P., 1955, *Catalogue of the Inscribed and Sculptured Stones in the Grosvenor Museum, Chester*

Rivet, A.L.F. and Smith, C., 1981, *The Place-Names of Roman Britain*

Robinson, R., 1979, *The Armour of Imperial Rome*

Rodwell, W. ed., 1980, *Temples, Churches and Religion in Roman Britain*, BAR 77

Ross, A., 1959, 'The Human Head in Insular Pagan Celtic Religion', *Proc. Soc. Ant. Scot.* 91, pp. 10–63

Ross, A., 1967, *Pagan Celtic Britain*

Ross, A., 1970, *Everyday Life of the Pagan Celts*

Rostovtzeff, M., 1947, *The Social and Economic History of the Roman Empire*

Ruud, J., 1960, *Taboo, A Study of Malagasy Customs and Beliefs*

Scullard, H.H., 1959, *From the Gracchi to Nero*

Scullard, H.H., 1981, *Festivals and Ceremonies of the Roman Republic*

Schoppa, H., nd., *Die Kunst der Römerzeit in Gallien, Germanien und Britannien*

Sherwin-White, A.N., 1967, *Racial Prejudice in Imperial Rome*

Sieveking, G. de, ed., 1971, *Prehistoric and Roman Studies* (BM)

Sjoestedt, M.L., 1949, *Gods and Heroes of the Celts*

Speidel, M.P., 1980, *Mithras–Orion, Études préliminaires aux Religions Orientales dans L'Empire Romain*, Vol. 81

Stead, I.M., 1965, *The La Tène Cultures of Eastern Yorkshire* (Yorks. Phil. Soc.)

Stead, I.M., 1967, 'A La Tène III burial at Welwyn Garden City,' *Arch.* 101, pp. 1–62

Stevenson, G.H., 1939, *Roman Provincial Administration*

Strong, A. Mrs., 1915, *Apotheosis and After-Life*

Syme, R., 1939, *The Roman Revolution*

Syme, R., 1958, *Tacitus*

Thévenot, É., 1968, *Divinitiés et Sanctuaries de la Gaule*

Tierney, J.J., 1960, The Celtic Ethnography of Posidonius' *Proc. Royal Irish Acad.* 60, sect. C, No. 5, pp. 189–275

Toynbee, J.M.C., 1957, 'Genii Cucullati in Roman Britain', *Latomus,* 28

Toynbee, J.M.C., 1962, *Art in Roman Britain* (Phaidon)

Toynbee, J.M.C., 1964, *Art in Britain under the Romans*

Toynbee, J.M.C., 1971, *Death and Burial in the Roman World*

Toynbee, J.M.C., 1973, *Animals in Roman Life and Art*

Vermaseren, M.J., 1977, *Cybele and Attis: The Myth and his Cult*

Vertet, A. and Vuillemot, G., nd., *Figurines Gallo-Romaines en Argile d'Autun*

Vries, S. de, 1963, *La Religion des Celtes*

Walters, H.B., 1908, *Catalogue of the Roman Pottery in the Department of Antiquities*, BM

Webster, G., 1975, *The Cornovii*

Webster, G., 1981, *Rome Against Caratacus*

Wedlake, W.J., 1982, *The Excavation of the Shrine of Apollo at Nettleton, Wiltshire, 1956–7*, Res. Rep. Soc. Ant. No. 40

SELECTED BIBLIOGRAPHY

Wheeler, R.E.M., 1943, *Maiden Castle, Dorset*, Res. Rep. Soc. Ant. No. 12

Wheeler, R.E.M., 1954, *The Stanwick Fortifications, North Riding of Yorkshire* Res. Rep. Soc. Ant. No. 17

Wheeler, R.E.M. and T.W., 1932, *Report on the Prehistoric and Post-Roman Site in Lydney Park, Gloucestershire*, Res. Rep. Soc. Ant. No. 9

Wightman, E., 1970, *Roman Trier and the Treveri*

Zwicker, J., 1934, *Fontes Historiae Religionis Celticae*

GENERAL INDEX

Note: Roman names are normally indexed under the *nomen*

Aachen, 124
Acesius, an epithet applied to Apollo, 54
acorn, symbol of fertility, 145 fn. 14
Actaeon, 44, 49, pl. 4
Ad Pontem (East Stoke, Notts), 55, 63
Adam, Fall of, 21
Addomarus, 71
Aedui, 25
Aelius Secundus, 79
Aeneas, 145 fn. 16
Aer, Celtic goddess of R. Dee, 73
aerial archaeology, 79
Aesculapius, 38, 113, 134
  staff of, 57, 129
Aesica (Hadrian's Wall), 151 fn. 22
Aetolian War, 50
Africa, North, 47, 48, 64
Age of Enlightenment, 21
Agricola, Julius, Gnaeus, 20, 138, 143
  fn. 9
Aire, R., 73
Akrisios K. of Argos, 149 fn. 117
Alator, an epithet applied to Mars, 54
Alauna, 136
Alcock, Dr Joan, 11, 52, 163 fn. 5
Alcock, Professor L., 164 fn. 29 fn. 30
Alexander (the Great), 19
Alexandria, 118, 173 fn. 2
Alexandrian School, 25
Alföldi, A., 172 fn. 203
Allason-Jones, L., 150 fn. 9, 158 fn.
  205, 162 fn. 59
All Hallows Eve, derived from Samain, 24, 31
almond, 'mystical', symbol of the flame, 127
Alpine cave, early burials in, 15
altars, images on the sides of, 125
  model, as votives, 127
  sacrificial rituals before, 126
Amand, Marcel, 160 fn. 1

Ambracia, 50
American, North – Indians, 21
Ammianus Marcellinus, 115, 130
amphitheatre, 48, 49, 51
  in timber, 50
amphorae sherd distribution on south
  coast, 120
  Welwyn burials in, 117
amulets, 118–36
  bezoars as, in the Middle Ages, 144
  fn. 18
Ancasta, Dea, 54
Ancaster (Lincs) a model cauldron from, 129, 154 fn. 99
ancestor worship, 17, 109, 115
anchor, model of, symbol of hope, 129
Andarta, 54
Anderson, A.C. and A.S., 160 fn. 12
Andescociuoucus, an epithet applied to
  Mercury, 54
Andraste, 54
Anextiomaro, an epithet applied to
  Mars, 54
Anglesea, 26, 107, 172, 163 fn. 1
animal masks worn by men, 98, fig.
  12D
  symbolism, 46
Annals (of Tacitus), 21
Annan, R., 76
Annianus, 136
Anniola, 136
Antenociticus, 73, pl. 16
anthropoid sword handles, 166 fn. 73
anthropomorphic features on pottery, 160 fn. 12
anthropologists, 21, 29, 118
anthropology, Victorian, 14
  changes in, 143
Antonine Wall, 64, 71, 163 fn. 2
Antoninus, a centurion of *Legio VI
  Victrix*, 77
Antoninus Pius, 169 fn. 139

182

origin of, 30, 130
Calleva, *see* Silchester
Callirius (or Calliriodacu), epithet
applied to Silvanus, 54
Cam, R., 73
Camerton (Som.), 40
Campestres (mother goddesses of the
parade ground), 64, 71
Campus Martius, 50
Camulodunum, *see* Colchester
Camulos, name derived from, 73
Camulos, Celtic God of War, 73
candles, lit to aid childbirth, 127
Canterbury (Kent, Durovernum), 156
fn. 161
cantharus, 48
Cantii, 80
Capitoline Triad, 33
Caratacus, 21
Carinthia, 66
Carlisle (Luguvalium), 146 fn. 43, 154
fn. 108
Belatucadros, 75
Cucullati, 68
cult pottery figure, 106, pl. 22
Tullie House Museum, 162 fn. 70
Carnavalet, Musée, 151 fn. 17
Carpentras, monumental arch at, 121
Carrawburgh, Coventina's Well, 78, 79
Mithraeum, 66, 154 fn. 110
cart burials in E. Yorkshire, 109, 116
Carthage, 47, 163 fn. 1
Cartimandua, Q., 116, 139
Carvoran (Hadrian's Wall), 71, 79
Casey, J.A., 123
Casey, P.J., 168 fn. 121
Cassius Dio, *see* Dio
Castle Loch, 76
Castlesteads (on the Antonine Wall), 64
Castor (Cambs.), 56, 144 fn. 123
cataleptic fit, 28
Catalin, 28
catasterism, 44
Catholic Church, 18
use of candles in, 127
Cato the Elder, 20
Catuvellauni, 71
cauldron-magic, of the Celts, 61
model of, from Ancaster, 129
cave burials in, 15
paintings, 15
Cavenham (Suffolk), 115
Celtic art, 161 fn. 47
burials in Britain, 61
calendar, 26, 30–5
craftsmanship, 72, 118
craftsmen, 53, 140
cult figures on pottery, 104–6
deities, classical, assimilation with, 58
epigraphic evidence for, 53

Sucellus, father of, 61
survival of, 52
triadic form of, 64
hero, 27–8
magic cauldron, 61
Magna Mater in Epona, 70
mythology, 20, 29, 144 fn. 5
potters in demand by Rome, 140
religion, 23–40, 53
sacred lakes or pools, 121–2
society, 52, 116, 120, 132
spoils of war, 120
swords, 146 fn. 30
Celtic temples and shrines, 111–15
at Stitchcombe (?), 60
continued to be venerated, 111
identification of, 108–9
Wycombe 104, fig. 14
warfare, seasonal, 120
war gear from Llyn Cerrig Bach,
121–2
water cults, 163 fn. 5
Cerberus, 38
Cernunnos, 42, 56–7, 151 fn. 18, fn.
22, pl. 5
Cétshamain = Beltine, 32
Chadwick, N., 144 fn. 16, fn. 9, 145 fn.
19, 146 fn. 47, 147 fn. 60
chariot, British, as described by Caesar,
22
burials, 116
reconstruction of, 122
Charlesworth, Miss D., 171 fn. 178
Chassaing, M., 63
Châteauroux, 56
chatelaine (*châtelain*), symbol of
marriage, 133, 134, 172 fn. 193
Chedworth (Glos.), model altars at, 127
Lenus-Mars temple at, 81, 93, 114,
124, 167 fn. 107
votive hand of Sabazios at, 129
Cheltenham Museum, 10, 167 fn. 106
Cherchel, mosaic from, 48
Chester (Deva), 55, 73, 126, 132, 140,
171 fn. 180
tombstones from, 168 fn. 126, pl. 4
Chesterholm (Vindolanda), a shrine to
Maponus at, 77
Chester-le-Street (Durham), 78, 99
Chessels, The, 167 fn. 106
childbirth, votive gifts for, 124, 125
Chi-Rho monogram, 48, 49
Christ, 48, 169 fn. 133
Actaeon, associated with, 49
Chi-Rho monogram of, 48
Orpheus, associated with, 47
Passion of, 46
Christian anchor, symbolism of, 129
Church, 47
confessional, 136

Tranquillus), 144 fn. 20, 145 fn.
22, fn. 24, 149 fn. 120, 156 fn.
166, 167 fn. 96, 173 fn. 6
Suleviae, 80, 159 fn. 222
Sulinus, a sculptor at Bath, 80
Sulis-Minerva, 42, 54, 78, 81, 104,
136
temple, 112, 150 fn. 11, 159 fn. 223
Sussex, 128
Swarling (Kent), 165 fn. 61
Aylesford, cemetery, 117
swastika on a votive axe from
Woodeaton, 126, fig. 16.5
as a symbol of motion, 130, 133
Switzerland, 120
symbolism, animals, of, 46
crosses, ring and dot motifs of, 63
Syme, Sir Ronald, 21, 143 fn. 10, 144
fn. 14, 171 fn. 169

taboo, 28–30, 133
corpse as, by Romans, 39, 40
mirrors, on, 171 fn. 181
sexual, before hunting, 44
Tacitus, Cornelius, 20, 21, 26, 121,
122, 130, 138, 139, 143 fn. 9, fn.
12, 144 fn. 13, 145 fn. 24, 166
fn. 88, 171 fn. 169, 173 fn. 7
Tamar, R., 72
Tamesis, R., (Thames), 72
Tanaris, (or Taranis), 16, 35, 53, 55–6,
90, 121, fig. 9F
wheel of, 129, 130, 134, 150 fn. 4,
fn. 13
Tasciovanus, 71
Taurus Trigaranus, 56
Taylor, Miss M.V., 157 fn. 170, 172 fn.
200
tazza, handled, with the symbols of
Sabazius from Friedburg, 129
telepathy, 17
Telesphorus, 67, 70, 155 fn. 120, 156
fn. 150
Tell Brak, 162 fn. 51
Tellus, 58, 64, 72
Tempelbezirk at Caerwent, 81, 112
at Springhead, 159 fn. 239
temple, Antenociticus, of, at Benwell,
73
banners and sceptres of, 134
bank, as a, 111
Bath, survival of, 112
Claudius, the deified, of, 137, 139
Cocidius, of, 75
curse tablets, inscribed at, 134–36
jewellery from, 132
Lydney, plan of, 113
metal workshops at, 123, 132
regalia, 114–15
Stitchcombe, at, 60

treasures seized by Constantine, 111
at Tolosa, 121
Temple de la Fôret d'Halatte, 121
Terra Mater on the Ara Pacis, 65
Tertullian, 169 fn. 144
têtes coupées, 39, 40, 99, 109, 166 fn.
73, fig. 11B
Entremont, at, 107
Teutates, 35, 53, 150 fn. 4
Thames, R., 72, 107, 161 fn. 25
Thebais of Statius, 145 fn. 19
Theodosianus, Codex, 136, 155 fn. 117
Thetford (Norfolk), Celtic temple at, 108
house at, 54
Thévenot, Émile, 61–3, 152 fns. 36,
153 fn. 57, fn. 61, fn. 68, 154 fn.
93–5, 156 fn. 152, fn. 153, 157
fn. 170
Thistleton (Rutland), 78, 79
Celtic temple, 108
Thompson, F.H., 166 fn. 85
Thor, 16
Thurneysen, R., 147 fn. 60
thyrsus of Bacchus, 63
Tiber, R., 36
Tiberius, 22, 56, 62, 119, 121, 143 fn.
12
expelled druids from Gaul, 27
Tiefenau, near Berne, 166 fn. 87
Tierney, Professor, J.J., 19, 20, 24, 143
fn. 7, 144 fn. 4
Timagenes, 167 fn. 90
Timotneus, a name on a curse tablet,
136
Tincommius, 71
Titus, 50
toe-rings found in the Maiden Castle
cemetery, 116
Tolosa (Toulouse), 121
tomb, circular as a prototype of the
Celtic shrine, 109
tombstones, cavalry of, 48, 72
dedications of, 125–6
lions, on, 38, 47
Tomlin, Dr Roger, 11, 135, 136
tools, model, as votives, 128–9, fig.
16.3
totemism, 15, 43
totems, 30
Toul, 63
Toynbee, J.M.C., 47, 51, 57, 59, 63,
65, 67, 68, 69, 70, 80, 104, 147
fn. 66, 148 fn. 83, fn. 86, 149 fn.
96, fn. 101, fn. 118, fn. 124, 150
fn. 128, fn. 7, fn. 12, 151 fn. 22,
152 fn. 41, fn. 44, fn. 46, 153 fn.
81, 154 fn. 97–9, fn. 103–5, 155
fn. 120, fn. 128, fn. 130, fn. 132,
fn. 133, fn. 136, fn. 138, 156 fn.
140, fn. 143, fn. 144, fn. 147, 160

INDEX OF CELTIC WORDS

INDEX OF LATIN WORDS

Where relevant, the plural form is shown in brackets

abaton, holy sleep, 113, 124

ad asciam dedicatum, dedicated under the axe, 125, fig. 15

amphora (-e), large pottery oil or wine container, 117

anguinium, serpents egg, 144 fn. 17

ara (-e), altar, 137

argenteus (-i), silver coin, 136

argentiolos, popular word for a small silver coin, 136

bardocucullus, a Gallic cloak, 154 fn. 112

bardus (-i), a bard, 26

beneficiarius consularis, a soldier seconded for duty on the Governer's staff, 64

bestiarius (-i), a professional fighter of wild beasts in the arena, 49, 50, fig. 3

Bona Deae, the good goddess, worshipped only by women, 58, 64

bractea (-ae), gold leaf, 145 fn. 16

caduceus, the snake-entwined wand of Mercury, 56, 90

Campestres, mother goddess of the parade ground, 64

cantharus, a large handled drinking vessel, 48

castus multiplices, taboo, 29

cella (-e), the house of the deity in a temple, 111

circus (-us), the long arena with rounded ends for chariot and horse races, 49

civitas (-ates), a tribe and its lands, 137

collegium, a guild of merchants or devotees of a cult, 112, 114

colonia (-e), a settlement for retired veterans, 79, 80

colossi, a term for the large wickerwork cages for Celtic sacrificial victims, 35, 164 fn. 18

commonitorium, an earnest reminder, 136

consilium, a council, 33, of the Three Gauls, 137–8

cornucopia (-ae), horn of plenty, 119

corona civica, the oak leaf crown, 145 fn. 14

cucullatus, a little hooded Celtic spirit, 42, fig. 11

cucullus, a Celtic hooded cloak, 66, 77, 98, 154 fn. 114, 158 fn. 115, fn. 116

culter, a knife, 168 fn. 131

cultrarius, a man who cut the throat of a sacrificial animal, 176

Deabus Matribus Omnium, the Mother Goddess of all nations, 64

Deae Matres, the Mother Goddess, 42

Deae Matres Tramarinis Patriis, Mother Goddess of the native lands and overseas, 64

Dea Nutrix, the nursing goddess, 39, 65

defictio, to curse, 173 fn. 209

defictus est, is cursed, 135

defixio, to fasten down, 173 fn. 205

denarius, a silver coin, 117

Deus, a God, 165 fn. 54

digitabalum, a hand-covering, 146 fn. 50

Dis, an early form of *Deus*, 165 fn. 54

Dis Manibus (a formula on tombstones), to the Gods of the Shades, 165 fn. 54

drunemeton, a sacred oak-grove, 145 fn. 14

dryadae, druids, 26

ensis hamata, a sword for bull-slaying, 127

fasces, a bundle of sticks and an axe

203